D0392876

100 Places in the USA
Every Woman Should Go

SOPHIA DEMBLING

TRAVELERS' TALES
AN IMPRINT OF SOLAS HOUSE, INC.
PALO ALTO

Travelers' Tales and Solas House are trademarks of Solas House, Inc.,
2320 Bowdoin Street, Palo Alto, California 94306. www.travelerstales.com

Art Direction: Stefan Gutermuth
Cover Design: Kimberly Coombs
Interior Design and Page Layout: Howie Severson
Author Photo: David Baumbach

Library of Congress Cataloging-in-Publication Data
Available upon request

ISBN-10: 1-932361-92-8
ISBN-13: 978-1932361-92-6

First Edition
Printed in the United States
10 9 8 7 6 5 4 3 2 1

*Dedicated to all the remarkable American women through history,
whose stories have only just begun to be heard.*

*I feel there is something unexplored about woman
that only a woman can explore.*
—GEORGIA O'KEEFFE

Table of Contents

SECTION II
AMERICANS' HISTORY

SECTION III
PARTICIPATE

Retreats and Spiritual Escapes

SECTION IV
X (CHROMOSOME) RATED

Just Kinda Girly

Home and Hearth

Introduction

WHEN I TOLD PEOPLE I WAS writing *100 Places in the USA Every Woman Should Go*, their first question was usually, "What are your criteria?" Or, less eloquently, "Sez who?"

A fair enough question, to which the answer is: "Sez me."

I did first poll friends and colleagues and got some excellent ideas from them, but in the end what we have here is an entirely subjective selection of American places I think are important or cool or fun or quintessentially American. Some are of particular relevance to women, some aren't.

So, who am I to say so? For one thing, I love traveling in the USA, and I've done a lot of it. I took my first cross-country road trip with two girlfriends when I was 19 years old. At that point, I had barely left my hometown of New York City—which, like Los Angeles, both defines America and barely resembles it. I was astonished and awed as much by cornfields as mountains. The solid farmers and their stolid wives we saw in diners and truck stops were wondrous as unicorns, and Iowa and Nevada were as magical as Oz. By the time we hit California, with the whole nation stretched out behind us, I was madly in love.

I've traveled the country extensively ever since—by car, by bus, by airplane, staying in luxury hotels and cinderblock motels. (Once, by choosing a motel because we liked its neon, my husband and I accidentally checked into a whorehouse.) I've been as far south as Key West and as far north as Seattle. (North Dakota, I've got my eye on you.)

My first published article in the mid 1980s, in the *Dallas Morning News*, was about touring the United States by Greyhound bus. My second was about touring the stars' homes in Nashville. I've written for the *Los Angeles Times*, the *Chicago Tribune*, the *Miami Herald*, and many other newspapers, magazines, and websites. For a couple of years, my friend Jenna Schnuer and I wrote a website called Flyover America, in which we shared our passion for America's out-of-the-way places.

I love the scale of America. I love her grand places and brash cities, her wilderness and forgotten hamlets. I love her breadth and depth and roadside attractions. I roll my eyes at world-traveling Americans who have never explored their own backyards—who have never seen a thunderstorm over Nebraska or the Atlantic pounding the coast of Maine, never eaten grits in the South or salmon in Alaska, seen real Western art or a jackalope trophy. I'm so passionate for travel in America, I even argue that Las Vegas is a must-see, no matter how highbrow you consider yourself.

After gathering a mess of suggestions, I cast a wide net of criteria to decide among them and which others to add. Some places are no-brainers—New York City, the Grand Canyon, that kind of thing. America's greatest hits, as it were. And I wanted to include sites related to women's history. From there, I moved on to sites relevant to the lives of prominent women writers and artists and some of America's toughest cookies. I included immigrant history because that's the story of all of us. There are places related to American music and places I consider Americana. There are girly-girl places and activities, adventures, spiritual places, places related to home and hearth, and silly, silly kitschy places. I tried to find a female story in everything I included, but didn't insist on it. Some places aren't places so much as activities (surfing, rafting), with suggestions for places to do them.

There is a lot about some states and not so much about others, but I tried to cover as much of the country as I could. I can't help it if a lot of really important historic things happened in New York and Massachusetts. I tried to include sites so big that you shouldn't miss them and so small you probably don't know about them.

And a note about the historical sections of the book: Some of the places included are not much to speak of. One is a mere plaque in a hallway—nothing to make a special trip for. It's more if you happen to be in Nashville. But it's a good story, and here is my thinking on things like that: If we go, they will build it. Tourism has a lot of clout for local economies. If we show interest in women's history sites, tourist boards and businesses will respond, and the ragtag sites full of fascinating women's stories will grow, pushing women's history aboveground.

I have been to the majority of the places in here. Many I visited in the past, others specifically for this book. But in saying every woman should go, I include myself. No matter how much travel I did, I kept finding other must-see places. I just ran out of time. Flat up against my deadline, I remembered Eudora Welty's home in Jackson, Mississippi. What a bummer that I didn't have time to go there and had to rely on research. Thank heavens for the interweb, but the photographs made me yearn to see it for myself, especially since I've never really been to Mississippi, only through it. Mississippi, I have my eye on you, too.

Naturally, there's no place or experience in this book that men wouldn't enjoy as well. Any American, male or female, who doesn't make a point of seeing Yellowstone National Park is a knucklehead, in my humble opinion. (People from other nations get a pass, but I know they're out seeing stuff like that anyway because I run into them all the time.)

Undoubtedly, every single person reading this would write a different version of this book. That's good and as it should be. Truth be told, I second-guessed myself until the manuscript was finally pried out of my hands. If I wrote this book five years from now, it would probably be different. Heck, if I wrote it next week it might.

So what are your must-sees? If you're so inclined, you can send a note to ttales@travelerstales.com and tell us about it.

See you on the road.

I

Get to Know America

1 Cross-Country Road Trip

AMERICA IS BIG.

Yes, you know that, but if you have never driven from sea to shining sea, then you don't really know that.

It's big.

Travel purists will tell you that the only way to know America is through her blue highways—small roads through small towns, where you can eat at the local diner and buy fruit from roadside stands. And yes, those kinds of drives are bliss, the best way to get an intimate experience of America.

But traversing the entire length of the nation on the Interstates is an education in America as a big hunk of geology.

I love the Interstate system, officially (and a little frighteningly) called The Dwight D. Eisenhower National System of Interstate and Defense Highways. The Interstates were built not just to move Americans around, but to efficiently move troops and weapons should the need arise.

These are big-picture roads, and that's one of my favorite things about them. They're big like America is big. I love the signs that direct you not from town to town, but from great city to great city: SOUTH—MIAMI; WEST—LOS ANGELES. These signs give me the same thrill as an international airport. I love the major interchanges, with underpasses and overpasses cutting through the sky, shuttling us around in our little pods. This is industrial art on a most massive scale.

The Interstates take you past farmland and desert and then plunge you into cities, where suddenly they are battered and rutted and everything speeds up. (Entering St. Louis from the south, on I-44, is among my favorite examples of that—the roads get potholed and confusing, traffic gets thicker, and then there's that crazy surreal arch, right there.) The Interstates cross rivers, follow railroad routes, weave aggressively through mountains. (Imagine the blasting that had to occur to build those highways. Just imagine.)

It doesn't matter what route you take, a cross-country trip on the Interstate system is like time-lapse photography. I like going right through the middle, from east to west, so the nation unfolds for me the way it did the first settlers. You watch the huddled hills of the East relax into the Plains, which then start furrowing like a worried brow before the ground heaves and the Rocky Mountains burst from its crust.

I'll never forget my first cross-country drive with a couple of friends when, after days of hypnotic corn fields, we spotted the first, barely discernible purple glimmers of the Rockies in the distance. "I've always wondered," one friend mused, "how the pioneers must have felt after weeks and weeks slogging across the prairies, then seeing...that."

My gosh, the Rockies are magnificent—claustrophobic in spots, then so grand and gracious they bring tears to your eyes. When you break through to the other side, the ground flattens again and parches as you reach the jagged western edge of the nation. And then, the Pacific Ocean and exotic lands beyond.

Going north-south is certainly fun, but it doesn't have the visual impact of east-west. And small road trips are wonderful, of course. I always choose driving if it's feasible for a trip. Someday, when I have all the time in the world, I'll take the blue highways across America.

But to take the full measure of our nation, for a wide view of everything America has, of her scale and breadth and splendor, we have our broad, bold, splendid Interstates. God bless 'em.

⋇

PLACES TO LEARN MORE

There are roughly 837 gajillion road trip books and movies out there. I am going to suggest just one: *Women's Diaries of the Westward Journey*, by Lillian Schlissel. It's academic in tone and gripping in content. These are the stories of women who crossed the country in wagons and by foot. You think not being able to find a rest stop when you need it is a road trip hardship? How about giving birth by the side of the road? Burying loved ones? If anything can make you grateful for the Interstates, these stories will.

2 National Parks

AMERICA'S NATIONAL PARKS ARE NOT NATIONAL PARKS for nothing. The acreage carved out for posterity is some of the most breathtaking beauty America has to offer.

The parks are all different, all spectacular, all appealing for their own reasons. So I asked a bunch of women about their favorite national park and why, to give you lots of ideas.

It's my book so I go first: Yellowstone National Park in the wintertime. Yes, it's lovely in the summertime but it's also crazy crowded. Getting stuck in a traffic jam in a national park is just wrong. But in the wintertime, when it's under a blanket of snow and it attracts far fewer visitors, it is—it's no use, I must use a cliché—magical. Great expanses blanketed in white are dotted with buffalo, who use their massive heads to push aside the snow and reach the grass beneath. Underground cauldrons roil under a layer of steam, mudpots burble ominously, geysers spew. (Did you know Yellowstone is essentially a big volcano? Try not to think about it.) Peak moment: after a day of snowmobiling, sitting in an outdoor hot tub at Mammoth Hot Springs Hotel when a light snow started falling.

Speaking of which, rules about snowmobiles are in perpetual flux, part of an ongoing tussle across the nation between park conservation and access. At the moment, you may snowmobile into the park, but check the park website for restrictions.

You can also take snow coach tours. I've snowmobiled in from lovely little Cody, Wyoming (see Chapter 23) and saw amazing things I wouldn't have seen if I'd arrived in a car. Still, I can take or leave the snowmobile, which is loud and seems terribly rude in such a pristine landscape. An alternative is to drive in and stay at one or both of the lodges; Mammoth and Old Faithful are open mid-December through mid-March. You can take snowmobile or snow-coach tours, cross-country ski, or snowshoe from there. And please do. Don't make it a drive-through visit.

I also suggest Badlands National Park because it's just so stunning and intense, and it's impossible to take a bad photograph there. The buttes and spires, desert and prairie go kaleidoscopic in changing light. It's the kind of place that makes your soul unfold to fill the space. A friend and I hiked out a while on Chimney Rock Trail, and it was like leaving the world as we know it behind. In a good way.

And a shout-out for Big Bend National Park in Texas, which is one of my favorite places in the world. It's desert, mountains, canyons, and hot springs. It's wild, kind of dangerous, and haunting. Out here, they say, the land is two-thirds sky. And they say out here, everything bites, sticks, burns, or breaks your heart. Also in a good way. The desert blooms in springtime and it's lovely, though you might want to avoid spring break if you're looking for solitude.

Now, for more inspiration, here's what other women have to say:

Glacier National Park, Montana: "Because of the mountains," says videographer Laura Mann. "The mountains are bigger there than in any other national park I've been to. It's like a wilder, less tourist-ridden Yellowstone."

Mesa Verde National Park, Colorado: "Mesa Verde was way more interesting than the usual 'hey, look at that cool tree/ mountain/river/etc.' stuff, and it was the first time I actually grasped the concept of people before 'modern' times," says Jennifer Medina, who grew up in Colorado and spent every childhood vacation going to national and state parks.

Rocky Mountain National Park: "For earth mama reasons," says Lara Mayeux, a psychology professor who vacations there with her young daughters. She takes them hiking. "The trail is covered in all kinds of tracks, and the girls like to try and identify them," she says. "They take very seriously the job of using binoculars to look up the mountain in search of bears. We listen to the birdsong and try to identify the flowers that are growing along the trail. We watch the bighorn sheep on the meadow."

Arches National Park, Utah: "Something there moved me to tears," says artist Therese Shirley Hardison.

Olympic National Park, Washington. "So foggy and spooky!" says Helen Anders, a travel writer.

Yosemite National Park, California: "In winter," says editor Robin Galiano Russell. "Just a Japanese tour bus...and us. *So* exquisite, and the 1920s lodge is amazing." (She's talking about the Ahwahnee Hotel.)

Cuyahoga Valley National Park, Ohio: "Not the jaw-dropper that some out west are, but it offers reassuring proof that nature manages to bounce back when we give it a break," says editor Jen Dennis. (An Erie Canal towpath has been turned into a walking/ biking/running trail here.)

Everglades National Park, Florida: "My favorite part was renting a canoe and paddling away on our own private bird-watching expedition," says travel writer Candy Harrington. "We saw herons, egrets, storks, spoonbills, and more. The area was just flooded with bird life—and a few gators too! Best of all, we only ran into a few other folks that day."

Finally, Amy Forbus, an editor, had a little trouble deciding which park to choose. She was just back from a trip to Mammoth Cave National Park in Kentucky, where she took the six-hour Wild Cave Tour, and to Great Smoky Mountains National Park in Tennessee and North Carolina (the most visited national park of the bunch), where she climbed Mount Le Conte, the tallest mountain in the eastern United States. "Yes, we feel like total bad-asses now," she says. But she also has a soft spot for Denali and Kenai Fjords national parks in Alaska. And Carlsbad Caverns National Park in Texas and New Mexico. "What can I say?" Amy says. "I'm becoming a national park junkie."

That's not hard to do. Bet you can't visit just one.

❧

PLACES TO LEARN MORE

The National Park website, www.nps.gov, is the place to start for information. And National Parks Traveler, www.nationalparkstraveler.com, is a great place for news and commentary about the parks.

The Ken Burns documentary series, *The National Parks: America's Best Idea*, is an exhaustive (and a little exhausting) exploration of the parks. The PBS website about the series has lots of links to click, www.pbs.org/nationalparks.

3 *Maine Coast*

MAINE HAS MORE COASTLINE THAN CALIFORNIA, and the Maine coast has two personalities: There's that whole Ye Olde Fudge Shoppe thing of touristy towns such as Ogunquit and Boothbay Harbor. These places are a fun and necessary component of a holiday on the coast of Maine. Most of the state's sandy beaches are in the southern part of the state. I spent many summers in among the pines at a sleepaway camp on a lake in southern Maine. Once a summer we went to Reid State Park, where the beach was big and wide and the water was so cold, my ankles went immediately numb when I waded in. (I waded out immediately.)

But beyond the outlet stores and cinnamon-scented gift shops, even beyond the harbors and lobstermen (mmm, lobster...) the Maine coast is deeply soulful. Here are crashing waves, rocky islands, tidal pools, and lighthouses. I'm going to stick my neck out and say that it is impossible not to be deeply affected by the Maine coast.

Acadia National Park stands on a collection of rocky islands that heaved from the Earth's crust in the aftermath of enormous glaciers passing through. Even the highest mountain within 25 miles of the shoreline between Nova Scotia and Mexico, Cadillac Mountain, had its top sheared off by glacial traffic, though it still stands: 1,529 feet of pink granite and pines overlooking the park. Acadia also has forests, lakes, ponds, wetlands, and tidal pools. Not so much beaches, unless you're O.K. with sea-critter skeletons mixed with your sand.

Park at Jordan Pond House Restaurant, and you can just stroll around the pond like Victorian ladies did, when the tradition of tea and popovers on the lawn began (it continues), or take up on foot or by bike on the network of carriage roads. "You'll lose most of the crowds pretty quickly," says Hilary Nangle, who lives in Maine and wrote Moon Handbooks to Acadia and Coastal Maine.

Hilary also suggests taking the ferry from Stonington to the Isle au Haut section of the park. "As a resident told me, it's the place where you can set yourself on a granite cliff, gaze out to sea, and all your questions will be answered," she says. Or, hike up to Great Head, a 1.4 mile loop through forests and over cliffs. It's a not-too-tough hike but you won't meet many people en route. "Even if you do, there are plenty of nooks and crannies on the ledgy summit where you can hide," Hilary says.

Schoodic Peninsula is the only part of the park that is on the mainland. "Begin at the point—watching waves crash on the pink granite slabs is mesmerizing," says Hilary. "Then hike up Schoodic Head and watch for eagles and osprey. Heaven!"

And then there are the islands, scattered along the coast like crumbs off a broken cookie. Monhegan Island has been an artists' colony since the 19th century. Robert Henri, George Bellows, Rockwell Kent, Edward Hopper (not yet famous when he summered on the island in 1916), and the Wyeths (see Chapter 57) and hundreds of other artists, famous and obscure, have painted the scenery of Monhegan.

Monhegan is still a magnet for artists, many of whom open their studios for visitors. You can pick up a schedule of studio openings near the dock. While you're there, pick up a hiking map too.

The Monhegan Museum is in the keeper's house and out-buildings of a still-working (but now automated) lighthouse. It includes exhibits on history, nature, and art. ("Cool fact about the art museum," Hilary reports. "It only shows the works of deceased artists because there are so many artists on the island. It would be a social/political nightmare otherwise.")

Monhegan is only 1.7 miles long and not quite half a mile wide, but they still managed to carve out 17 miles of hiking trails. And the island is on the Atlantic Flyway migratory path, so bird-ers love it. You could see more than a 100 species on a long weekend in season. Monhegan may be reached via ferries from Boothbay Harbor, New Harbor, and Port Clyde. (And, by the way, these are also good places to get on a puffin tour and see colonies of those fine little fellows.)

From up and down the craggy, peril-ous coastline, lighthouses cast protective beams. You could make a vacation of view-ing all 60 lighthouses, perhaps starting with the Portland Head Light, a little north of Portland. It was America's first light-house, commissioned by President George Washington and built in 1787. If you're truly passionate, Maine's annual Open Lighthouse Day is in September, when dozens of real, functioning lighthouses are opened to the public.

www.visitmaine.com

4 Cape Cod, Massachusetts

If you're fond of sand dunes and salty air
Quaint little villages here and there
You're sure to fall in love with Old Cape Cod

So sang Patti Page in the popular 1957 song. And she's right, you know.

Cape Cod, a beckoning finger of land that reaches out into the Atlantic and wraps around Cape Cod Bay, exudes an aura of away-from-it-all-ness even in the middle of summer, when it's full of sun-baked tourists. Cape Cod has various personalities, from the festive gay mecca of Provincetown on its tip; to the laid-back vibe of Martha's Vineyard, a one-time hangout for James Taylor and still a favored getaway of his former wife, Carly Simon; to the upscale ever-so-everness of Nantucket, and the raw glory and great, rolling dunes of Cape Cod National Seashore.

Cape Cod inspires poetry from its devotees.

"I love how the trees gradually turn craggy as you head down Route 6A, like Van Gogh's apple tree drawings," says Jill Goodman, a painter. "The crooked little streets are on a human-size level and have an intimacy about them. Then there's the solitude of the dunes, which I can't get enough of. Oh, and the gorgeous patches of color everywhere, as nearly everyone has a garden or window box. The Cape is where I want to retire. I'd live there now if I could."

"I love the light and the air and walking barefoot in the surf and falling asleep on a sand dune," says Debby Kaspari, also an artist. "And steamed clams," she added.

The Pilgrims first landed on what is now Provincetown before heading across the bay to settle Plymouth. In 1848, trains started running from Boston to Sandwich, and by 1873, they were running all the way to Provincetown, establishing the Cape as one of the nation's first summer resorts. President Kennedy summered here, but he was not the first U.S. president to do so; a few decades earlier, President Grover Cleveland had a summer home in Bourne. More recently, presidents Bill Clinton and Barack Obama (and families) have vacationed on Martha's Vineyard.

Explore Cape Cod's great outdoors on the Shining Sea Bikeway or the Cape Cod Rail Trail. Take a sunrise or sunset tour of its windswept dunes. Hike nature trails at the Cornelia Carey Sanctuary (The Knob), named for the woman who donated the land for protection. Meet local fauna at the Wellfleet Bay Wildlife Sanctuary and the Monomoy National Wildlife Refuge. Explore the Great Salt Marsh in Barnstable by kayak. Visit the Nauset and Highland lighthouses. The lighthouse grounds are open all year, and you can visit the Nauset tower during periodic open houses May through October; guided tours of the Highland are offered daily in season.

The Old King's Highway (Route 6A that Jill mentioned) is a must-do meander through the Cape's sweet historic villages. Frequent stops for exploring and shopping are required.

And, of course, there are beaches every which way. On the Atlantic Ocean side, the Cape Cod National Seashore is more than 40,000 acres of pristine nature—40 miles of coastline, marshes, ponds, and uplands for swimming, biking, hiking, or contemplating. Here the surf is grand and pounding, and the water is *brrracing.*

Look for the collection of interesting shacks perched on the dunes and built from the '20s to the '50s. Exuding history but perpetually threatened with demolition (many have been), they recall the Cape's freewheeling days, when artists, writers, and other iconoclasts used the remote getaways to escape and create. And party. Today you can sample the life with an overnight stay offered through various residency programs.

The water lapping the beaches on Cape Cod Bay is less tempestuous and therefore more kiddy-friendly, and warmer, though still chilly, averaging in the 60s and 70s in summertime. Water on the Nantucket side is warmest because of the Gulf Stream.

People who love the Cape all have their favorite beaches, or favorite beaches for various activities. The only way to find the right beach for your style is to research and sample, which is hardly a hardship (except parking, which can be challenging).

Cape Cod is a tourist magnet, and its beaches and quaint towns can be busy and crowded in high season. Yet somehow, the magic of the Cape manages to transcend the throngs.

www.capecodtravelguide.com

PLACES TO LEARN MORE

The Big House: A Century in the Life of an American Summer Home by George Howe Colt is a moving memoir about the declining WASP lifestyle and the evolution of a summer resort, told through the story of a big, old house on the Cape.

5 Tallgrass Prairie National Preserve, Flint Hills, Kansas

I AM IN LOVE WITH THE great American prairie.

I love its grand vistas and its wildflowers and butterflies. I love the changing shadows and colors of the grasses in shifting light and passing seasons. I love the green, earthy fragrance and birdsong. I particularly love the prairie at twilight, when the sinking sun turns the scene impressionist.

The prairie reminds me of the desert. It appears bland and monochromatic, still and lifeless at first glance. But when you slow down and really look, you see it's full of color and variety and life.

Only a sliver of virgin native prairie remains in North America, and few people give it much thought. Lawns and ranchland seem reasonable facsimiles. Prairie plants might strike us as weeds. Even for those of us who came of age in the 1960s and 1970s, when the modern conservation movement began, the prairie is sort of a deep cut—not as flashy as the ocean nor as darkly seductive as the forest primeval. Like the rain forest, it cleans our air, but it is the most endangered ecosystem on the continent.

But we're coming around, and passionate grassroots groups (in an almost literal sense) between the Appalachian and the Rocky Mountains are snatching up remaining fragments and protecting them.

In 1996, the National Park Service joined the effort, establishing the Tallgrass Prairie National Preserve in the Flint Hills of Kansas. One of the nation's newest national preserves, it protects almost 11,000 acres of tallgrass prairie.

I have visited the preserve in late spring and late autumn. I've seen it under the baking sun, I've sprawled on the ground as twilight brought out the deer and coyote howls before melting into a long, Technicolor sunset.

Free bus tours are offered from the end of April through the end of October. My tour was led by dry-witted park guide Jeff Rundell, who explained the prairie as we bounced along dirt roads in a bus painted with prairie scenery.

The grasses were knee-high at best in June. In autumn, in a good year with lots of rain, grasses on the rich bottomland can grow to eight feet high. Most of the preserve is upland prairie, where the soil is thin, and grasses grow merely to chest high. This thin, unhelpful soil, with limestone just inches below its surface, helped preserve the prairie by chasing off farmers who tried to settle here—though many pioneers during the Westward expansion didn't bother.

"Kansas was considered a wasteland, just something you had to get through to get to the good stuff," Jeff said.

Over time, farmers gave up and ranchers moved in, and the bison that originally grazed the prairie gave way to cattle. About 5,000 head of cattle still graze here. So do bison; the park started a herd in 2009 with 13 Plains bison.

The prairie also hosts about 140 species of birds. Listen for the piping warble of the meadowlark—both Eastern and Western. Barn swallows fly hieroglyphics around the old stone ranch headquarters on the property. And about 500 species of plants grow here. Purple was abundant during my spring visit, in the clusters of ironweed blossoms and spiky pom-poms of wavyleaf thistle. Bergamot (or bee balm) blooms coral-red. Grasses—too numerous to name—provide an undulating green-and-gold backdrop. The lone trees scattered among the grasses mark natural springs; there are hundreds on the preserve, thousands in the Flint Hills.

The prairie is lovely and varied and important and complex, and I am not alone among its passionate fans.

"If you go past it at 70 miles an hour, it's just another pasture," Jeff said. "But get out and take a look. I have actually stopped the bus for a dung beetle."

www.nps.gov/tapr/index.htm

6 *Grand Canyon*

TO CELEBRATE HER 60TH BIRTHDAY, MY mother's oldest friend fulfilled a lifelong dream and rafted the Colorado River in the Grand Canyon. Naomi is gone now, but that image and spunky decision have been inspiring to me. Perhaps I'll follow her lead for my 60th (which doesn't seem nearly as old as it used to).

Though I have visited the Grand Canyon several times, I've never seen it from the bottom looking up, only the top looking down. This is a big hole (no pun intended) in my American education. But at least I've seen it, and from both the South Rim and the North Rim.

I'm always a little bit shocked to meet Americans who have never seen the Grand Canyon. If you are among them, then I insist you put this high on your life list. Really. No matter what you imagine it's like, you are wrong. It's more than that.

The Grand Canyon is a National Park and a UNESCO World Heritage Site. It encompasses 1,218,375 acres. Go ahead, imagine that. Can't be done. It's 6,000 feet deep at its deepest point, averages 4,000 feet deep throughout its 217 miles, and is 15 miles wide at its widest point. It is a record of 3 of our 4 geological eras and contains 5 of North America's 7 life zones and 3 of the 4 desert types.

Imagine that.

No one can. You have to see it.

If the best you can do is take a look from the South Rim—and that's a mighty busy place in summertime—then so be it. The North Rim, which receives only 10 percent of the park's visitors, is considered by many people (myself included) to be the more beautiful. Though the rims are only about 10 miles apart as the California condor flies (the largest land bird in North America and highly endangered, is being reintroduced at the Grand Canyon), it's a five-hour drive between them, because you have to circumnavigate the canyon. But if you're ever in the neighborhood of the North Rim (say, during that visit to Best Friends Animal Sanctuary, Chapter 82), be sure to take a peek. It is, by the way, open only mid-May through mid-October; the South Rim is open all year.

While you're at the South Rim, a night at Bright Angel Lodge can be your tribute to a groundbreaking woman. This National Historic Landmark was designed by architect Mary Jane Colter. Colter was chief architect and designer at the Fred Harvey Company, which built the famous Harvey Hotels along the then-new interstate railways. In her 40 years with the company, Colter designed a number of national park buildings, including all the Grand Canyon buildings. (She also designed La Fonda, on the plaza in Santa Fe, see Chapter 16.) Her style of Native American motifs and carefully executed rough edges came to be known as National Park Service Rustic. Colter, who died in 1958 at the age of 88, was not listed as architect on many of her buildings and didn't receive the recognition during her lifetime that her male peers, such as Frank Lloyd Wright, did.

Even if you don't stay at Bright Angel Lodge, you will check in here if you sign up for a Grand Canyon Mule Ride. You can take either a two-and-a-half-hour ride to the Abyss Overlook, or a one- or two-night overnight to Phantom Ranch. A caveat:

Mules are sure-footed, but traveling a narrow canyon trail may still be just a wee bit terrifying for some people.

If you're not a hiker, you can join one of the short interpretive ranger-led programs, some of which include walks along the rim; the park website also includes a downloadable interpretive podcast. Hikers (or aspiring hikers) can look into the nonprofit Grand Canyon Field Institute, which offers a schedule of multi-day hiking and camping experiences, including some for women only. Of course, you can always hike independently—although, as the NPS points out on the website, "The difference between a great adventure in Grand Canyon and a trip to the hospital (or worse) is up to YOU," and (in red), "There are no easy trails in and out of the Grand Canyon!" Know what you're doing, and you can have a grand adventure; NPS has podcasts to help you prepare and stay safe. (The website GORP.com is also a good place to check for hiking information.)

My friend Rebecca Brasher, an artist, hiked with friends down to the waterfalls and remote Indian village of Havasupai for five days of camping, and highly recommends that. And, she says, they hiked in during a full moon. "If at all possible, that's the best way to do it," she says.

www.nps.gov/grca

7 Storm Watching on the Oregon Coast

MOTHER NATURE HAS BEEN FLEXING HER muscles all over the country in the past decade, but if you're still not 100-percent convinced of her power, then take a trip to Oregon during winter storm season, roughly December to April, give or take.

Even on calm days, the Pacific is treacherous: signs along coastal trails warn of "sneaker waves"—sudden large waves that  can sweep people away. And on stormy days, the waves don't sneak; they crash and churn and sometimes overwhelm those who underestimate their power. People get washed away all the time.

With respect for the havoc they can wreak, I find big storms thrilling. Mother Nature's libido, I call them. A good storm is at once humbling and exhilarating. There's no stopping it; you can only ride it out. It reminds me how small we really are in this huge universe. As a metaphor for life, a passing storm may not be soothing, but it is apt.

Storm watching has become a popular winter pastime in Oregon. If you're the kind who prefers to stay dry and cozy, you can check into a hotel on the coast with windows on the water and watch from there. Or, as long as you're smart about it, you can suit up and head out to feel the storm's power for yourself.

Even when there's no stormy weather, you can get an idea of nature's power at the South Jetty in Port Stevens, a military installation that dates back to the Civil War and is now a 3,700-acre state-run park. The Columbia River and the Pacific Ocean meet here with a crash. More than 2,000 vessels have met their end here, earning the intersection the name "Graveyard of the Pacific." Tempestuous waters batter the jetty violently, and even on the clear day my husband and I visited, I was fearful for a man who had climbed atop the massive wood structure.

If you're lucky, your storm-watching trip will include a real storm. After several misty but calm days on the coast waiting for some weather, my husband and I were finally rewarded with a storm. A big one. About a seven on a ten-point scale, a local told me later.

And so we put on our rain gear and drove up a lookout at Ecola State Park, near the town of Cannon Beach. After we pulled into a parking space, I leapt out of the car, and the wind nearly blew me off my feet.

I abandoned my plan to walk out and look at the ocean meeting the rocks below. That would have been too dangerous, and I couldn't have made it anyway. As I stepped a couple of feet from the car, a sudden gust had me lunging for the door handle to steady myself. Across the parking lot, a man clutched the luggage rack on top of his car, clearly as exhilarated as I. (Our respective spouses stayed inside the cars, shaking their heads.) When another gust of wind almost took me, I jumped back into the car. I have video my husband shot of that moment. I'm wet and unkempt, and I have an enormous, giddy grin plastered on my face.

Mother Nature totally kicks butt.

www.traveloregon.com

8 Pacific Coast Highway, California

THE FIRST TIME I DROVE THE Pacific Coast Highway was also the first time I'd seen the West Coast. I was 19 years old and with a couple of friends had driven all the way from New York City. Now, at the end of our journey, skirting the craggy western edge of the nation, I had a strong sense of the rest of the country stretched out to my right—desert, mountains, cornfields, and coast—and the rest of the world somewhere out there, beyond the crashing waves and the mysterious deep of the Pacific Ocean.

From sea to shining sea. I got it.

Strictly speaking, the PCH proper is limited to the Central Coast of California, from Monterey to Morro Bay, about half-way between Los Angeles and San Francisco. The rest of the road is just plain old Route 1. But what's in a name? It's all gorgeous, and you could plan an entire vacation around the drive, starting in San Diego and ending in San Francisco (or beyond—the coasts of Oregon and Washington are no less spectacular).

And oh, the things you'll see and do! The first part of your drive, going south to north, is more fun than spectacle and can be slow going because of California's infamous traffic. But take a deep breath and enjoy. Check out the Queen Mary in San Diego; watch the surfers (or surf yourself, Chapter 72) at Huntington Beach in glamorous Orange County—the OC in TV lingo. While the road itself doesn't hug the coast through the

Los Angeles area (see Chapter 17), you should factor in time to check out the kooky scene at Venice Beach and have some fun at the Santa Monica Pier.

In Malibu (the name alone conjures Hollywood glamour, doesn't it?) you can stop at Malibu Lagoon State Beach, and watch more surfers tackle the waves at Malibu Pier. From here, the views start getting seriously spectacular and the driving seriously scary. If you're traveling with a companion, you might want to take turns driving because with the hairpin turns and the narrow road wedged between cliffs and a sheer drop to the ocean below, the driver will have to keep eyes fixed firmly on the road, missing the must-see scenery.

Detour to visit San Simeon, aka Hearst Castle (see Chapter 98). Slow down to soak in Big Sur, perhaps with a hike at one of the state parks. And don't miss the chance for a meal or at least a glass of wine at Nepenthe, a longtime (since 1949) institution perched high above the Pacific. Time your Nepenthe visit for sunset if you possibly can.

Tony Carmel-by-the-Sea considers itself an artists' colony, albeit for very wealthy artists (which might be an oxymoron). The pretty town is a celebrity magnet; Clint Eastwood was mayor of Carmel in the 1980s. Still, Carmel clings fiercely to its version of old-timeyness. To this day, residents of Carmel must go to the post office to pick up their mail because there is no house-to-house delivery. There also are no addresses, parking meters, streetlights, or sidewalks except in the downtown area. But there is shopping. Always shopping. And galleries.

Just to the north, Monterey's big draw is the marvelous Monterey Bay Aquarium. Stop in and visit the giant Pacific octopuses, invertebrates so intelligent the aquarium has an enrichment program for them. Who knew?

Now you're coming to San Francisco, where you can end the adventure or keep going—Redwood National Park lies beyond, yet another spectacle, just before you reach Oregon, and yet more magnificent coastline (see Chapter 7). Sometimes stopping is the hardest part.

www.visitcalifornia.com

9 *Hawai'i Volcanoes National Park, Hawai'i*

MY VISIT TO HAWAI'I VOLCANOES NATIONAL Park was aborted by my husband's unexpected altitude sickness. Someday I hope to return and see it, but until then, I will rely on the word of an expert to tell us about its greatness.

"Hawai'i is made of volcanoes!" says travel writer, ukulele player, and aficionado of Hawai'i, Pam Mandel. "There's nowhere on the islands to get a better feeling of the role geology played—plays, rather, the islands are still growing—in the creation of this archipelago in the middle of the Pacific.

"Visiting HVNP puts your feet literally in an active landscape where the shape of the islands are being changed while you stand there. In some places, you can feel the warmth of the earth beneath your feet. In others, you can see the steam and gasses escaping from inside the planet. Yellowstone (see Chapter 2) is the only other place I've been where you so completely feel that the earth is a living, breathing being."

So that's one reason to visit Hawai'i Volcanoes National Park. The woman-centric reason is Pele, the passionate, dangerous Hawai'ian goddess of volcanoes, fire, lightning, and wind. (More goddesses in Chapter 77.) Legend has it she lives in Halema'uma'u Crater in the caldera of Kilauea, a volcano that has been erupting since 1983—the longest eruption in recorded

history. Kilauea has destroyed almost 200 structures, including
a park visitors center. Or was that Pele?

But despite her fire and brimstone, Pele can touch a visitor's
heart.

"Many years back, before the vent was as active as it is today, I
watched hula dancers in bright orange pareos dance to the rising
steam of the crater," Pam recalls. "I thought, 'Wow, Pele is real
for them!' and somehow, seeing those dancers made Pele more
real to me.

"I didn't think much more about it, but then, I was in a junk
store in Washington state, and I found a little carved *menehune*—
little person—made of lava rock, probably a 1960s souvenir. 'She
doesn't belong here,' I thought. 'She is one of Pele's children.' I
bought her, and I brought her back to Hawai'i where I gave her
to a Hawai'ian friend to return to the land where she belongs."

The park has lots of overlooks, but wind and volcanic activity
will determine where you can go to do your overlooking. Pam
likes the Jagger Museum where the observation deck is. "It looks
out over a vast crater, and I'm a sucker for dated hands-on science exhibits," she says.

She also recommends the Thurston Lava Tube. "To get
there, you walk through a dripping green rainforest choked
with all kinds of plants, and the air is full of bird song. Visiting
there and any of the open places on the upper flanks of the volcano totally brings home the range of ecosystems in the park,
not to mention on the islands. If you've got the time, take a
ranger-guided hike. The rangers are really well-informed,
and they help you gain a deeper understanding of the park.
And the art center showcases some of the best in island arts
I've seen anywhere on all five islands. It's a great place to buy

a souvenir if you're looking for something really of Hawai'i to bring back home."

And better to buy a souvenir than to just pick one up.

"I've heard that the park receives hundreds of lava rocks mailed back to them every year from around the world from people who take them as souvenirs," says Pam. "I was as surprised as anyone to find myself affected enough by being in Pele's presence that I would rescue a little stone souvenir and carry it around with me for months before finding exactly the right place to return it."

Apparently Pele works in ways mysterious.

www.nps.gov/havo

10 *Seward Highway, Alaska*

JENNA SCHNUER, WHO IS PASSIONATE ABOUT road tripping and Alaska (among many other things) calls the drive from Anchorage to Seward "one of the greatest drives I've ever taken."

This 127-mile stretch of road has been named a USDA Forest Service Scenic Byway, an Alaska Scenic Byway, and an All-American Road, which is a big thumbs-up from the feds. It is spectacularly beautiful even by Alaska's very high standard of spectacle and beauty. It has no billboards and just a few towns and (take note) gas stations. It's the most dangerous road in the state, winding between cliffs and steep drops to the cold, cold Pacific, and it attracts a dangerous combination of impatient speeders and poky RVs.

Worth it, Jenna says.

 Worth it for views of snow-covered mountains, crystalline blue lakes, wetlands and waterfalls, cliffs and fjords. Worth it, too, to spot eagles and whales, moose, Dall sheep, and seals. Worth it for the bird watching and fishing, the wildflowers and glaciers. The road climbs from sea level up 1,000 feet and back down again.

You could drive the highway in a few hours but why would you? The better plan is to take your time so you can stop frequently for view appreciation, to peer into the waters of

Turnagain Arm looking for the white glow of beluga whales, to take photos that probably won't do real justice to the magnificence before you and around you.

www.dot.state.ak.us/stwdplng/scenic/byways-seward.shtml#high

11
Washington D.C.

THE FIRST BEST PIECE OF ADVICE I can give you about visiting our nation's capital is to bring comfortable shoes. More than one pair. The second best piece of advice is to take any and every opportunity to sit down. And I'm not just saying this because I'm old. The city was mall-to-mall class trips when I was there last, and I heard teenagers moaning about their aching feet.

The sites and sights of Washington D.C. are on a grand scale, and there is so much. So very much. So, so, so much. My feet start hurting just planning my last trip.

Of course, Washington D.C. is very much a no-brainer as a must-go. The seat of our government, it throbs with power. It's a thrilling place, a hotbed of icons, from the Capitol dome to Archie Bunker's chair.

Everything is wonderful. The Lincoln Memorial—stately and awe-inspiring, although you'll have to work to get your awe on if you visit when it's thronged with tourists. Try stopping by late at night, when all the class trips have gone off to their hotels and the monument is lighted so that Lincoln glows behind the building's massive columns.

The Supreme Court building is as imposing and important as it should be; viewing it in the distance from the terrace of the Newseum gave me chills. I even got a geeky thrill seeing the

National Archive, although only from the outside. The line to get in was daunting. Next time.

And when a caravan of motorcycle cops, sirens blaring, and gleaming black SUVs speed past the National Mall, all tourist activity pauses to watch. What famous person was rushing where? (I'm told that if it's the president, you'll always see an ambulance in the caravan. Kind of grim, but I get it.)

And it's fascinating that when you visit a place with your focus set on finding women's stories, how many you'll find. Emancipation Hall, the cavernous, clamorous visitor center for the Capitol, is lined with statues, many of them women. Helen Keller I know, and Sarah Winnemucca, but who was Maria Sanford, whose base identified her only as the "Best Known and Best Loved Woman in Minnesota"? She was, Google explained to me later, a professor and teacher circa 1880s. Do even Minnesotans know that?

By far the highlight of a tour of the Capitol is getting to see the elaborate interior of the building's great dome, but here's a nifty tidbit I learned: the newest statue in the hall of statues is Rosa Parks, who stands (well, sits, actually) where Robert E. Lee's statue once stood. Sweet irony. Oh, also, the statue of Abraham Lincoln that stands in the Rotunda was sculpted by Vinnie Ream, who was just 18 years old at the time and was the first woman to receive a commission for a sculpture from Congress. (For more about women artists you've never heard of, see Chapter 55.)

You have to pick and choose what you'll see here, and you'll have to miss far, far more than you see. It can't be helped. The National Portrait Gallery, or the National Gallery of Art? Either one could fill a full day or more. The Smithsonian Museum of

American History or of Natural History? The Smithsonian National Air and Space Museum or the Newseum? Only you can make these decisions; I can only provide women-centric suggestions.

To my mind, the most affecting memorial on the National Mall—possibly anywhere—is the Vietnam Veterans Memorial, designed by Maya Lin, who was a mere 21 years old at the time, an architecture student who entered a contest. The wall lists the names of more than 58,000 servicemen and 8 women who died or went missing in the Vietnam War. Alongside each name is a little diamond or a little X; the X means that the individual is still missing. (An interesting note I learned on a park ranger-led tour of the monuments: the Tomb of the Unknown Soldier at Arlington cemetery, which should contain remains of soldiers from every war, contains no one from the Vietnam War because the remains that were interred there were ultimately identified and brought home by the family.) Poor Maya Lin was put through terrible trials when her design was selected. People found it too stark, too abstract, and thought it inappropriate that the memorial should be designed by a woman of Asian descent. (Lin was born in Ohio, her parents were Chinese immigrants.) To mollify the objectors, a more traditional statue of soldiers was placed nearby, but nobody predicted the emotional healing Lin's design would provide veterans and their families. Though it happens less frequently than it once did, you may still find flowers, flags, and photos placed by the wall in memory of the young men who never came home.

One former Vietnam nurse, interviewed in the affecting documentary *Vietnam Nurses*, said, "I have never cried, but I burst into tears at the Vietnam wall. If it weren't for us, the wall would be much wider and much higher."

Many women served and died in the Vietnam War, but it was a long time before they got their due. (It was a long time before any of the women who served throughout history were acknowledged, see Chapter 46.) In 1993, a statue by Glenna Goodacre honoring the women who served in Vietnam was dedicated. The sculpture depicts one nurse holding a fallen soldier, her hand pressed to his heart to staunch the bleeding, and another looking to the sky for helicopters that were harbingers of more horror, work, hope, and grief.

I went to the Newseum because I have a background in newspapers. It's a massive media assault—there's a reason tickets are good for two days. Just viewing and reading the stories behind Pulitzer-winning photos could take hours. Women are all over the museum, from Nellie Bly to Wonkette Anna Marie Cox—a list of exhibits and artifacts significant to women is included in the museum's visitors guide. One small moment that struck me was in a gripping film of interviews with reporters who covered the 9/11 bombing. WNYC radio reporters Beth Fertig and Marianne McCune found each other amidst the chaos and, in their interviews, commented how they couldn't have gotten through it all without each other. This struck me as a touching moment of sisterhood and tend-and-befriend, often considered the womanly version of fight-or flight.

At the Smithsonian Museum of American History, which also has a brochure about artifacts related to women, you can dish with other women over the collection of First Ladies' gowns. "What was she thinking?" said one woman, viewing Rosalyn Carter's brocade housecoat. More to her liking was Pat Nixon's trim yellow gown and sparkly bolero jacket. I was particularly partial to Eleanor Roosevelt's simple dusky blue column. (For more first ladies, see Chapter 43.) Helen Taft was the first First

Lady to donate her inaugural gown to the museum. She also was the first First Lady to ride with her husband in his inaugural parade, and she was instrumental in bringing Japanese cherry trees to Washington, starting a beloved spring tradition (and, I'm told, annual mob scene). Quite a woman, that Helen.

Here, too, you can view the enormous flag about which the Star-Spangled Banner was written. It was made by Mary Pickersgill, who was paid $405.90, which was more than most Baltimoreans earned in a year in 1813. And/or take a look at Bette Davis's costumes from *Dark Victory* and *Now Voyager*.

Washington D.C. has a lifetime of things to see—important, moving, fascinating, educational, awe-inspiring, fun, distressing, stirring. You name it, you'll feel it. And then, you can grab a bench on the Mall and watch the people go by and rest your aching feet.

᠔

PLACES TO LEARN MORE

Maya Lin: A Strong Clear Vision traces the artist's career and won an Academy award for best documentary.

Otherwise, there is a lifetime's worth of movies that are in or about Washington D.C.: *Mr. Smith Goes To Washington*, *All the President's Men*, *Wag the Dog*, *Thank You for Not Smoking*, *The American President*, *Primary Colors* and many many more. You're on your own there.

12 New York City

O.K., I'M BIASED BECAUSE I GREW up in New York City, and even though I moved away decades ago, I will consider myself a New Yorker until my last breath.

I don't think anybody should have to be persuaded to visit New York City. It too is a no-brainer, one of those important, exciting places. It's also the creative pulse of the nation. (Well, Los Angeles too, but La La Land is movies and TV, whereas NYC is everything else.) New York has a whole lot of something for everyone and then some. But since I'm talking to women here, let's talk about some womanly things in this great, gray, bustling, energetic, complicated, crazy, expensive city.

Did you know that women in the U.S. attend theater more than men do? It's true, according to research by the National Endowment for the Arts. Yay us, keeping theater alive. And although there's all sorts of wonderful theater happening all over the country, New York City is the magnet, the Mecca, the ambition of every aspiring stage actor. So, go. See a show.

If you have a particular show in mind, buy your tickets ahead of time to avoid disappointment. If you aren't picky, grab a spot in line at one of the TKTS discount tickets booths at Times Square, South Street Seaport, or downtown Brooklyn (if you happen to venture that far from the epicenter of Manhattan, and no reason not to, Brooklyn is cool). There can be long lines for tickets at Duffy Square especially, so get there early for the greatest selection. Don't worry: New York is never boring and just waiting in line can be fun. And don't pooh-pooh Off-Broadway or Off-Off-Broadway plays. With the cost of staging Broadway shows these days, producers tend to be cautious and conservative about what they produce, so a lot of the real innovation occurs off the Great White Way; tickets to Off and Off-Off shows also are available at the half-price booths and are usually more affordable in general.

(While you're in the theater district, look for slender beauties in black hurrying in and out of 4 Times Square, home of the offices of *Vogue, Glamour, Architectural Digest, House & Garden*, and other Condé Nast publications.)

Now, museums. The Metropolitan Museum of Art is a NYC must-see, but the Impressionist galleries have a particular connection to a particular couple of women: Suffragette Lousine Elder Havemeyer and her husband collected Impressionist works under the guidance of painter Mary Cassatt (Havemeyer called Cassatt "my inspiration and my guide"), and when Louisine died in 1929, she left the collection to the Met. (For more on the Met, see Chapter 87.)

Now, the other story here is that according to feminist activist group the Guerrilla Girls, the best way for women to hang in the Met is to pose naked. At last count, in 2004, less than 3 percent of the artists in the Met's modern art galleries were by women, but 80 percent of the nudes were female.

So in some ways, the Met isn't a modern-thinking institution and never has been. In 1928, the museum said "no thanks" to the offer of a collection of modern art amassed over 25 years by socialite and sculptor Gertrude Vanderbilt Whitney. Whitney was a champion of living American artists, and she both collected and provided exhibition space for them. In 1931, after the Met turned its nose up, Whitney opened the first iteration of today's Whitney Museum of American Art, with her friend Juliana Force as director. While Whitney wrote the checks, Force "moved poker-backed and sharp-eyed among American artists, watching for someone who might make another 'Whitney' first," according to a 1949 article in *TIME* magazine. These days, the Whitney Biennial is the institution's signature event, and it tends to rouse all sorts of interesting squabbles and indignation among critics.

The Museum of the City of New York is not on many tourists' radars, but it's been a favorite of mine since I was a girl. Collections include homely historic artifacts and items of domestic life in the city—furniture, teapots, textiles, clothing, toys. While you're there, on the very Upper East Side, cross Fifth Avenue into the Conservatory Garden in Central Park, at 105th Street, and look for the Frances Hodgson Burnett Memorial Fountain, which depicts Mary and Dickon, characters from the Victorian author's most famous book, *The Secret Garden*.

On the subject (sculpture and Central Park), the Angel of the Waters atop the park's famous Bethesda Fountain is by American sculptor Emma Stebbins, a feminist lesbian long before that kind of thing was cool. The sister of the president of the Board of the Commissioners of Central Park, she also was the first woman to receive a commission for a sculpture in New York City.

While Lady Liberty is the city's most famous female sculpture (see Chapter 20), amazingly, the city's only public sculpture of a real American woman is Gertrude Stein, who sits (in

a greatly reduced state—just 33 inches high) in Bryant Park,
behind the main public library on Fifth Avenue and 42nd St.
The park is an inviting oasis of chairs and tables and trees and
people and things.

Fashion and New York City have long been wed, although
the garment district, in the neighborhood surrounding the
original, flagship Macy's on 34th Street and in the shadows of
the Empire State Building, is not what it once was as the heart of
the "rag trade." In those days, pre-1980s, when gentrification
hit the city, you were at risk of being plowed down by bellowing
men pushing racks of clothing through the streets. Now, with
skyrocketing rents and new zoning, manufacturing has moved
out; you'll no longer find fabric and trim stores on every side
street. Still, Macy's is worth a visit, and then you can continue
your stroll through retail history along Fifth Avenue from 34th
Street to 57th, stopping into the original Lord & Taylor, which
was given landmark status in 2007; Henri Bendel; Tiffany and
Company (see Chapter 86); and Bergdorf Goodman. (A fan of
Sex in the City or just expensive shoes? Take a quick detour to the
Manolo Blahnik store, which is on 54th Street between Fifth and
Sixth Avenues.)

Although Soho has pretty much jumped the shark—lost all its
edge years ago—it can be fun shopping for cheap trendy junk.
The Upper West Side, which used to be artsy but now is upscale,
has lots of interesting boutiques.

I have to admit, though, I don't do much of any of this when
I visit New York City. My favorite thing to do in New York is
just goof around. I adore the street theater of New York and can
spend hours just wandering and looking. I always spend some time
in Central Park; on Sundays in particular it's a carnival of New
Yorkers at play. I love Riverside Park, where I played as a child.

I walk and walk and walk. I tool around on the subway. (Yes, you must. It's a quintessential New York experience.) I cram in with the crowds at Katz's Delicatessen on the Lower East Side (read about one of Katz's celebrity turns in Chapter 85) for a pastrami sandwich or maybe corned beef. I eat pizza and falafel. I buy stuff from street vendors.

But, you know. That's my New York. New York is different things to different people. You'll find your own.

www.nycgo.com

PLACES TO LEARN MORE

In the book *New York Theater Walks*, former Daily News theater critic Howard Kissel walks you through the theater history, throughout the city.

Stuffed: Adventures of a Restaurant Family by Patricia Volk is just one woman's memoir about a New York restaurant family, but it captures beautifully a moment in time in New York.

Inside the Apple: A Streetwise History of New York City by Michelle and James Nevius manages to be enlightening even to New Yorkers and includes 14 walking tours.

13 *New Orleans, Louisiana*

ARTIST REBECCA BRASHER BISH LIVED IN New Orleans for a little more than two years. She moved to Tucson more than fifteen years ago, but still can't bear to even visit New Orleans because she misses it so keenly. "I miss the aromas and odors of our old uptown neighborhood," she told me. "Creole and Cajun seasonings wafting through the air, mixing with the odor of the 'cheese barges'—which are garbage barges hauling stuff down the Mississippi. P.J.'s Coffee House roasting dark French roast two blocks away, that dank loamy smell of rotting wood emanating from the abandoned Victorian, wet asphalt after a good rain—almost daily, it seemed....Oh, I've just gotten started and already my heart hurts."

That's what it means to miss New Orleans.

Karen Tate, who grew up in New Orleans and has written a guidebook to goddess sites, considers the Vieux Carre among them (see Chapter 77) for its accepting spirit and inclusiveness (among other things). And indeed, New Orleans does seem more feminine than masculine, with its torpid climate, love for the culinary arts, extravagant wrought-iron, lush gardens, and that whole *laissez les bons temps rouler*. There's nothing Type A about New Orleans. Everything's O.K., baby. Enjoy. (Well, O.K., Katrina wasn't O.K.. Not one little bit. But the French Quarter was unaffected, and the storm did little to quell tourists' passion for the city.)

New Orleans is pretty much one long festival. There are small festivals almost all the time, and then there are a few killer fests. If you like raucous crowds, you're a Mardi Gras girl. This storm before the calm—a last blowout before the deprivation of Lent—tracks back to Europe, but was brought to Louisiana by French settlers. By the mid-1800s, the traditions of public revelry that continue today started emerging.

Although the Mardi Gras parade was traditionally the domain of men, you know that couldn't last. The Krewe of Iris, founded in 1917, is the oldest of the all-female krewes, and it's a traditionalist bunch in masks, white gloves, and gowns. The Krewe of Muses, founded in 2000, is decidedly untraditional. Among its annual floats is the bathing beauties float: a giant bubble bath filled with Muses. And each year, they choose a woman who has made a significant contribution to New Orleans, make her an honorary Muse, and put her on the fabulous fiber-optic shoe float.

Or, you might prefer to get your crowds at the New Orleans Jazz and Heritage Festival, aka Jazzfest. This 40-year-plus tradition has multiple stages and attracts hundreds of acts, most but not all from Louisiana, and ranging from small local Dixieland bands to big time stars like Bonnie Raitt and Bruce Springsteen, whose popularity helped buoy the fest in 2006, after Katrina nearly wiped it out along with the city.

I found my fest with the Tennessee Williams Literary Festival, which celebrated its 25th anniversary in 2011. This springtime fest is considerably more sedate (though in no way stuffy) than the others. It includes theater (plays by Williams and others), speakers, panels about writing and the publishing industry, a Stella bellowing contest, cocktails and bon mots in a shady courtyard, and more.

Of course, food is key to the NOLA experience. Hit the big players—Galatoire's, Emeril's, Broussard's, Arnaud's, etc., and/or check out some small favorites. I've enjoyed Mother's, Coop's, and the Coffee Pot. New Orleans Culinary History Tours offers walking and tasting tours of the city to help you understand all the influences that come to bear in classic New Orleans cooking.

The Southern Food and Beverage Museum offers interesting programs, though the museum exhibits on foods (rice, beans, corn, bananas) and specific dishes (King's Cake, chicken fried steak) are still developing. Housed in the same space, The Museum of the American Cocktail is a gorgeous collection of cocktail-abilia tracing the history of all things cocktaily.

You can visit the grave of Marie Laveau, who was the Queen of Voodoo in New Orleans in the mid-1830s. Voodoo grew from African traditions among slaves, and Laveau was a Quadroon whose blood was African, Indian, and Caucasian. A hairdresser by trade with access to some of the city's richest and most powerful women, she was admired for her devout Catholicism, which helped her gain both power and respect. Performing sexy, mysterious ceremonies, using lots of snakes, a splash of Catholicism, and some show biz, she removed curses, told fortunes, read minds, and helped establish New Orleans' deep Voodoo roots. Her grave, in St. Louis Cemetery #1 on Basin Street, is a popular stop for both spiritualists and tourists, and many believe that on June 23, St. John's Eve, her spirit rises. Blue candles burn continually in memory of Marie Laveau in the New Orleans Historic Voodoo Museum on Dumaine Street.

Another woman who has both given a female face to New Orleans and promoted its more mystical side, author Anne Rice offers a virtual tour of "Anne's New Orleans" on her website, www.annerice.com.

As long as you avoid the drunken stupidity of Bourbon Street, you may find that New Orleans is one of the most soulful places in the country.

❧

PLACES TO LEARN MORE

The Booklover's Guide to New Orleans is by Susan Larson, former book editor of the New Orleans Times-Picayune. *Why New Orleans Matters*, by Tom Piazza, is a rigorous defense of the city's culture, published post-Katrina. *Gumbo Tales: Finding My Place at the New Orleans Table*, by Sara Roahen, is one food writer's love affair with the city and its food. *A Confederacy of Dunces* by John Kennedy Toole is a novel that captures the city and its spirit. *A Streetcar Named Desire* by Tennessee Williams (book & movie). Of course. Duh. *Treme* is a post-Katrina HBO drama following struggling musicians and other locals in a historic African-American neighborhood.

14 Detroit, Michigan

FOR SOME REASON, I THOUGHT THE decay and ruin of Detroit was something you have to seek out. Silly assumption, considering that haunting photographs of Motor City's decline and blight have become so commonplace, they've come to be known as "ruins porn."

But I was unprepared for the ubiquity of ruins. They are so commonplace as to be confrontational. Shuttered and graffiti-covered businesses and industrial spaces. Weedy blocks, clinging to life as neighborhoods, studded with charred husks of burned houses. So many burned houses...the result of accidents, arson, downed power lines, absentee owners, and a city that can barely afford its fire department, much less tear down every burnt, abandoned home.

Apartment buildings are a patchwork of broken and boarded-up windows. Sofas and car bumpers, boxes and brush pile up on street corners, in empty lots. The massive Michigan Central Railroad Station is a spectacle, a grandiose and hulking Beaux Arts shell, designed by the same team that designed New York City's pampered and feted Grand Central Station. On my visit, the also opulent historic Wayne County Building had a "For sale/lease" sign in front of it.

I found it deeply moving.

I wrote about Detroit's decline for a blog a few years ago, and the response was large and heartfelt—mostly wistful emails from people who had left Detroit but yearned to return.

Detroit has a population of about 700,000, down from a peak of 1.8 million in the 1950s. It has some 70,000 abandoned buildings. The city's decline has been so steep and pervasive that in 2010, Mayor Dave Bing talked about relocating people from nearly abandoned neighborhoods and letting parts of the city revert to farmland, saving the city the cost of providing services like trash pickup and police to barely populated areas.

This sort of decline can't be hidden. Blight has become one of the city's trademarks. Actually, in 2012 a developer proposed turning part of downtown Detroit into "Zombieland"—a zombie theme park where people could pay to be chased through the ruins by flesh-eating hordes. (As of this writing, it was all just talk.)

And yet under that blight, Detroit has beautiful bones. Wide avenues are lined with once-grand homes. Downtown includes a collection of once-opulent Gilded Age skyscrapers (many in great peril) as well as Comerica Park, where the Detroit Tigers play. Opened in 2000, the ballpark is a dazzling funhouse of a structure, liberally decorated with enormous snarling tigers.

Detroit ain't dead yet, though. Midtown, nestled between downtown and New Center, is the young professional part of town, encompassing Wayne State University and the Detroit Institute of Arts. Here are the coffee shops, galleries, and boutiques. Residential Corktown, Detroit's oldest neighborhood, has retained many of its historic homes and is seeing signs of life, with new businesses opening in long-shuttered spaces. The city has been tearing down derelict structures and cleaning brush and trash in empty lots—which counts as positive progress in neighborhoods littered with despair. An empty lot is a vast improvement over a derelict building, and some are becoming community gardens. Organizations all over the city are coming up with plans for economic development and community rebirth. In 2012, the state took control of Detroit's economy to try and stop the downward spiral.

As it is, Detroit seems almost a reproach. Are we, Americans, going to stand by and let a once-great city crumble?

"How Detroit Became the World Capital of Staring at Abandoned Old Buildings," read a headline in *The New York Times Magazine*. Yes, well, Detroit might not be crazy about this, but they might as well make the best of it. You make do with what you have. Tourism can be a great force for good and if you go to Detroit just to look at decay (and stay in a hotel, and have a few meals), you contribute to the economy.

I took almost no photographs in Detroit. I saw no need or reason to add to the ever-growing stream of ruins porn. And I hope, deeply, that someday, all those haunting photos of despair will be just interesting documentation of what Detroit once was, before its future miraculous renaissance.

www.visitdetroit.com

※

PLACES TO LEARN MORE

Some of the best ruins porn is by French photographers Yves Marchand and Romaine Meffre, and you can see a sample here: www.marchandmeffre.com/detroit

8 Mile, Eminem's critically acclaimed film about a white hip-hop artist in an African-American-dominated genre, takes place in Detroit.

15 Chicago, Illinois

I MARRIED INTO CHICAGO.

My in-laws grew up there, a couple of Catholic school city kids in a close-knit neighborhood called Rogers Park, near Loyola University and blocks from Lake Michigan. Though they moved around in the early years of their marriage, by their 50s, they were back in Rogers Park, where they have lived happily again for 20 years and counting.

I probably wouldn't have given Chicago a second thought if not for that. I always thought of it (with typical New York provincialism) as a NYC wannabe. But over years of visits there, I've come to love Chicago on its own virtues. It's thoroughly urban but with an easygoing Midwestern character. It's a lively art city, music city, theater city, sports city. It's a melting pot. It's confident but not bombastic. In the summertime it's even an outdoors city, standing as it does on the shores of Lake Michigan.

Chicago is a city that matters. With the lake, the river, and then the railroads, Chicago developed as an important and prosperous trade center. And that's kind of where architecture comes in. You can't talk about Chicago without talking about architecture.

Chicago was nearly wiped out by the Great Fire of 1871, but by the 1880s, the city had bounced back economically, and it was becoming the powerhouse of the Midwest. Land values were skyrocketing, making building upward attractive.

49

In 1885, William Le Baron Jenney built the world's first sky-scraper in Chicago, the nine-story Home Insurance Building. (The building, while technologically innovative, was reportedly not so great looking. In 1931, in a shocking show of disrespect, it was demolished.) The burgeoning steel industry saw opportunity in this new type of structure, and a tradition of innovative, exciting architecture was born in Chicago.

 The Chicago Architecture Foundation has a huge menu of tours, and they train and educate their guides stringently. I'm partial to the river tour, since a boat ride is an awfully nice way to spend a summer afternoon. My mother-in-law, Jo Ann Battles, also recommends a walking tour. "You see marvelous old buildings that you wouldn't think to go into unless somebody is guiding you."

I get that. On our last visit, my husband and I wandered semi-cluelessly into the Chicago Cultural Center, in an old library, and were flabbergasted by the opulent marble staircase and extravagant Tiffany dome. (We also saw some very cool and unusual art.)

Out of curiosity, I made a point of stopping into the ornate former Carson Pirie Scott Building, which was designed by Frank Lloyd Wright's mentor, Louis Sullivan. The building has been polished to a fresh gleam and now houses, surprisingly, a two-story Target. It's a bit disorienting—the exterior is elaborate, the interior is...Target. But good for Target for giving the building love, and the building always has been a department store, so it's true to its roots.

Sullivan, Wright, Ludwig Mies van der Rohe, and lots of other name-brand architects are represented in Chicago, right up to the present. The beautiful new modern wing of the Art Institute of Chicago was designed by Renzo Piano, and Frank Gehry did his kooky thing for the bandshell in wonderful Millenium Park, a swell place to hang out in general; take a picture of yourself in the giant reflective bean.

Chicago also has a tradition of outdoor art; Picasso, Miro, Calder, and Dubuffet are among the artists represented on the city streets.

If you stay downtown, you can walk to a lot of what you'll want to see, including the Art Institute, the park, and Michigan Avenue between the river and Oak Street, which is known as the Magnificent Mile. Here is the Fifth Avenue, the Champs-Élysées of Chicago. The venerable Drake Hotel is here; for a fancy night out, the hotel's Cape Cod Room restaurant is a long tradition. "It's been there since we were kids," Jo Ann says. "Even longer." Look for Marilyn Monroe and Joe DiMaggio's initials carved in the bar.

The elaborately gothic Tribune Tower is kind of an albatross for a struggling former news empire; it stands in the center of town, by the river, a once-proud symbol of the central role newspapers played in a city.

The circa 1869 Water Tower, one of the few downtown structures to survive the Great Fire, is now a mall, because most of all, the Magnificent Mile is about shopping. Lots of high-end shops and the obligatory chains: Victoria's Secret, Eddie Bauer and others. (But, Jo Ann says with a sigh, "Lord & Taylor is gone, which hurts me deeply." The store closed its doors in 2007.)

You will not run out of things to do in Chicago. Each visit, my husband and I try to get baseball tickets and join the throng riding the El train to historic Wrigley Field, which is smack-dab in the middle of a residential neighborhood. From the train you can see the rooftop decks in the neighborhood, where people hang out to watch the games.

We've caught student stand-up and improv in Donny's Skybox Theater at Second City, where some of the nation's most famous comedians get their start. We hear live jazz—my favorite spot is the historic Green Mill, over 100 years old and still swingin'.

We walk by the lake, usually near the family manse, which is a pleasantly scruffy urban beach. But elsewhere, the lakeside parks are groomed and inviting. "You can walk along the lake practically forever," Jo Ann says. "Start at Oak Street and go north."

We haven't done that yet, or dined on the Riverwalk, which is being developed, "...and it just keeps getting better and better," says Jo Ann. But we have hung out in Lincoln Park and watched a peewee T-ball game. We've dined in Greektown (the flaming cheese, Saganaki, is a Chicago-born tradition). Of course the Art Institute, old and new wings, and the Field Museum. Tom sometimes meets a brother or old friends on State Street for a beer or two. We've been to Navy Pier, built for commerce and entertainment in 1916 and now a full-out funplace. We've been to the excellent National Museum of Mexican Art and Chicago History Museum.

My image of Chicago before I got to know it was of a serious grey place huddled against a biting wind.

And it does get cold in winter. Very. Also windy. Also dark. That's why we try to visit in spring and summer, when Chicago is vibrant, colorful, and fun—which are three words I didn't associate with Chicago until I got to know it.

www.choosechicago.com

&⁊

PLACES TO LEARN MORE

Dozens and dozens of movies have been filmed in Chicago, gangsters (*Scarface, The Untouchables*) to modern manners (*About Last Night*). Upton Sinclair's novel, *The Jungle*, is set in Chicago's meatpacking plants and, though fictional, exposed the abuses of that industry. *The Devil in the White City: Murder, Magic, and Madness at the Fair That Changed America* by Erik Larson is one of my favorite books of all time, a true story written like a novel that weaves together the World Exposition of 1893 in Chicago and the movements of a serial killer.

16 Santa Fe, New Mexico

WHEN I THINK OF SANTA FE, one very specific image springs to mind: bright, sun-drenched yellow lilies against red adobe.

I saw it in the courtyard of my hotel on a spring morning, and the image has been burned into my mind. That was the kind of rich, liquid light and vivid color that have contributed to the area's attraction for artists. And others. Everyone loves Santa Fe. When I polled women about places to include in this book, Sante Fe was the clear winner.

"It's healing and so walkable," says editor Linda Crosson. "You can wander downtown and up the side streets and always find your way back, even if you're not much of a walker."

"I love the vibe of Santa Fe," says writer Sue Russell. "First visit not so sure, second time it felt special. In an ethereal, spiritual kind of way, and the near-daily rain shower refreshed my dusty brain."

"It's a very feminine place," says psychologist Deborah Boelter. "The way Canyon Road winds around, all the art..."

Santa Fe is the epicenter of Southwestern style (howling coyotes and Kokopelli, denim, turquoise, and silver). In Santa Fe you can shop or hike, see an opera under the stars at the world-famous Santa Fe Opera House, visit a spa, shop for art or cowboy boots, mountain bike or just sit in front of a fire in your hotel room. Santa Fe manages to be earthy and tony at the same time.

Old Town is an intimate maze of adobe Spanish-Pueblo style buildings (thanks to zoning laws established in 1958) housing high-end shops, galleries, and restaurants (also some souvenir shops). Outside the Palace of the Governors, Native American artists sell jewelry and other beautiful hand-crafted items, and you can meet and speak to the artist before you make a purchase (yes, they do take credit cards).

Every culture that has passed through this city has been preserved here. Santa Fe's first inhabitants were Pueblo Indians. The Spanish settled in thirteen years before Pilgrims landed on Plymouth Rock, making Santa Fe the oldest European community west of the Mississippi. In 1610, Don Juan de Oñate, Governor-General of New Mexico, moved his capital to Santa Fe, making it the oldest capital city in North America. The American flag was raised over Santa Fe in 1846, during the Mexican-American War, and New Mexico became a state in 1912.

Artists drawn to New Mexico's light and landscape have established the city as a mecca for the arts. Curvaceous Canyon Road is the heart of Santa Fe's artist's colony, though its old adobe homes were once farmhouses; the oldest date to about the 1750s. The city hosts numerous art fairs and markets, including the huge annual Santa Fe International Folk Art Market and the contemporary art fair ART Santa Fe, in the newly renovated Railyard District.

Georgia O'Keeffe is perhaps the most famous artist to find her muse in New Mexico. O'Keeffe lived the last couple of years of her life in Santa Fe, until her death in 1986. The Georgia O'Keeffe Museum is the most visited museum in New

Mexico. (More on O'Keeffe, Chapter 61) Santa Fe is a wealth of museums in general, including the New Mexico Museum of Art and the new (2009) New Mexico History Museum. My personal favorite is the Museum of International Folk Art, where the womanly arts of samplers, rugs, clothing, and quilts are treated with the respect they deserve. The Girard Wing alone requires multiple visits; it contains more than 100,000 folk art objects collected over a lifetime by architect and textile designer Alexander Girard and his wife Susan. The exhibit, designed by Girard himself, is an explosion of color and whimsy.

Santa Fe also is a foodie, celebrity-chef kind of place, with its own green chile cuisine. The Santa Fe School of Cooking, which has been offering cooking classes for 31 years, also offers restaurant tours.

And Santa Fe nestles at the foot of the Sangre de Cristo Mountains, making it a great base for outdoorsiness, like mountain biking and hiking. The nearby Aspen Vista Trail is the most popular in the Sangre de Cristos, appealing to hikers in summer and cross-country skiers and showshoers in winter; it's closed to snowmobiles. Many of the trails are easy enough for hiking hobbyists, others require more commitment.

For an easy little trek, hit the Dorothy Stewart trail, a three-mile loop named for an artist whose work, which focused on Native American life, has mostly dropped from view. But here's the sweet story about the trail: The property allowing access to other trails was owned first by Stewart, then by Irene Von Horvath, a preservationist honored in 1998 as a "Santa Fe Living Treasure." A fan of Stewart's work, Von Horvath donated the property for trail access with the stipulation that the trail be named for Stewart. So it's kind of a trail tribute to sisterhood.

www.santafe.org

PLACES TO LEARN MORE

Santa Fe Style, by Christine Mather and Sharon Woods looks at the origins and current forms of Santa Fe's distinctive design.

17 Los Angeles, California

Los ANGELES IS ONE OF THOSE love-it-or-hate-it kinds of places. I fall into the love-it camp, and although I understand the haters, I maintain that LA is a must-see. After all, much of the image of America that goes out to the world has been filtered through the lens of Hollywood, making LA quintessentially American even though it bears little resemblance to anyplace else in the USA.

And really, if you haven't seen the Hollywood sign, have you really seen America?

Yes, traffic. A thousand times yes. You will get stuck in it. But relax and soak in the vibe of the original, quintessential car culture. As city streets are to New York, highways are to Los Angeles. Consider: the Petersen Automotive Museum on Wilshire Boulevard is four floors of everything automotive, including movie star cars and even Hot Wheels.

Yes, beaches, too. And bodies. Oh, those beautiful California bodies. Hit wide, white-sand Santa Monica Beach, which is always abuzz with glamour: sleek, sun-bronzed people play beach volleyball; sunbathers risk cancer for that golden glow; surfers challenge the Pacific; bikers, joggers, and roller-bladers stream back and forth the 22-mile paved Ocean Front Walk, commonly called "the boardwalk," although it isn't.

Head south on the boardwalk, and you'll reach the patchouli tie-dye happyface hippie hangout of Venice Beach. Here are artists selling their art, street performers doing their thing, beach bums bumming around, and a whole lot of color swirling around the scene. Oh, and Muscle Beach is here too, and, yes, there will probably be muscular people doing muscle-y things there.

Don't be ashamed to do the touristy stuff. Take a Warner Brothers studio tour; it's not a theme park like Universal Studios. It's an honest-to-god tour around the back lots. Walk Hollywood Boulevard's Walk of Fame (and wonder about all the famous people you've never heard of). Go to the TCL Chinese Theater (once Grauman's, then Mann's), and try fitting your hands and feet into the handprints and footprints of famous people.  There is something touchingly immediate and homely about the handprints and footprints of long-gone stars—Marilyn Monroe, Rita Hayworth, Mary Pickford.

While you're in the neighborhood, stop into the original (though no longer on the original site) Frederick's of Hollywood and browse the naughty underwear. Push it up, pad it out, cinch it in—that's what it's all about.

(By the way, if you get to North Hollywood, look for the Amelia Earhart statue in North Hollywood Park. Earhart lived in North Hollywood from 1928 until she vanished. More about her in Chapter 52.)

You'll want to shop on Melrose Avenue and window shop (at least) on Rodeo Drive. And while you're in Beverly Hills, spring for a meal at the gorgeous old Beverly Hills Hotel. The Polo Lounge has long been known as a power breakfast spot, but I'm partial to the sinuous, circa 1949 counter in the Fountain Coffee Room, where you can have a spot of breakfast or a light lunch. It's a pleasant, not-too-pricey way to get a peek at the iconic hotel.

Keep an eye out for movie stars while you go about your business. You might spot them just about anywhere locals hang—at the hot new restaurant du jour or the longtime beloved institutions. Stay alert and keep in mind that movie stars can look a lot less glamorous when they're off duty. Goldie Hawn once sneezed on my shoulder at a Malibu restaurant, and it wasn't at all glamorous. Diana Ross's elbow bumped my husband's noggin as she sashayed past our table at the original (now gone) Spago restaurant.

You might spot celebs at the Rose Bowl Flea Market in Pasadena, held the second Sunday of every month. Even if you don't, you should find some cool stuff. Or try hiking the Runyon Canyon Loop trail. This isn't a wilderness experience, but it's great for people watching, possibly celebrities, and for great views. Also free yoga classes daily.

Live celebrity sightings are never guaranteed, of course, so if you're determined to have a brush with fame, you might have to settle for dead movie stars. At "Hollywood Forever" cemetery (once named the more dignified Hollywood Memorial Park Cemetery), you can see Mel Blanc's famous "That's all, folks," headstone. Also the graves of Fay Wray, Jayne Mansfield, Estelle Getty, Vampira (Maila Nurmi), Hattie McDaniel. And I'll throw in, for no particular reason, Don Adams.

Bette Davis is buried at the Forest Lawn Memorial Park in the Hollywood Hills. So are Sandra Dee, Dorothy Lamour, Jill Ireland, Julie London, Isabel Sanford. Also Liberace and Rodney King and a whole bunch of other famous people. Stan Laurel. Marvin Gaye. Andy Gibb.

And at Forest Lawn Memorial Park in Glendale, you can say "goodnight Gracie" to Gracie Allen. Joan Blondell is buried here, as are all three Andrews Sisters, costume designer Edith

Head, and evangelist Aimee Semple McPherson. Liz Taylor is here too, though not in a public area. Same with her tragic little buddy, Michael Jackson.

And speaking more of movies, if you're the type of person who likes this kind of thing, you can stop in to the Margaret Herrick Library, which is the library of the Motion Picture Academy of Arts and Sciences, and browse original scripts: *It's a Wonderful Life*. *Mildred Pierce*. *Pretty Woman*. *Halloween*. Whatever turns you on.

Of course, LA also has the Getty Museum and LACMA (Los Angeles County Museum of Art) and the Walt Disney Concert Hall, a hallucination of a building designed by Frank Gehry. (Another hallucinatory structure: the Watts Towers, seventeen steel structures built by one man possessed over 30 years, starting in the 1920s. Worth a pilgrimage.)

No, it's not all swimming pools and movie stars. But you can't go to La La Land without indulging in some of that silliness. That would be wrong.

www.discoverlosangeles.com

❧

PLACES TO LEARN MORE

The 1992 Robert Altman movie, *The Player*, is a whodunit full of Hollywood insider jokes, for a flavor of the town. The documentary, *Tales from the Script*, is an insider look at the life of the screenwriters, as is the William Goldman classic book, *Adventures in the Screen Trade*. And *You'll Never Eat Lunch in This Town Again* by Julia Phillips is an autobiography of the late producer's Hollywood adventures in the 1970s and '80s.

18 Seattle, Washington

WRITER TARA AUSTEN WEAVER DIDN'T PLAN on living in Seattle. She arrived in spring 2007 to spend just the summer there, working on a book. But when summer ended, she couldn't tear herself away.

"I didn't know a city could be so intertwined with nature," she says. "From the lakes and hills that shape the topography, to parks that feel like forests, mountains and islands, and the fishing and boating that make up life in this area...there are community gardens scattered everywhere, organizations that volunteer to harvest excess fruit off backyard trees and donate it to food banks, and in the spring, people line up for the annual plant sale. Maybe it's the rain, the green, but this is a community rooted in nature."

I've visited Seattle a couple of times and frankly, I don't know what all this talk about rain, rain, rain is about. Both times I visited, it was all sunshine, all the time. (No, but really, Seattle gets rain about 50 percent of the time. I visited in July and August, the city's driest months.)

Water is Seattle's defining element. A major port, it stands between Puget Sound to the west and Lake Washington, and paying tribute to H2O is on the must-do list during your visit. "Take a ferry out to Bainbridge and feel the salt air in your hair, rent a kayak on Lake Union or a canoe from the University of Washington and paddle past houseboats or through the Arboretum," Tara says. "This is an area so defined by water—what with the rain, lakes, fishing, shipping, islands—you almost cannot understand its nature and history if you stay on dry land. Also, it's loads of fun." At the very least, she says, go hang out by the Ballard Locks and watch the boats go by, some Alaska-bound, some just tooling around.

And visit Seattle's parks—there are hundreds of them. Discovery Park is 534 acres of natural gorgeousness overlooking Puget Sound and with views of the Cascade and Olympic mountain ranges. It has cliffs, forests, dunes, meadows, and tidal beaches. Hard to believe it's in a major American city. You can fly a kite in Gas Works Park—once an industrial site now remade into grassy green hills perfect for picnicking—with stunning views of Lake Union and downtown skyscrapers.

Olympic Sculpture Park was also once an industrial site; now it's a nine-acre park under the jurisdiction of the Seattle Art Museum and studded with works by Alexander Calder, Mark di Suvero, Ellsworth Kelly, and other notables. "In most other cities, prime land like that would have been used for luxury condos," Tara boasts, with understandable civic pride.

Speaking of industry, although Boeing's world headquarters have moved from Seattle to Chicago, its aircraft are still in the civic blood and are assembled in nearby Mukilteo. Take a factory tour and see how they build the big birds. Or, stay close to Seattle Center and visit the Museum of Flight at Boeing Field (still a working airport), just a few miles south of downtown.

You probably know about the Space Needle, a city trademark. You can visit the Observation Deck, 520 feet up, or the revolving SkyCity Restaurant (500 feet), or remain earthbound and visit the Chihuly Garden and Glass, a kaleidoscopic display of art glass by one of the world's most beloved (and prolific) glass artists. Nearby, in that crazy Frank O. Gehry building/hallucination, is the Experience Music Project, Microsoft co-founder Paul Allen's massive collection of music and pop culture memorabilia. Fans of edgy architecture will also want to visit the wild, glass, love-it-or-hate it Central Library with its crazy angles and "Book Spiral" of continuous shelves of nonfiction books.

Seattle is a foodie city too, so you will want to ingest delicious things. Of course, everyone has to pop into Pike Place Market (see Chapter 99), but, says Seattle local Noelle O'Reilly, serious foodies should visit the Sunday farmers market on Ballard Avenue. "Superstar chefs wander around doing their shopping along with the rest of the neighborhood," she says. "There's also a concentration of excellent restaurants and bars on the street. Stop in and have brunch during the market, or have cocktails afterwards. There are also several up-and-coming breweries within walking distance."

For more dining and for shopping, Noelle suggests Capitol Hill, location of the famous Elliot Bay Book Company (for more bookstores, see Chapter 80), and Melrose Market, a new but classic-style shopping arcade—great for people watching too.

And to get to know the funky side of Seattle, head for Fremont, a neighborhood that was defined by artists and iconoclasts. A sign welcomes you to "Fremont—Center of the Universe" and suggests you set your watch five minutes ahead. Get your bearings at the Guidepost to the Center of the Universe at 35th Street N and N Fremont Ave., and you must pay your respects to The Troll under the George Washington Memorial Bridge (aka Aurora Bridge), one of many public artworks in this quirky 'hood.

Seattle doesn't have a knockout, category-killer, must-see attraction. It is, rather, a city of many seductive pleasures—the kind that might entice a person to come for a visit and stay for a lifetime.

www.visitseattle.org

PLACES TO LEARN MORE

Along with Starbucks coffee and Boeing airplanes, grunge rock music is one of Seattle's most famous imports. *Grunge Is Dead: The Oral History of Seattle Rock Music* by Greg Prato tells the story in the words of people who were there.

You'll see scenes of Seattle in the Tom Hanks, Meg Ryan romantic comedy *Sleepless in Seattle*, of course. And the infamous *Fifty Shades of Grey* series of erotic novels is set in Seattle.

19 San Francisco, California

SAN FRANCISCO IS ONE OF THOSE cities that inspire passion and poetry, not to mention quite a few songs: Jeanette MacDonald implored it to open its Golden Gate, Tony Bennett left his heart there, Rice-A-Roni boasted that it was the San Francisco treat with unbeatable flavor. My friend Ashley Powell, who is from Dallas, Texas but has lived in San Francisco at various points of her life, waxes rhapsodic about, "The possibilities. There are so many possibilities there—whoever you are, whoever you want to be, it's the city that allows people to have their space to do whatever they want. And there's so much creativity."

And Helen Anders, a travel writer who lives in Austin, Texas, cites it as her favorite city and visits twice a year. She loves it first of all, for the weather. "It's almost always cool, and that's huge for Texans. Also, it's an easy city. Very walkable, and there's a ton to do—museums, parks, neighborhoods, and I always feel comfy on my own. The locals are nice, too. Just a great, highly diverse city—cool in every way."

 San Francisco *is* walkable, so even if you start your visit with the obligatory ride on the city's beloved cable cars, which are a national historic landmark, wear your comfy shoes for the rest of your explorations. You might even walk to the Cable Car Museum on Washington and Mason streets.

It's located in the Cable Car Barn & Powerhouse, a marvel of 19th-century engineering still operating today.

For an overview of the city, hike up to Coit Tower, which was built with money bequeathed by Lillie Hitchcock Coit, a quintessential San Francisco eccentric: volunteer firefighter, cigar smoker, and trousers wearer (before women did that kind of thing) who dressed like a man to gamble in the men-only establishments in North Beach. On the ground floor, you can see beautifully restored murals, a Public Works of Art project from 1934. The left-wing, Marxist imagery of many of the artworks was a little scandalous, although the one female artist represented here, Suzanne Scheuer, painted nothing more controversial than newspaper production in her mural, "Newsgathering." (Another woman, Edith Hamlin, has a mural "Hunting in California" on the second floor, but this may be viewed only during Wednesday and Saturday morning tours.)

Oh, and by the way, don't feel compelled to visit the tower observation deck. "You have to pay to go to the top," Helen points out, "and the view's not that much better than you get on the ground, absolutely free."

Also free, the observation deck at the Hamon Education Tower at the de Young Museum in Golden Gate Park has a helluva view and should be added to any visit to the de Young or the California Academy of Sciences across the plaza.

Otherwise, strolling around the diverse neighborhoods is what to do in San Francisco.

Helen loves North Beach, "the garlic-infused" Italian neighborhood that, of course, has no beach. "Lie in the grass in Washington Square Park and watch locals cavort with their dogs, then go grab some Italian food at one of the area's many fine restaurants," she says. One idea: Pizza from Tony's Pizza

Napoletana eaten in the parklet (that's a mini-park) outside. Other ideas: In the morning, watch elderly Chinese people doing Tai Chi in Washington Square, have a coffee or glass of wine at Mario's Bohemian Cigar Store at Union and Columbus, or at Caffe Trieste at Grant and Vallejo. Peruse and patronize the fun old shops up and down Grant Avenue.

From North Beach you can stroll into Chinatown, stopping first at the famous City Lights Bookstore, founded and still owned by beat poet Lawrence Ferlinghetti, which more or less straddles the neighborhoods. Then, plunge into the bustle of Chinatown. "It smells terrible but it's great," says Ashley. "And it has some really great tea shops—sort of like wineries for teas. They have tasting menus and everything." (For more on tea, see Chapter 91.)

Haight Ashbury, the epicenter of the hippie counterculture world in the 1960s and early 1970s, is still colorful and has tons of fun vintage shops, says my sister-in-law, Christine Battles, who consulted with my niece Elizabeth (who just moved to San Francisco for her first real job) to come up with some of their favorite things. "It's so much fun to get lost in time, with all the treasures," Christine says (although Ashley contends the Goodwill on Haight Street beats any of the shops).

Christine continues, "There's also an Amoeba Music store, where you can spend hours perusing the record albums especially. And Amoeba has artists like Camper van Beethoven and Silversun Pickups stopping by to perform."

The one place all my correspondents agree on with equal enthusiasm is the Ferry Plaza Farmers Market on Tuesdays, Thursdays, and Saturdays. "I always wind up wishing I had a kitchen to cook in," Helen says. Ashley and the Battles girls both point visitors to Cowgirl Creamery (cheese and artisanal breads) and Hog Island Oyster Company. "Sitting there and having a dozen oysters and a glass of chardonnay, that's just the perfect day in San Francisco," Ashley said wistfully.

In the Tenderloin, the "Sunday Celebrations"—music, dance, sermons, and lots of joy—at Glide Memorial Church are so popular, you'll need to arrive well before the 9 or 11 a.m. start times for a spot in the sanctuary. The church was founded in 1929 by Methodist Lizzie Glide, but was limping along when it went through a transformation from conservative to loose, free-spirited and inclusive under the guidance of Cecil Williams, then a young African American minister. He and poet and activist Janice Mirikitani (who eventually married Williams) steered the church through some turbulent decades, providing outreach to troubled communities of the Tenderloin. The church is still going strong, and Williams and Mirikitani still help steer it.

Afterwards, perhaps while away Sunday afternoon with a stroll around Stow Lake in Golden Gate Park, or rent a pedal-boat. Take a walk at Land's End in the forest on bluffs high above the crashing Pacific, part of the Golden Gate National Recreation Area, and a place so wild you won't believe you're in a major American city (also see if you can find the labyrinth on an outcropping with views of the Golden Gate Bridge, Marin Headlands, and the Pacific Ocean). Expansive Ocean Beach is ideal for a walk in good weather or bad. Or visit Dolores Park in the Mission District. "Weekends it's hipsters galore," says Ashley. "Anything goes. The food trucks come out, the Dolores Park playground—you have to have kids with you—is unbelievable."

Dolores Park also is the starting point for the San Francisco Dyke March each year during the city's annual, enormous Gay Pride festival. The march ends in the Castro, the epicenter of

San Francisco's LGBT community (and San Francisco could be considered the epicenter of the nation's LGBT community).

The people of California are generally very outdoorsy, and San Francisco is no exception. Ashley, a marathoner, loves trail running in the Presidio, a national park of nearly 1,500 acres of forest and coastline studded with historic buildings (it was an army post for Spanish, Mexican, and American soldiers). Christine says there are more great hiking/jogging spots than she can name, but among her favorites: Starting at the Embarcadero and the Bay Bridge and heading toward Crissy Field. "The view is the beautiful San Francisco Bay all the way, ending at Fort Point and the spectacular Golden Gate Bridge." It's about six miles if you start at the Ferry Building or three-and-a-half if you begin at the Hyde Street Pier. "But you lose yourself in the beauty and don't really think about the mileage or the time," she says. And you can stop at Greens in Fort Mason, a vegetarian restaurant with views of boats and the bridge. The food is great, and it's run by Zen monks and provisioned by their gardens. And walking across the bridge, rain, wind or shine, is always spectacular—rushing fog on days of no visibility, stunning vistas of the headlands, city, bay, and ocean when the sun shines.

"Another amazing hike—and you can make it as challeng- ing as you want—begins in the Sea Cliff area, home to famous and wealthy San Franciscans, including Robin Williams and Metallica drummer Kurt Hemmerer. Elizabeth and I walked all along the Coastal Trail of Land's End, with breathtaking views of the Golden Gate Bridge. On this strenuous trail, you're among cypress trees and native plants and wildflowers. The cliffs are high, overlooking the Pacific—be careful not to look down!" On this hike, you can visit the ruins of the once-spectacular Sutro Baths—an ostentatious project of Adolph Sutro, who opened to the public the world's largest swimming pool establishment in 1896. Among other glories, it had seven baths: one freshwater and six saltwater. But times change, and the thing got way too expensive to maintain; following a big fire in 1966, there are only ruins, which remain a curiosity and a sad loss. "We hiked to the Cliff House," Christine says, "and after a challenging hike like that, it was time to indulge in oysters, peppered prawns, and a glass of sauvignon blanc with an incredible view overlooking Ocean Beach."

And this is where I'll leave you.

PLACES TO LEARN MORE

Armistead Maupin's series of novels, *Tales of the City*, written in the late 1970s and early 1980s, takes place amidst San Francisco's counterculture. (Although in San Francisco, counterculture is actually kind of mainstream.) *San Francisco's Telegraph Hill* by David Myrick covers the history of one of the city's most famous hills, while *The World Rushed In* by J.S. Holliday chronicles the Gold Rush, which prompted explosive growth and turned San Francisco into an instant city. *Travelers' Tales San Francisco*, a collection of 41 true stories from many writers, covers lots of ground and includes a long suggested-reading list.

Woody Allen's 2013 movie, *Blue Jasmine*, though not the impassioned love letter to the city that his New York City movies are, takes place in San Francisco. The city has starred in lots of films over the decades, including the 1936 *San Francisco*, a story involving the 1906 earthquake starring Clark Gable, Jeannette MacDonald, and Spencer Tracy; Bogart and Bacall's

The Maltese Falcon; Alfred Hitchcock's *Vertigo*; *Bullitt*, starring Steve McQueen, and Clint Eastwood's *Dirty Harry* for gritty mean streets; and, more recently, *Mrs. Doubtfire, The Pursuit of Happyness* and *Milk*, among others.

www.sanfrancisco.travel

20 *Statue of Liberty, New York City*

"If it weren't for the French," says writer Kerry Medina, "the most well-known symbol of the U.S. could well be the faces of four white, middle-aged men carved into the side of a mountain. (See Chapter 34.) And so every American woman should make the pilgrimage and pay her respects to this tiara-wearing woman, purposely put on a pedestal, and remember that *she* continues to be the face of our nation."

Well said, Kerry!

Of course, every American (and every visitor to America) should see the Statue of Liberty—at the very least, from the Staten Island Ferry, which is a free ride. But as Kerry points out, women can take particular pride that arguably our nation's most powerful symbol is female, and a goddess at that. The chains and broken shackle at the statue's feet as she strides forward symbolize her as "a goddess free from oppression and servitude," as the National Park Service puts it. (More about goddesses in America, Chapter 77.)

"Some people refer to her as the political goddess," says Karen Tate, author of *Sacred Places of Goddess: 108 Destinations.* "Not only is there historical relevance for it being a goddess site, there are also ideals and benchmarks, and political, cultural, and social beliefs attached. She represents harmony, justice, tolerance. The goddess does not exploit people or nature."

That's how we see it now, but America wasn't sure about the whole thing at first.

The Statue of Liberty was a gift from the French to celebrate America's first hundred years of independence and the friendship between France and America, forged during the Revolutionary War.

Actually, the statue was a joint project: the French created Lady Liberty, America agreed to build her pedestal. But America had a hard time getting motivated to kick in the money necessary to hold up its end of the deal. The rich weren't interested in funding the pedestal, the middle class thought the rich should cough up the dough, and everyone wondered why Americans were being asked to pay for a statue from France.

In fact, the famous words, "Give me your tired, your poor/ Your huddled masses yearning to breathe free," were part of the fundraising effort for the pedestal. Emma Lazarus, a well-connected poet, wrote the sonnet "The New Colossus," from which they were drawn, for an art auction.

Still, France had the statue finished before America had enough money to build the pedestal on which to put her. Finally Joseph Pulitzer, publisher of the *New York World* (and the Pulitzer in Pulitzer Prize) used his newspaper to scold and shame Americans into ponying up, and the pedestal was built.

Sculptor Frederic Auguste Barthold titled his creation, "Statue of Liberty Enlightening the World." (Alexandre Gustave Eiffel—the Eiffel in Eiffel Tower—added engineering expertise to the massive undertaking.) Lady Liberty is made from copper hammered to 3/32 of an inch thick, about the thickness of two pennies. Her torch symbolizes enlightenment;

the seven points of her crown symbolize the seven seas and seven continents; the 25 windows in the crown symbolize gem-stones and the heaven's rays shining over the world; and the tablet she holds represents the law.

The statue was shipped in 350 separate pieces packed in 214 crates. It took 4 months to put her together and she was dedicated on October 28, 1886—10 years after the centennial she celebrated.

The Statue of Liberty gained much of her symbolic potency during the great wave of immigration at the turn of the last century. For European immigrants fleeing poverty, starvation, or genocide—or just seeking their fortunes in this brash, young nation—she was a stirring sight, standing there at the gateway to the Port of New York.

Today, although she is 151 feet tall from toe to torch, the Statue of Liberty is dwarfed by the towering skyline of Manhattan. Yet that doesn't lessen her impact in the least. She stands tall, torch held high, representing for us the finest of our ideals. She is one powerful dame.

www.nps.gov/stli/index.htm

21 Brooklyn Bridge, New York City

IT'S AN AMERICAN ICON, A MASSIVE, granite monument to American ingenuity and hubris. It was an engineering marvel of its time. Its great Gothic arches tower 275 feet over the East River; about 145,000 vehicles cross it daily.

And it has a woman's touch all over it.

The bridge was conceived by John Augustus Roebling, who died from tetanus in 1869, before construction even started. His son, Washington Augustus Roebling, took over the project, but got a near-fatal case of decompression sickness—"the bends"— supervising underwater construction on the bridge. The bridge took a toll on its builders—about 27 men died during construction.

Ill and weakened, Washington Roebling could not actively continue his work on the bridge project. That's when his wife, Emily Warren Roebling, stepped in. For the next 11 years, Emily, who had studied math and science in an era when women were typically barely educated, was the conduit between Roebling and the construction; she essentially acted as chief engineer on the bridge. Though her husband remained official chief engineer, Emily was not a figurehead. She was on the site daily and educated herself about stress analysis and cable construction and other engineerish things. When the bridge opened, on May 24, 1883, Emily rode with President Chester Arthur, the first people to cross the mighty span. It was the first land route to Brooklyn from Manhattan, and it began Brooklyn's development from farmland to the urban hipster hangout it is today.

Walking across the Brooklyn Bridge is a time-honored and delightful activity. There's a wide wooden walkway, benches along the way, and marvelous views of the skyline, the hustle and bustle of boats on the East River, the Statue of Liberty in the distance (see Chapter 20). It doesn't matter whether you want to go to Brooklyn or not (although it is recommended), walking across the bridge and back is an end in itself.

Oh, by the way, Emily Roebling went on to get a law degree from NYU at the age of 56. So right on, Emily.

❧

PLACES TO LEARN MORE

The definitive history of the Brooklyn Bridge is David McCullough's *The Great Bridge: The Epic Story of the Building of the Brooklyn Bridge.*

Ken Burns's first PBS documentary was *Brooklyn Bridge*. It was nominated for an Oscar in 1982.

www.nyc.gov/html/dot/html/bridges/brooklyn_bridge.shtml

22 Berkeley Springs, West Virginia

FIRST OF ALL, WEST VIRGINIA IS one of the nation's undiscovered jewels. It's just so lovely. It's said that if you flatten out West Virginia, it would be the size of Texas. That's not actually true, but it's still a good way to get a sense of the state's terrain. West Virginia is deep-green mountains, rollicking rivers (see Chapter 71), and historic 19th-century towns like Berkeley Springs. (Actually, the town is much older than that, but fire wiped out a lot of its 18th-century structures.)

Berkeley Springs has been a resort town since it was a town, claiming the title of America's first spa. Native Americans took the warm mineral waters here before Europeans arrived, and the springs were first mapped by Thomas Jefferson's father as Medicine Springs in 1747.

For a time, Berkeley Springs was a sinful spot, with gambling and brothels. We don't know or aren't saying if George Washington partook of any of this sinning during his visits, but in 1769, he spent five weeks in the area, and in 1776 he was among the first to buy land in the newly established town of Bath. That's still the town's official name, but everyone calls it Berkeley Springs.

The springs flow at a constant 74 degrees. At the historic Roman Bath House, in 4.5-acre Berkeley Springs State Park, they heat the water to 102 degrees, making it a nice place for a hot dip. The historic bath house is open to the public daily year-round and five-by-nine-foot tubs may be rented by the half hour and shared with someone of the same sex. The main bathhouse also offers massage, with men on one side and women on the other. Like the old days.

The town does have modern spas as well and lots of shopping on its pretty ye olde streets. You can take a self-guided walking tour of its historic sites (including the location of George Washington's original two lots, where a private home now stands).

And take a moment to view Berkeley Castle, a delicious example of Victorian excess, built by Colonel Samuel Taylor Suit for his young wife, Rosa Pelham, daughter of an Alabama congressman. Suit, who made his fortune selling whiskey in a little brown jug, hired the architect responsible for U.S. State Department and Treasury buildings to design the edifice, and construction kept 100 German stonemasons busy from 1885 to 1891. Suit didn't live to see it completed, but stipulated in his will that Rosa had to complete it to inherit his fortune. She did complete the castle and went on to host lavish parties there, sometimes renting entire railroad cars to bring her fancy guests to town. Her profligate ways eventually caught up with her, though, and by the time she was 50, she was out of dough. In 1909, the castle was sold at public auction. It was open to the public for many years but no longer is, although it can be rented for weddings and other events.

Berkeley Springs and surrounding area are rich with history, and while you're in the neighborhood (because really—how often are you going to be in West Virginia?), you should also drive about an hour northwest to Harpers Ferry National Historic Park, location of, among other things, abolitionist

John Brown's final insurrection, when he tried to raid the federal armory there. He was captured, tried, and hanged in nearby
Charles Town, but his act was one of the sparks that ignited the
Civil War. West Virginia is the only state to form by secession,
when it broke away from Virginia to join the Union. Which is
another cool reason to visit.

www.berkeleysprings.com

23 Buffalo Bill Historical Center, Cody, Wyoming

I HAD AN EPIPHANY ON MY first visit to the Buffalo Bill Historical Center in Cody, Wyoming.

Until visiting the BBHC, all I knew of western art was (Charles) Russell and (Frederic) Remington, who painted and sculpted cowboys and Indians in narrative works that are both skillful and, to my eye, kind of hokey.

The BBHC was my first in-your-face encounter with western art that captures the fascination and spectacle of the West, before it was settled, when it was still a thrilling, unknown land. (O.K., it's still thrilling but it's mostly pretty known.)

Artists were among the first Europeans to see these wild places, following or traveling with the trailblazing explorers. The images they brought back East excited imaginations and helped spur the Westward Expansion.

The gallery has lots of Russell's and Remington's action-packed set pieces, which still didn't do a lot for me, but also Albert Bierstadt's awe-inspiring landscapes; George Catlin's sensitive portraits of Native Americans; John James Audubon's meticulous renderings of the birds of the West. The collection winds its way to the present and changed my understanding of western art.

Cody has a population of just 10,000, but this is no small-town collection. The BBHC is five spectacular museums, launched with East Coast money. The original Buffalo Bill Museum, opened in 1927, was just a log cabin full of memorabilia. In 1929, artist/rich chick Gertrude Vanderbilt Whitney donated a sculpture she made of Cody. It sat alongside the cabin/museum until her son Cornelius founded the Whitney gallery in 1959 and moved the sculpture and museum there. And the place just keeps growing.

As well as the Whitney, the BBHC includes the Buffalo Bill Museum, which includes show posters, costumes, and more about the showman's life. It was expanded and jazzed up to be modern and multimedia in 2012. Look for Buffalo Bill's female counterpart Annie Oakley here (also Chapter 49). The Museum of the Plains Indians is a wide and deep collection of not only artifacts of the tribes' lives in the past, but also art and objects up to the present. Women are more widely represented here than in the Whitney gallery, since so many Native American arts are historically womanly arts like pottery and beading.

The Draper Museum of Natural History opened in 2002. It focuses on the natural history of the region, especially nearby Yellowstone National Park (more on that in Chapter 2), and includes a live raptor program. The Cody Firearms Museum has a particularly large collection of Winchesters.

All told, these sophisticated museums provide all kinds of context for a visit to the West—and Yellowstone, our first national park, where the landscape is little changed from Bierstadt's day. Between Cody and the park is Shoshone National Forest, still studded with historic guest ranches, which followed the artists, once people back East got a load of what the West looked like and wanted to come to see for themselves.

www.bbhc.org

World's Longest Yard Sale, Michigan to Alabama

CAN YOU CALL IT A YARD sale if it spans 675 miles and five states?

Every year, on the first Thursday through Sunday of August, people along Highway 127 schlep their stuff out and display it by the side of the road, on their front lawns, in vendor tents. From the Ohio/Michigan border, to Gadsden, Alabama, the Highway 127 Corridor Sale—aka The World's Longest Yard Sale—started in 1987 as a way of luring people off the Interstate. And it worked. The crowds and yard sale have grown over the years. Traffic slows to a crawl as people scan the tables looking for whatever is on their mind that day. Antique bottles. A crock pot. 1970s board games. Baby clothes. Or whatever just catches their eye. There's a lot of stuff, junk to crafts. There also are funnel cakes and boiled peanuts and fried Oreos, because this is a big yard sale party.

And, if you're inclined to meet people, there are lots of folks to visit with as you pick over boxes of old doorknobs or flip through someone's old collection of Perry Como albums.

The route runs from northern Ohio down to the Appalachians' last ripples. It's a hilly green landscape with the Cumberland River running through it. Lakes, parks, and trails along the way suggest relaxing detours.

Leave your Type-A self behind for this—this weekend is for poking along and poking around and shootin' the breeze.

It's a good idea to plan way ahead if you want to shop this Mother of All Yard Sales. Some motels are booked a year in advance. "Don't just show up and expect to find lodging, you won't," says my friend Jenna Schnuer, a travel writer and dedicated shopper who has shopped the 127 Corridor Sale.

Some people bring trailers to haul home the loot, but if you're that serious (shopping for furniture, perhaps), you're better off finding someplace to park the trailer while you treasure hunt by car. Big trailer, small roads, traffic, parking problems—lots of headaches in that mix.

Jenna says your sale survival kit should include lots of $1 and $5 bills; shopping bags; bubble wrap; Wet Naps; and friendly haggling skills. Also tissues or toilet paper. "And really, use clean restrooms where you find them," Jenna advises. "Avoid the Porta Potties at all costs." And water. Drink lots of water. It's August. It's hot.

"There is no shame in just driving part of the route, or in skipping over parts of it via faster highways," Jenna says. But be sure and take the Lookout Mountain stretch of the road (a small portion of the route veers off 127). "The goods are great and the prices are fair."

And yeah, although there are treasures, there's also a lot of junk in the mix. "It's not unusual to see random old clothes ($1 per shirt) hanging on a clothesline in somebody's yard," Jenna says. "Share sale intel with other shoppers on the route. It's the best way to find top shopping spots."

www.127sale.com

25 Cadillac Ranch, Amarillo, Texas

THEY'RE RIGHT OFF THE I-40 SERVICE road. Just pull over and walk across the dusty plain to reach them, ten vintage Cadillacs, covered with graffiti, buried nose down in the earth, where they have been since 1974.

The Cadillac Ranch, an artwork created by a group that called itself the Ant Farm, is the most famous of the many witty art projects funded by multimillionaire Stanley Marsh 3. A controversial but mostly beloved Texas eccentric with piles of oil money, Marsh is having a tough time in his twilight years, having been accused of paying vulnerable teenaged boys for sex. This has resulted in discussion about dismantling the Cadillac Ranch if he is found guilty. I understand the sentiment, but fervently hope cooler heads prevail. The man is not the art. He didn't even make the art. He just paid for it. It should be left standing as one of America's essential images.

Stand among the cars, hair whipping in a hot wind, and you can only to appreciate the imagination and ingenuity that put them in the hard Texas dirt. This is a perfect roadside attraction. The cars span years, from a 1949 Club Coupe to a 1963 Sedan de Ville, their trademark fins stark against the big panhandle sky. You can't take a bad photo of the Cadillac Ranch. Or, add your graffiti to the cars, which are periodically painted over to give the next army of graffitists a fresh canvas.

85

Destroying this artwork would be a grievous mistake. Besides, cars are only made of metal, and they are already starting to perish in the punishing climate. In time, and unless someone takes up the task of maintaining them, they will eventually be only skeletons of rusted metal anyway. Just thinking about that makes me sad.

ॐ

MORE PLACES

I haven't seen Carhenge near Alliance, Nebraska, but it's on my list. This replica of Stonehenge is built of 38 cars, some welded together to form arches. The whole thing is spray painted gray. Carhenge was conceptualized by artist Jim Reinders as a memorial to his father; in 1987, 35 family members gathered to construct it. Other sculptures, also from cars, have been added to the site over the years.

26 Endangered Historic Places

EVER-STRIVING AMERICANS LOVE TEARING THINGS DOWN and building new things. Bigger, better, slicker, sleeker! We are not, speaking very generally, preservationists. Sometimes even if we don't tear things down, we leave them to molder, just building our bigger and better someplace else. We have lots of space, why worry?

Well, somebody has to, and since 1988, the National Trust for Historic Preservation has released annual lists of the nation's 11 Most Endangered Historic Places, bringing attention to treasures that need TLC and, more importantly, cash money. The good news is that all but a few of these 200-plus places have been saved. Some are success stories by any measure; some are successes only in that the site still stands, even if it is no less endangered by development or neglect.

Some examples:

* The grand old bathhouses of Bathhouse Row in Hot Springs, Arkansas were built around the turn of the last century for people who came to take the waters for their health. They were standing but in sorry condition when they were listed as an endangered place in 2003. Today the bathhouses are being rehabbed and repurposed—as a museum, a spa (different from the olden days spas, but you can still take the waters), a bathhouse museum and visitors center. They live again.

❋ Designer Eero Saarinen's futuristic 1962 TWA Terminal at JFK airport in New York was already a national landmark when it was listed in 2003, but at that time there was talk of slamming on a hulking addition to the building, compromising its fabulous design. In 2005, the terminal was placed on the National Register of Historic Places (tax incentives on the rehab!), and the Port Authority of New York and New Jersey put $20 million into a building buff and puff. As of this writing, a boutique hotel was under discussion.

❋ The Antietam Battlefield, site of the bloodiest battle in the Civil War, was threatened by encroaching development and made the list three years in a row, from 1989 to 1991, but now is considered a victory for preservation, because not only the battlefield itself has been preserved, but the surrounding land has also been preserved by concerned civic organizations, so that the battlefield wouldn't become a patch of history surrounded by shopping centers.

Tourism is an interesting economy that can save historic places when it's done right, or destroy them when it's done thoughtlessly. But sometimes just proving to local governments and businesses that endangered sites are of genuine interest and could conceivably contribute to the local economy can inspire a new attitude.

The National Trust website has a list of all current and past endangered sites. It also has a list of what it calls National Treasures, which are "places of national significance," that also are endangered, places such as the Sweet Auburn Historic District, a historically African-American commercial district in Atlanta, Georgia; and the Washington National Cathedral.

While you're touring endangered places, stay at one of the Historic Hotels of America, a program of the National Trust. The hotels range from the fabulous Hotel Valley Ho, a mid-century modern gem in Scottsdale, Arizona,; to the opulent Gilded Age Brown Palace Hotel in Denver, Colorado; to the breezy seaside Victorian frou frou of the Chalfonte Hotel in Cape May, New Jersey.

It's a matter of paying respect to our elders. Appreciate them while they're around.

www.preservationnation.org

27 *Las Vegas, Nevada*

MANY PEOPLE WILL PART COMPANY WITH my opinion here...they wouldn't go to Vegas if you paid them. I understand that. Vegas is silly and tacky, it represents aspects of America that, let's face it, aren't necessarily things we're proud of. (So we can build a replica of a Venice's Grand Canal inside a casino...this is something to brag about?) Not only that, but Vegas has its roots in organized crime, it allows—encourages—all manner of bad behavior, and then urges us to cover it up. ("What happens in Vegas stays in Vegas"—an all-time great ad campaign.)

I stand my ground: Everyone should see Las Vegas at least once for exactly the reasons above. The silliness, tackiness, even the decadent indulgence of it are among the elements that make it quintessentially American. It is bigger than it needs to be, brighter than it needs to be, full of whiz-bang and ha-cha-cha. You don't have to like it, but you might. It's O.K. I like it. You just have to know how to do it.

First of all, no more than two nights. Any more than that, and you will end up hating it and yourself. Trust me. Two nights of staying up late, drinking weak casino drinks and losing money is plenty. Not that I'm much of a gambler—an hour of slots or video poker and I'm done. And that's not unusual. While 80 percent of visitors to Vegas gamble, almost half of them do so for just a couple of hours a day. Which brings me to my second rule of Vegas:

Stay someplace with a nice swimming pool. This is especially important if you're not a gambler and are traveling with someone who is. A lounge chair, a cold drink, and a trashy novel (or highbrow nonfiction, if that's the way you roll). You can stay at hotels, such as the Four Seasons, that have no casino or kitschy Vegas vibe, or check into a  theme hotel casino with a theme pool. I'm partial to Caesar's Palace and its Garden of the Gods Pool Oasis. It's a whole collection of pools, tranquil and not-so (you can play swim-up blackjack at the Fortuna Pool). Plus, Caesar's Palace is full of gladiators in skirts.

Although you must see the Strip, where all the most over-the-top casinos are (catch the "Sirens of TI" show outside Treasure Island, ride the roller coaster in New York, New York, see the talking statues at The Forum Shops, the shopping arcade at Caesar's Palace), you also must visit Downtown for a whole different vibe. This is old Vegas, not as glitzy, more sincere, if such a term can be applied to such a place. (In addition, for what it's worth, some gamblers swear the slots are looser downtown.)

The Fremont Street Experience is a sound and light show in the canopy that covers Downtown's main drag. Every hour on the hour, everyone stops and looks up for the six-minute spectacle, which might be a tribute to Kiss, or to Don McLean's *American Pie*. In addition, ten neon signs from the past have been renovated and are displayed along this stretch, including Aladdin's lamp and the horse and rider from the Hacienda

Hotel. Las Vegas also has a Neon Museum, where all the great neon signs of the past go to their final rest.

And please, eat well. Unless you left all your dough at the craps tables, there is no reason to dine at the cheap buffets. You think all those fancy-shmancy celebrity chefs are going to ignore a city, however tacky, that attracts people just dying to get rid of their money? You got your Nobu, you got your Charlie Palmer, you got your Tom Colicchio...dining is a big deal in Vegas.

And finally, the best advice I can offer for a good time in Vegas: Go with friends. Vegas is festive and silly and indulgent, and with a gang, you can just drop all and any pretensions and take it all in the spirit of middlebrow, middle American fun. Get over yourself.

www.vistilasvegas.com

PLACES TO LEARN MORE

You can get a little highbrow about Vegas by watching *American Experience—Las Vegas—An Unconventional History*, a PBS documentary available on DVD or VHS.

28 Disney World, Orlando, Florida

MANY PEOPLE ADORE WALT DISNEY WORLD in Orlando, Florida. It gets about 700 million visitors every year. Some people make annual trips. Adults without kids, even. About 1,500 couples every year love it so much they get married there. From the altar of the Disney wedding chapel, a bride can look out on Cinderella's castle, that classic icon of the pink-and-frilly princess tsunami that swamped a nation of little girls.

A lot of other people hate Disney World.

"It's cheesy and there are too many weeping, tired kids," says my friend Helen Husher.

"Shudder," says my friend Helen Anders. "John and I have informed all our children that as much as we love our grandchildren, we will NOT be accompanying them to Disney World or Land."

Those of you reading this who love Disney World don't need to be persuaded to go, so I'm going to write to everyone else. The haters.

I get it. I've been to Disney World twice, and I wouldn't call myself a fan. It's too loud and rambunctious for me. It's also way too commercial, and it has people in giant cartoon character heads wandering around, which I find a little creepy.

And yet, like Las Vegas, it's something to see for all it says about America—all that money, all that creativity, all that idealism. It's brash and over-the-top. Disney's inventions are among America's most pervasive exports, and Disney World is, really, an astonishing accomplishment.

Disney World was the vision of Walt Disney, but he died in 1966, before it was realized. The project was shepherded through its first stage by Walt's brother Roy, who died just three months after the park opened.

I remember the dazzled reports of Disney World when it opened in 1971—a more ambitious version of wee 450-acre Disneyland in California. Early Disney World was just one theme park, the Magic Kingdom, and two resort hotels, surrounded by thousands of Disney-owned acres awaiting more magic.

Today, Vacation Kingdom (behold, the conquering tourist!) is 40 square miles, four theme parks (Magic Kingdom, Epcot, Disney's Hollywood Studios, and Disney Animal Kingdom); 23 resorts; a couple of big water parks, shopping, dining, blah, blah, blah.

And the parks continually reinvent themselves. Though some rides are now and forever ("Small World," and "Pirates of the Caribbean," which Disney parlayed into a whole new franchise), others adapt and change according to whim, fashion, and market forces. In 2009, Disney's Hollywood Studios added an American Idol Experience—an "immersive experience" to let you feel the thrills (and humiliations?) of competing. The grand prize winner wins a guaranteed reservation to audition for the real show, for as long as that lasts.

Disney World is the largest single-site employer in the nation, and the corporation's famously controlling attitude towards its 62,000 "cast members" is part of the fairy dust. If you work there, you are part of the show and of Disney's vision of an unthreatening America. Men were not permitted to wear mustaches until 2000, and in 2010, women were finally excused from wearing pantyhose—probably losing that industry the very last of its customers.

The flowers are always blooming in Disney World. The streets are swept and people smile and you're never far from an ice cream cone. The rides are sophisticated and glitzy, and at Epcot they even take a stab at educational: Audio-animatronic Frederick Douglass and Alexander Graham Bell tell you what they're about; a virtual Ellen Degeneres explains the Big Bang Theory. And if you want to travel around the world by visiting the international pavilions, what's so terrible about that?

The first time I visited Disney World was on assignment for a newspaper. I got a behind-the-scenes tour of the greenhouses and storage sheds and a room lined floor to ceiling with giant Disney character heads, hung up to dry. ("Don't even think it," the publicist said when she saw my hand twitch towards my camera.)

The second time, I tagged along when a couple of special youngsters in my life (and their mom, an old friend) wanted to go. None of us was particularly snockered by the place, but we had a great time together, and I don't think any of us regretted a minute of it. I'm glad I've seen Disney World because it's really something to see. And that's why it's on this list.

I won't try to tell you what to do in Disney World—you'll have to find your own way. Instead, here are some random facts that will either inspire you to visit, or convince you to stay away.

More than 75 million Cokes and 13 million bottles of water are consumed at Disney World each year, washing down 10 million hamburgers, 6 million hot dogs, 9 million pounds of French fries, and more than 300,000 pounds of popcorn.

The attraction Honey I Shrunk the Audience "may be scary for children and those with animal phobias."

Rock Hudson narrated the first Christmas Parade.

In 1989, the late Harvey Korman welcomed the park's 300-millionth guest.

Nixon made his "I am not a crook" speech at the Contemporary Resort at WDW in 1973.

To spend one night in every resort guest room on the property would take more than 68 years.

www.disneyworld.disney.go.com

PLACES TO LEARN MORE

The Complete Walt Disney World by Julie Neal and Mike Neal is fat and glossy and thorough.

Mousejunkies! by Bill Burke is irreverent and entertaining and full of tips and other useful information.

29 South Beach, Miami, Florida

SOME THINGS, WHEN YOU THINK ABOUT them, are absolute no-brainers, and you have to wonder why they took so long to happen.

So it is with the renaissance of South Beach in Miami. First swampland and mangroves, then farmland, this stretch of land between the Atlantic and Biscayne Bay started developing as a resort in the early 1900s. By the 1920s, it was a playground for the super-rich with names like Firestone and J.C. Penney, and it blossomed in the 1930s and 1940s with the addition of a collection of stylish Art Deco hotels along Ocean Drive.

In the 1950s and early 1960s, a couple of TV's earliest stars, Jackie Gleason and Arthur Godfrey, drew more attention to South Beach, taping shows at the Fontainebleu and Eden Roc hotels. But by the late 1960s and early 1970s, South Beach was a retirement community for mostly Jewish retirees from the Northeast, and it grew tatty and rundown. And dangerous.

We can thank the late Barbara Baer Capitman for saving the Art Deco hotels of South Beach. Passionate about Art Deco, she was president of the Art Deco Society of America. She moved from New York to Miami in 1973, and in 1976, she and a friend founded the Miami Design Preservation League. In 1979, she got South Beach on the National Register of Historic Places, which meant not only protection, but also tax incentives for restoration.

In the 1980s, *Miami Vice*, the hugely popular pastel-hued TV show, brought new attention to the area. And then, finally, came the money. Lots of it. And the celebrities. And the Europeans. And the supermodels. The old hotels were buffed and puffed, painted and pampered and neon-ed up, and South Beach blossomed again into a playground for the über-fabulous.

Oh-so-very fabulous.

This is a sexy, sexy place.

It's big buff boys in little shorts. It's gorgeous women in barely-there bikinis. It's convertibles and roller blades. Palm trees and cocktails. Beach and sunshine. It's swimming pools and movies stars. Julia Roberts, Rosie O'Donnell, Shakira, Gloria Estefan, and many other celebs have homes here, and many more come here for the scene. It's fabulous (expensive) restaurants and glitzy all-night-long nightclubs. It's a throbbing disco beat. It's decadence under the sun. And it's fun.

www.miamiandbeaches.com

PLACE TO LEARN MORE

Miami Vice is available on DVD and for streaming and can give you a glimpse of South Beach before the glitterati arrived.

30 *Weeki Wachee Springs State Park, Florida*

I FEEL GOOD ABOUT THE WORLD because the live mermaid show at Weeki Wachee Springs is still going. It's retro and silly and kinda sexist, but it's a quintessential roadside attraction, and it brings me great joy.

I saw the mermaid show in the early 1990s, incredulous even back then that the attraction had survived. My Weeki Wachee Springs snow globe is still a prized possession.

Since 1947, Weeki Wachee Springs has presented live mermaid shows: pretty young women wearing fish tails in an underground theater/giant fish tank fed by a natural spring. Their long hair wafting in the water, the mermaids smile, dance, sing, and blow kisses, periodically sucking in air from tubes.

Weeki Wachee Springs was the vision of Newton Perry, a former Navy man who trained SEALS to swim underwater. He designed the underwater breathing system and opened his roadside attraction.

When the attraction opened on U.S. 19, there was so little traffic that when the mermaids heard a car, they would hurry into their bathing suits to try and lure the drivers in for the show. But the show's acclaim spread, and it was a popular tourist stop through the 1950s. ABC Broadcasting bought the attraction in 1959, expanded the original 18-seat theater to 500 seats and updated the shows. Half a million people a year, from all over the world, saw the mermaids. (Trivia question: What do Elvis Presley, Don Knotts, Esther Williams, and Arthur Godfrey have in common?)

Today, Weeki Wachee Springs is a state park (good job, Florida!) and also a city in its own right—with a former mermaid as mayor. The attraction (which includes a water park and other stuff) has been spruced up. And each year, former mermaids reunite at Weeki Wachee Springs for a Former Mermaids show—an SRO event. Because once a mermaid, always a mermaid. And who wouldn't want that?

We're not like other women, they sing.
We don't have to clean an oven
And we never will grow old,
We've got the world by the tail!
And all is right with the world.

(And, yes, the answer to the trivia question is that they all saw the mermaids at some point.)

weekiwachee.com

31 Mall of America, Bloomington, Minnesota

THE FACTS ABOUT THE MALL OF America are a little bit stagger-ing. For example, more than 650 million people have visited since it opened in 1992; about 40 million each year. (That, the mall boasts, is more than the combined populations of North Dakota, South Dakota, Iowa and Canada. I'm not sure if that impresses me or makes me a little sad.)

The Mall of America is reportedly the number one tourist attraction in the Midwest; 4 out of 10 visitors to the mall are tourists, who come from all over the world. More than 5,000 couples have been married in the mall, which has its own wedding chapel. It also has a 7-acre Nickelodeon-branded theme park, giant American Girl and LEGO stores, an 18-hole miniature golf course, a 1.2 million gallon aquarium, home to sharks and seahorses and Brutus, a 60-year-old alligator snapping turtle. It has trees and gardens and a comedy club. It even has a campus offering ESL and high school credit classes for local teens. And the mall hosts hundreds of events each year, including celebrity appearances—New Kids on the Block, Paula Deen, Stephanie Meyer and the cast of *Twilight* have attracted thousands of fans.

Oh yeah, shopping. Macy's, Nordstrom, Bloomingdales, and Sears anchor the mall and then there's...well, pretty much anything else you might want. Eddie Bauer. Hot Topic. Williams Sonoma. J. Crew. Marshall's. Best Buy. Barnes &

Noble. Sephora. Fredericks of Hollywood, a Barbie shop. Also, Minnesota has no sales tax on clothing and shoes.

The mall is just outside Minneapolis/St. Paul. You can practically day trip to it from anywhere in the country: it's just five minutes from the airport, and a train runs between the mall and the airport about every ten minutes. Most of the more than thirty nearby hotels offer free shuttles to and from the mall, including the Sioux-owned Mystic Lake Casino Hotel in Prior Lake, Minnesota, in case you need another way to rid yourself of money.

Really, once you're in the area, it's almost impossible to fight the Mall of America's gravitational pull.

www.mallofamerica.com

32 *Junk Food Museums*

WHAT IS MORE AMERICAN THAN JUNK food? We invent it, ingest it, and export it. We might as well pay it respect with a pilgrimage to a museum dedicated to our guilty pleasures. Admit it—you sometimes turn to one of these when you need the comfort only fat and calories can provide.

It's hard for me to wrap my mind around the thought of SPAM as a viable dinner alternative, but I understand that some people actually like SPAM, which is made of pig bits I don't want to think about. Enough people are SPAM fans for Hormel to justify building the SPAM Museum across from its plant in Austin, Minnesota (a couple of hours from Minneapolis). View the mighty wall of SPAM cans. See a replica of a SPAM conveyor belt and a mock assembly line where visitors may can their own SPAM, if they can. You may get a SPAM snack while you learn about the evolution of the SPAM can, peruse vintage ads, get some new recipes at SPAM cooking demos. All free!

www.spam.com

If any food product could be accused of aiming for world domination, it would have to be Coca-Cola. Or has it already accomplished said domination? Decide for yourself at The World of

Coca-Cola in Atlanta, Georgia, a 60,000-square-foot interactive museum befitting the world's most popular drug. It's a fizzy wonderland. You can view a movie, *Inside the Happiness Factory*, about "the magic that goes into every bottle of Coke." You can meet the Coca-Cola polar bear. You can see ads over the years and watch Coke being bottled, see a "4-D" movie (a little chair shaking) about the secret ingredient, and visit a pop culture gallery of Coke-inspired art and design. Annual passes are available. Which is a little bit mind-boggling, when you think about it.

www.worldofcoca-cola.com

Considering how shmancy the Coca-Cola museum is and the SPAM museum's investment in its own legend, the McDonald's #1 Store Museum in Des Plaines, Illinois is surprisingly humble. The original store was razed, so the building is a replica built from the original store blueprints, with some modifications. The sign is original. Inside, mannequins wearing paper hats man (literally—they are all male) vintage food-prep equipment.

www.aboutmcdonalds.com

My favorite exhibit in the Dr Pepper Museum in Waco is the advertising room. If there's one thing soda pop companies do right, it's irresistible advertising. Pepperabilia is colorful and fun. *I'm a Pepper, he's a Pepper, she's a Pepper, we're a Pepper, wouldn't you like to be a Pepper too?* (Now, good luck getting that out of your head.) Dr Pepper was invented in Waco, Texas. The Dr Pepper Museum is in the 1906 Artesian Manufacturing and Bottling Company building, which is on the National Register of Historic Places. The nifty museum, which includes a replica of the drugstore where the drink was invented, gets support from but is not owned by the corporation.

www.drpeppermuseum.com

A few others: Ben & Jerry's Ice Cream factory in Waterbury, Vermont offers factory tours that include a movie history of the company and a look at the ice cream production floor. (If you're unlucky and arrive on a day when they're not making ice cream, your guide will narrate a movie of the process.) It all culminates in a sample of the flavor of the day. The Jelly Belly Factory in Fairfield, California (about an hour north of San Francisco) also has factory tours (and samples). M&M's World in Las Vegas is more candy and gift shop on steroids than museum, but it does include a timeline of the M&M's characters, if that counts as history.

33 Graceland, Memphis, Tennessee

AMONG MY DIRTY LITTLE SECRETS IS that I can kinda take or leave Elvis Presley. I understand and recognize his greatness, but I've heard enough of him to last me, thanks.

And yet I've still visited Graceland twice. This ridiculous, heartbreaking, heartfelt, extravagant man-boy mansion is as American as Mount Rushmore. Elvis is both a dazzling success story and one of our most potent cautionary tales; his death ushered in our era of celebrity tabloid journalism.

Elvis's taste was common, even allowing for the fact that the mansion is frozen in 1977, which explains the color palette (green, gold, orange). The living room is old lady fussy, with mirrors, white overstuffed furniture, peacock stained glass windows and a (to-die-for) sunburst clock over the fireplace. The TV room is like life in the future as imagined in 1970, with three old tube TVs set in the wall and a wraparound sofa.

But best of all is the Jungle Room, with its chunky, Trader Vic's exotic furnishings, faux animal skins, and floor and ceiling covered with green shag carpeting.

Your tour ends up at Elvis's grave—which, after the kitschfest of the mansion, is quietly moving, as any gravesite is. You also can tour Elvis's Car Museum and the Lisa Marie, the private jet he had customized.

Here's another confession: On my last trip to Memphis, I skipped the mansion but made a pilgrimage to the glittering complex of over-the-top Elvis gift shops across the street. They're a total kitschgasm, although you have to spend kinda serious money if you want to carry an Elvis handbag ($50 and up) or tote Elvis luggage (in the $100s).

www.elvis.com/graceland

PLACES TO LEARN MORE

Really, how can you not know about Elvis? He's ubiquitous. But for a quick Elvis education—perhaps you're taking a young person—I'd suggest starting with the movie *Jailhouse Rock*, then one or two of the happy-go-lucky movies like *Girls, Girls, Girls* or *Blue Hawai'i*, and then finish off with *Elvis on Tour*, a documentary from the 1970s, at the precipice of his descent to dissolution.

34 Mount Rushmore, Keystone, South Dakota

MOUNT RUSHMORE IS ONE OF THOSE things you've seen a million times in photos, movies, postcards, and such, but you've never really seen it until you've really seen it.

I try to be reverent about Mount Rushmore, since those four presidents were pretty righteous dudes, but the audacity of it just makes me giggle. Mount Rushmore is the pinnacle of American kitsch.

If you don't believe me, visit the vast gift shop. There's the standard fare and lots of it—postcards and jewelry and T-shirts and key chains and little personalized license plates that never have my name on them. But then they just kept going, slapping Mount Rushmore on anything they could get their hands on. There's a wall of Mount Rushmore socks alone. Mount Rushmore salt water taffy? Why? Because it's Mount Rushmore.

The sculpture is actually a little hard to make out at first, as you approach from the parking lot, passing through stone portals and walking a broad boulevard flanked by columns displaying flags of the 50 states. Then you pass the gift shop and step out on a viewing platform, and there it is, totally Mount Rushmore! It's a little farther away than I expected, and it's difficult to get a sense of its hugeness, but it is no less its amazing self.

The sight is surreal not only because it's four giant heads carved into the side of a mountain, but also because it's so iconic, so familiar. I have a hard time tearing myself away, as I struggle to morph together the familiar image and the reality. There it is. There it really is.

To an extent, Mount Rushmore National Memorial was conceived with tourists in mind. It was dreamed up by a state historian named Doane Robinson to bring people to South Dakota, and in 1924, he contacted sculptor Gutzon Borglum to get the crazy scheme started. But not so crazy, too, as local and state politicians got on the bandwagon. Congress said, "Sure" to carving the memorial on federal land in the glorious Black Hills of South Dakota, and President Calvin Coolidge signed over some federal funds to get things rolling.

By 1927, the carving was underway. More than 400 people worked on the sculpture before it was completed in 1941. Remarkably, there was not a single death, even though 90 percent of the carving was done with dynamite, and men were raised and lowered along the rock face in bosun chairs, which are little more than a piece of wood and some straps. But this was the Depression, and for $8 a day, risking death to carve a president's nostril was a good job.

This entire region is remote, but one of America's greatest deep cuts. The Black Hills are lovely. If you need schlock and gambling, you have Deadwood. And Custer State Park is a magical slice of mountains and prairie, and a necessary sight to see in its own right.

www.nps.gov/moru

❧

PLACES TO LEARN MORE

Mount Rushmore's most famous film appearance is at the
climactic ending of Alfred Hitchcock's 1958 thriller, *North by
Northwest*, with Cary Grant and Eva Marie Saint.

MORE PLACES

The Black Hills are sacred to the Lakota Sioux, who were more
than a little miffed when white guys came along and carved those
big ol' faces in their mountains. But now, while you're in the
neighborhood, you can check out the Crazy Horse Memorial,
another massive undertaking to honor the Lakota warrior—and
even more ginormous than Mount Rushmore. So far, there's a
(very impressive) face, a lot of dreams, and not a lot of money.
A rambling museum starts with an excellent exhibit of Native
American art and artifacts, and, as you wend your way deeper,
gets a little weird, culminating in a spooky collection of sculptor
Korczak Ziolkowski's odds and ends. Good gift shop for Native
American art and tchotchkes.

II

Americans' History

35 Ellis Island, New York City

WHEN I WAS GROWING UP IN New York City in the 1960s and 1970s, Ellis Island was a glowering, abandoned hulk in the river to which most New Yorkers gave little thought. In retrospect ...how odd, especially considering how many of our families (mine included) entered the country through the building's then-moldering halls.

Since 1982, and more than $500 million later (all raised from the private sector), Ellis Island and the Statue of Liberty (more on that in Chapter 20) have been beautifully restored, and Ellis Island has been developed into one of our nation's most moving museums, focused on the great wave of immigration at the turn of the 19th century, when about 25 million people came to the United States to escape starvation, persecution, poverty, or just to chase the American dream.

The main building itself is a magnificent sight. The Great Hall, where immigrants waited to be registered and inspected, has been exquisitely restored, down to reproductions of the inspectors' desks. Alongside the big story of how immigrants were processed, the museum is peopled with thousands of photos and artifacts, written and oral histories, telling individual stories of coming to the New World. It is all too much to absorb in one visit, but the overall effect is deeply moving and evocative.

One of my favorite exhibits is in the Baggage Room: a long stretch of the suitcases and baskets, trunks and boxes people brought with them, filled with the things they couldn't leave behind. They are so homely, so concrete and imbued with the lives of people long gone. The Treasures from Home exhibit on the third floor displays what might have been carried in those receptacles, dirndls to bibles.

Ellis Island comprises hundreds and thousands of stories that make up one enormous story. Ellis Island is the story of families, of generations, of parents and children and grandchildren and great-grandchildren. Its Great Hall seems to still hold echoes of the babble of thousands of immigrants speaking a thousand dialects (give or take).

The immigration station opened in 1892, and the first person processed was young Annie Moore, who arrived from County Cork, on December 31 and was granted entry the next day. She was one of 148 steerage passengers on the S.S. *Nevada*, including her two younger brothers. Ellis Island's bronze statue of Annie Moore honors her arrival and the beginning of the great migration; another statue of her stands on the other side of the Atlantic, at her point of departure in Cobh, Ireland.

Over the next 62 years, more than 12 million immigrants passed through Ellis Island, undergoing an inspection that took 5 or 6 hours before they were either released to their new adventures or, for an unhappy 2 percent, denied entry.

Among the notables who passed through Ellis Island either as immigrants or returning to the U.S. after traveling are (to name just a few): Claudette Colbert; Rudyard Kipling; Israel Beilin (Irving Berlin); Leslie Hape (Bob Hope); Carl Jung; Theodore Roosevelt; Herbert Hoover; Albert Einstein; F. Scott Fitzgerald; George Gershwin; and Tobias Wendy and Fannie

Kaftal. (O.K., those last two are my grandparents. So not-so famous.) The Ellis Island list of famous arrivals includes only a couple of women, including notably Colbert and a couple of Titanic survivors.

The museum feels very personal if your ancestors were among those who entered the country via Ellis Island. You can search for their records and names on the ship manifest, even see a photo of the ship they sailed in on, on computers or online. And, if your family paid for the privilege, look for their names on the American Immigrant Wall of Honor outside the museum.

www.ellisisland.org

36 Angel Island State Park, San Francisco, California

IT'S BEEN A COUPLE OF DECADES since my visit to the Angel Island Immigration Station, but I recall perfectly the haunting emotions stirred by Chinese characters carved into the walls of one of the detention barracks.

"It was like ghosts were in there," said park ranger Alex Weiss who, in 1970, was the first to notice the characters in many languages, but mostly Chinese. These were poems and cries of lament, despair, and anger carved into the walls by detainees.

I wish I could travel on a cloud far away, reunite with my wife and son.
How was I to know I would become a prisoner suffering in the wooden building?
The barbarians' abuse is really difficult to take.

At one point in its history, Angel Island was less an immigration station than a prison for people guilty only of being Asian.

The first wave of Chinese immigrants came to the States during the Gold Rush (1848-1855); a second wave arrived in the 1860s, when they were recruited to help construct the transcontinental railroad. But as the Chinese population grew and prospered, so did prejudice against them—a bigotry ultimately sanctioned by the United States government with the Chinese Exclusion Act of 1882, which put strict limitations on immigration from China. To be permitted entry to the U.S., Chinese immigrants had to prove they had family here awaiting them. As the West Coast portal to the nation from 1910 to 1940, Angel Island was point of entry for newcomers from China, as well as Japan, Korea, India and other points east of America.

At first, immigrants were detained in a ramshackle and unsanitary shed on a San Francisco wharf. Eventually the feds decided that they needed a building especially for this purpose, and Angel Island, at 740 acres the largest island off the coast in San Francisco Bay, was selected. In 1910, the Angel Island Immigration Station opened. It was not all that much better than the old, and the new buildings were immediately inadequate, overcrowded, and unsanitary. Nevertheless, perhaps 100,000 immigrants (the exact number is unknown) were processed here between 1910 and 1940. Along with the Chinese immigrants came other Asian arrivals, including Japanese "picture brides," who waited at the station for their betrothed to claim them.

Detainees here were carefully and painstakingly scrutinized, examined, and interrogated. Detention could last weeks, months, or, in one case, two years. Most of the immigrants were ultimately afforded entry to the country, but barbed wire, armed guards, and isolation from loved ones were a poor introduction to their new home.

A fire destroyed the station's administrative building in 1940, and the remaining immigrants were moved. After the station was closed, it was allowed to fall into ruin and disrepair. In 1954, Angel Island became a state park. The history of the station continued fading from memory, and plans started taking form to demolish it for park facilities.

Alex Weiss helped bring the shaky position of the station to the Asian-American community, who then lobbied the state to preserve it. Today, the deteriorating buildings have been restored, the carvings stabilized, and the immigration station is open for tours. You may visit the grounds any time the park is open and see exhibits and interpretive panels, or take a guided tour of the detention barracks. Though not our proudest moment, this chapter of our history should not be forgotten.

www.aiisf.org

PLACES TO LEARN MORE

Island: Poetry and History of Chinese Immigrants on Angel Island, 1910–1940 by Him Mark Lai, Genny Lim, Judy Yung

37
Galveston, Texas

I ABSOLUTELY, POSITIVELY CANNOT THINK OF Galveston without hearing Glen Campbell singing the famous Jimmy Webb song, *Galveston*. It perfectly captures the sort of windblown bittersweetness of the complicated, historic, battered little island.

As a major port of entry for immigrants, Galveston predates Ellis Island. From about 1845 to 1924, immigrants from all over came through the Port of Galveston, helping settle Texas and the Midwest. From 1907 to 1914, the Galveston Movement purposefully diverted Eastern European Jews away from the crowded ghettos of New York City and through Galveston instead.

The Germans and Czech immigrants who came through Galveston have given Central Texas much of its distinctive flavor, including barbecue and kolaches (which come in many flavors, all of them delicious). The Texas Seaport Museum, at the Galveston pier, includes a searchable database of immigrants who came through it to America.

Sultry, semitropical Galveston was a prosperous port city. The Strand—named for the London street and once called "the Wall Street of the Southwest"—is several blocks long and lined with Victorian buildings that housed shipping offices and other businesses. (Today it's more gift and snack shops.) Galveston's one-time high-rollers lived in what is now a beautifully preserved collection of historic mansions. The imposing Bishop's Palace, the Moody Mansion, and others are open for tours.

On September 8, 1900, when Galveston was the fourth largest city in the nation, a monster hurricane swept across the low-lying island, killing approximately 8,000 people and wiping away two-thirds of the city. The Pier 21 Theater on Galveston has a good documentary about the Great Storm. The gulf-side seawall that now acts as a barrier against a repeat of the disaster was built as a result of this storm. In 2008, twelve hours of pummeling by Hurricane Ike did formidable damage to Galveston, but the seawall held, preventing even greater disaster.

But inflicting more lasting damage on Galveston than the 1900 storm itself was the opening of the Port of Houston in 1909, while Galveston was still reeling. This struck an economic blow from which Galveston never completely recovered.

Galveston grew seedy through the 1970s, but then historians stepped in, and the island rebuilt itself on tourism. Things were going along quite nicely until Ike hit in 2008, but the city is rising from the puddles again—although some losses are forever, like grand old trees that lined the boulevards, many of which were irretrievably damaged by salt water.

Of course, for many Texans, history is the least of Galveston's attractions—they're in it for the beaches. In truth, probably only Texans feel that way about Galveston beaches, which hold potent childhood memories for many. But you have to grade on a curve here when it comes to beaches. They're nice enough, but they tend to erode and have little problems with jellyfish and tar balls washing ashore. Nevertheless, a beach is a beach, and that's good. It helps the history go down easy.

www.galveston.com

PLACES TO LEARN MORE

Isaac's Storm: A Man, a Time, and the Deadliest Hurricane in History by Erik Larson is a gripping account of the 1900 hurricane that nearly took Galveston off the map.

The Galveston That Was is an absolutely gorgeous book of photographs taken by such luminaries as Henri Cartier-Bresson and Ezra Stoller in the 1960s, of the city's then-fading beauty.

If you can get your hands on it, the re-enacted documentary *West of Hester Street* is the story of a Russian immigrant who enters the U.S. through Galveston. It's also narrated by my great-uncle Sam Jaffe, a character actor in movies and television. Uncle Sam was born in 97 Orchard Street, which is now the Tenement Museum (see Chapter 92).

38 National Civil Rights Museum, Memphis, Tennessee

TODAY, IT'S HARD TO WRAP MY brain around the stuff that went down.

Men had to wear signs saying "I Am a Man" to make that point? Really? Eating a sandwich at a lunch counter was an act of civil disobedience? Really? Hotels refused to accommodate even big stars on tour because they were the "wrong" color? Really?

Can all this be true? Really?

Yeah, it's true. All of it. And it wasn't that long ago.

Of course, I know all this, and you probably do too, but I am shocked and saddened every time I am confronted with it anew.

The National Civil Rights Museum isn't fun. It's a confrontation with a painful past in a location permeated with sadness and shame: The Lorraine Motel, where Dr. Martin Luther King, Jr. was assassinated.

The two-story building, no different from any other run-of-the-mill '50s-era motel, was a heartbeat of the black community in Memphis. Artists from Stax Records (see Chapter 68), who  were barred from other hotels all stayed here: Ray Charles, Otis Redding, Aretha Franklin, Wilson Pickett, and many others. (And can you imagine what a cool scene that must have been?) Martin Luther King, Jr. stayed here many times before April 4, 1968, when he was gunned down on the motel balcony. Today, a wreath marks the spot, and the Lorraine Motel is a designated historic site, a shrine, and part of the National Civil Rights Museum.

Gentrification is creeping into the historic industrial neighborhood four blocks south of the Mississippi River, where the museum is located. At the time of this writing, the main museum was undergoing an extensive renovation, to reopen in 2014, but centerpiece experiences from the old exhibits will remain. The museum takes you inside the civil rights movement, with photos, recordings, and inside stories.

You can, for example, sit on a bus next to a statue of Rosa Parks, who triggered the first serious exercise of black power, in Montgomery, Alabama. In Montgomery at that time, 70 percent of bus riders were black women, mostly maids. So when they boycotted the buses, the bus companies felt it. And the boycott lasted 13 months, abetted by the fact that white women started carpooling to get the domestic help on whom they depended back on the job. The boycott didn't end until (white) bus drivers started getting laid off.

You can also stop at a lunch counter sit-in, and watch a film that was part of required training for students who wanted to participate in the protests. You'll learn about the Freedom Summer and the March on Washington, where expat showgirl Josephine Baker was the only woman invited to speak on the official roster. (Other women were relegated to unpaid, unofficial turns on the stage.)

You can also look into the motel room where Martin Luther King, Jr. had a pillow fight with the Reverend Ralph Abernathy and Andrew Young a little while before stepping out on the balcony to chat with Jessie Jackson, Jr. That's when James Earl Ray took aim.

The Legacy Museum across the street is in the boarding house where Ray built his sniper's nest (which is recreated here). Exhibits here focus on the search for King's killer, the aftermath of the assassination, and the inevitable conspiracy theories that followed. The exhibits end hopefully, focusing on people who fought or fight for civil rights of all kinds.

Pausing to fully grasp the reality of history is affecting. Even if you know the stories with your head, museums like this help them reach your heart.

www.civilrightsmuseum.org

❧

PLACES TO LEARN MORE

Eyes on the Prize, a PBS documentary, is a 14-hour overview of three decades of civil rights history.

39 Salem, Massachusetts

WHEN HISTORIAN CAROL F. KARLSEN, AUTHOR of *The Devil in the Shape of a Woman*, started analyzing what went on in the New England colonies, back when women (and a few men) were being tried and hanged as witches, she found a depressing consistency in the types of women accused and convicted: They were mouthy women, over-40 women, business women, women without husbands or brothers and therefore in line to inherit money or property. You know—uppity women.

And in Salem, Massachusetts, between June and September 1692, 14 of them were set swinging in a hysteria that was a grim milestone in the nation's history, so significant that it has entered our lexicon: Everyone knows what a "witch hunt" is.

Today, the town of Salem makes lemonade from a bitter chapter in our history. Old Town Salem is a charming village of brick streets and century-old buildings housing shops attracting the flamboyant and free spirited and magical: Wiccans and witches and pagans. "There are lots of gay people and women, middle-aged women, who wear flowing robes,"' says my friend Christine Wicker, who wrote a book called *Not In Kansas Anymore: Dark Arts, Sex Spells, Money Magic, and Other Things Your Neighbors Aren't Telling You.* "There's a lot of fortune telling and New Age shops. It's a town where you have license to be extravagant. It made me realize how drab the rest of the world is."

Oddly, this colorful extravagance has somehow become one of the few remnants of a really grim tale. (A tale told with narration and life-sized figures at the Salem Witch Museum.) The only remaining structure related to the trials is the 1675 Corwin House (aka the Witch House, 310 Essex Street). This was home to Judge Jonathan Corwin, who presided over the trials; you may also visit his grave at the Broad Street Cemetery. His fellow magistrate John Hathorne is buried in the Charter Street Cemetery. (His great-great grandson Nathaniel Hawthorn, author of *The Scarlet Letter,* added the "w" to his name to distance himself from his ignominious ancestor.)

And you can look for markers at locations of significance throughout town. The Salem Witch Trial Memorial on Liberty Street includes granite benches inscribed with the names of the accused and their date of execution. The town also has named a Gallows Hill, although the location of the original hill is unknown, as are the locations of the graves of the executed.

Time heals all wounds, and today, Salem has embraced the witch as a mascot; there's even a Witchcraft Heights Elementary School. Blame (or credit) the TV show *Bewitched*, which shot episodes in Salem and helped crank up the town's tourism. Today, a statue of Samantha Stevens/Elizabeth Montgomery stands in Lappin Park.

Of course, Salem does have more than witches, and there is a contingent in town that would like you to know that—they hope to bring the city's rich sailing history to the forefront, too. There's no witch kitsch to the Peabody Essex Museum (161 Essex

Street), but it does have a renowned collection of maritime and historical artifacts, for when you've had your fill of hocus-pocus.

www.salem.org

❧

PLACES TO LEARN MORE

If you can't find a staged version of *The Crucible*, Arthur Miller's dramatization of the Salem Witch Trials, you can rent the 1996 movie, starring Daniel Day-Lewis and Winona Ryder.

The Heretic's Daughter is written by Kathleen Kent, who is a descendent of Martha Carrier, the first woman accused and ultimately hanged for alleged witchery. In this novel, her story is told in the voice of her daughter Sarah.

Women's Rights National Historic Site, Seneca Falls, New York

HERE, AMID THE ROLLING FARMLAND, LAKES, gorges, and waterfalls of upstate New York, revolution fomented. In this tranquil setting, the women's suffrage movement was born.

Seneca Falls is one of the pretty former factory towns that developed along the Seneca River in the early 19th century. Today, it is home to The Women's Rights National Historic Park, and the things I learned here filled me with shame for knowing as little as I knew.

Growing up during the second wave of feminism, I knew from Gloria Steinem, Betty Friedan, Helen Gurley Brown. But for some reason, I'd given no thought to the women of the first wave, the ones who fought for the most basic of civil rights: to own property, to vote, to sign contracts.

Before Elizabeth Cady Stanton, Lucretia Mott, Susan B. Anthony (see Chapter 41), and others rolled up their sleeves and hiked up their cumbersome skirts, a married woman was helpless to prevent herself from being bankrupted by an intemperate husband (a link between the women's rights and temperance movements); women could not retain custody of their children in divorce; and they had no say in the governance of the nation or its laws. Women were expected to marry, and when they did, they ceased to exist.

Upstate New York has always been a magnet for freethinkers and iconoclasts. The women's movement was hatched by progressive thinkers and Quakers, whose religious tenets include complete equality for all people.

These beliefs linked the Quakers with the abolitionist movement, and Elizabeth Cady Stanton and Lucretia Mott met at an abolitionist conference in London. Ironically (yet not surprisingly), women at this conference were denied status as full delegates. This pissed off Elizabeth and Lucretia and got them talking.

Several years elapsed before happenstance put the two women in the same place again. When Lucretia Mott visited Seneca Falls, her friend Jane Hunt threw a party to introduce her to other local smart ladies, including Elizabeth Cady Stanton. The gears started turning, and the idea of the First Women's Rights Convention was born. Soon after, Stanton, Mott, and others convened around Mary Ann M'Clintock's parlor table and drafted the Declaration of Sentiments, which said (and I paraphrase), "Party's over, boys."

About 300 men and women attended the First Women's Rights Convention, on July 19 and 20, 1848, at the Wesleyan Chapel in Seneca Falls. After debate and discussion, the gathering ratified the Declaration of Sentiments, and the fight was on. A mere 72 years later, women won the right to vote.

I sorta kinda knew all this, but history often is a lot easier to comprehend when you stand on hallowed ground.

The Women's Rights National Historical Park opened in 1980. "It was the first of its kind to talk about women's rights," said park ranger Andrea Dekoter. The park incorporates what's left of the Wesleyan Chapel, which is being rebuilt from the one remaining original wall (it's been a furniture store, doctor's office, opera house, roller skating rink, car dealership, and apartments); the Elizabeth Cady Stanton House, where she lived for 15 years and gave birth to four of her seven children; the M'Clintock Home, where the Declaration of Sentiments was drafted; and a very excellent interpretive center, where you can watch a film, view exhibits, and join ranger tours. The park service also owns the Hunt House, which is not currently open to visitors. "It's still in all its 1970s glory," Andrea said.

The houses themselves don't have a lot to see. They're mostly an opportunity to hear the women's stories and think about what these feminist foremothers accomplished. The Stanton house contains memories and a piano and little else, but requisite ranger-led tours shed some light on the woman. And our ranger gave a shout-out to Stanton's husband, who supported his wife's political involvements. Not so her father, who considered her an embarrassment.

The M'Clintock House includes a display about the Quakers. The M'Clintocks were devout and firm in their beliefs; Thomas M'Clintock refused to sell slave-made products in his store. Here, too, is the parlor where those first suffragettes gathered to draft the Declaration of Sentiments. The table on display is a replica; the original is in the Smithsonian Institution.

www.nps.gov/wori

MORE PLACES

Also in Seneca Falls, the National Women's Hall of Fame needs a powerful infusion of cash. Plans to relocate are bogged down by a bad economy, but slow down, read the plaques, and pause to think about the women honored here. There are women you know—Oprah Winfrey, Georgia O'Keeffe, Amelia Earhart, Willa Cather, Maya Lin. There are women you might have heard of but didn't know it, such as Virginia Apgar, who developed the widely used Apgar score, to determine right after birth if a newborn needs immediate medical care. And there are women you might not have heard of but who will impress you nonetheless, such as Nettie Stevens, who discovered that males and females have different chromosomes; Marjory Stoneman Douglas, whose activism saved the Everglades from development; and Ida M. Tarbell, a pioneer in investigative journalism.

www.greatwomen.org

41

Susan B. Anthony House, Rochester, New York

ALTHOUGH THE WOMEN'S HISTORY NATIONAL HISTORICAL Park is a work in progress, the Susan B. Anthony House in nearby Rochester is stopped in time. Even the gorgeous old horse chestnut tree outside the front door has been there since Anthony's day. "It's the last living witness to the Anthony family," said Annie Callanan, the director of programs and visitor services.

Not only that, but Anthony was famous (to some, infamous) in her lifetime, so her life is well documented, and much of it occurred in the neat brick house, where Frederick Douglass was a frequent visitor, as were friends such as Elizabeth Cady Stanton, to whose children Anthony was "Aunt Susan." (See Chapter 40.)

Anthony's sister Mary, a teacher, owned the house, and the sisters lived there for many years. Mary provided unwavering support for her sister's mission-driven life. After Susan died in 1906 and Mary in 1907, the house passed out of family hands for forty years. But the Rochester Federation of Women's Clubs bought it in 1946, and when they did, the artifacts of Anthony's life starting returning to the house—even the alligator purse that children sang about in a jump-rope rhyme.

The rosy, doily-strewn parlor, recreated in the house, is where in 1872, when she was 52 years old, Anthony was arrested for illegally casting a vote. Her plan was to challenge the constitutional definition of "citizen" in the recently passed 14th Amendment. Election officials debated mightily before letting her and about 20 other women cast votes, but ultimately accepted the ballots. Anthony was arrested anyway, tried, convicted, and fined $100 and court costs, which she never paid.

One of her dresses is displayed in the home—she was hurt by media's depictions of her as ugly and mannish, Annie said. "She was not ugly, she was not masculine. She was very pretty and had a good heart." She also took great pains with her clothes and toilette and urged other suffragettes to do the same, so as not to feed the misrepresentation. Evidently, the hairy-armpit braless feminist stereotype was born at the same time as the feminist movement.

Anthony traveled to Congress every year for decades to put the law up for a vote. But she didn't live to see success. Annie choked up as we stood by Anthony's deathbed, and she told my friend and me about Anthony's last trip to Congress and the last words she spoke publicly: *Failure is not an option.* "She passed away a month later, after having just seen the law voted down one last time," Annie said.

That was 1906. Women won the right to vote 14 years later.

www.susanbanthonyhouse.org

PLACES TO LEARN MORE

After you watch Ken Burns's documentary, *Not for Ourselves Alone: The Story of Elizabeth Cady Stanton and Susan B. Anthony,* "you couldn't even miss a school board election without feeling bad," said Annie.

Iron-Jawed Angels, starring Hillary Swank, picks up where Susan B. Anthony left off, telling the story of Alice Paul and other suffragettes in 1918 who finished the job Anthony started. Brace yourself: men who opposed the women's suffrage got rough. It's not pretty.

42 Tennessee State Capitol, Nashville, Tennessee

REALLY? I'M GOING TO SUGGEST YOU stop in a small lobby, near a ladies' room in the Tennessee State Capitol, to look at a plaque? Really?

I know, I know. But it commemorates a pretty nifty moment in American history, and it never hurts to pause to remember an unsung hero. While you're in town.

It was 1920, a mere 72 years after the Seneca Falls Convention. Susan B. Anthony and Elizabeth Cady Stanton were dead. Suffragists had been suffering slings and arrows for decades.

At 24 years old, Republican Harry Burn was the youngest legislator in the Tennessee House. On this day in August, Tennessee legislators gathered to vote on the 19th amendment. Burn sported a red rose in his lapel, signifying opposition to the amendment. Burn was up for reelection in the fall, and the majority of his constituents in McMinn County objected to women's suffrage. Pro-suffragists wore yellow roses.

The first vote was whether to simply table the amendment until the next legislative session, after fall elections. Burn voted with the other antisuffragists, to table the amendment, hoping to delay the most important decision he had to make about the amendment: whether to vote to please his constituents, or his mother.

Because in his pocket, Burn carried a letter from his mother, a tough-minded, well-informed farmer's widow and a suffragist.

The newsy letter was seven pages long, but it also included an admonition for him to "be a good boy" and vote for suffrage.

The first vote, to table the amendment, deadlocked at 48-48. So the speaker of the house had no choice but to put the 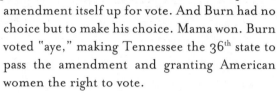 amendment itself up for vote. And Burn had no choice but to make his choice. Mama won. Burn voted "aye," making Tennessee the 36th state to pass the amendment and granting American women the right to vote.

You can visit the spot where this historic vote took place. The chamber of the House of Representatives in the Tennessee Capitol is as stately as one might expect, all crimson and chandeliers. The plaque commemorating the event? That's down the hall, by the ladies room. Presumably they hung it there to catch the eye of passing ladies and educate them on a little history they might not know, although the plaque, which was designed by a man, has exactly one woman depicted in the crowd of men. So, you know, whatever.

ॐ

PLACE TO LEARN MORE

For more on the story of Harry Burn and his mom: www.teachamericanhistory.org/File/Harry_T._Burn.pdf

43 First Ladies National Historic Site, Canton, Ohio

BET YOU DIDN'T KNOW THAT SEVEN of America's first ladies were born or lived in Ohio. Me neither. But one of those women's homes is now part of the First Ladies National Historic Site.

Ida Saxton McKinley, daughter of a successful banker in Canton, Ohio, married a young lawyer and Civil War vet who went on to become 25th president of the United States from 1897 until his assassination in 1901. Today, the Ida Saxton McKinley House is both a house museum and museum dedicated to Ida and all the rest of the 45-and-counting first ladies.

There wasn't always a lady in the White House. Jefferson, Jackson, and Van Buren were widowers who managed to get by without. It was Dolley Madison who helped establish the position of first lady as the White House hostess-in-chief, who gives the home the womanly touch. Before moving into the White House with her own husband, Dolley Madison helped President Thomas Jefferson when an event required a lady co-host. Her hostess skills were legendary, and she launched the country's ongoing fascination with our first ladies.

The National Historic Site, which also includes a separate education and research center with rotating exhibits, is located in the heart of a pretty, historically eclectic, downtown—although Canton is a seen-better-days kind of place, like so much of America's Industrial Belt these days.

A costumed docent leads you on the (required) tour of the McKinley house, gossiping about the family while showing off the kind of fussy home you would expect of a well-placed family in the Victorian age. Ida's story is interesting, but I was eager to get to the first ladies part, which is in the third floor ballroom, where a collection of first lady photographs and bios hangs along with a few artifacts, mostly belonging to Ida.

Like the Women's Hall of Fame (see Chapter 40), this exhibit has a sort of makeshift, make-the-best-of-it air. (Much of the exhibit is from the collection of one Craig Schermer, who is a prominent collector of first lady memorabilia and portrays several of the first ladies in educational one-man/woman shows.)

Still, it's a good reminder that history is chock full of interesting women, going about their business behind the wall of male dominance. We all know about Eleanor Roosevelt, Jacqueline Kennedy, and Betty Ford, but there are plenty we don't think about, and a lot of them have good stories, too.

Florence Harding of Marion, Ohio, for example, whose marriage to Warren Harding was her second, after eloping when she was 19 in a short-lived union that, records suggest, may have been no more than a common-law marriage. Warren Harding owned a newspaper when they married, and later, when he was taken ill and the paper's business manager quit, Florence stepped in and whipped that newspaper into shape—including hiring the state's first female reporter. And when her husband ran for president, Florence was the first candidate's wife ever to speak to the press and the first who was able to vote for her husband.

"I know what's best for the President," she said once. "I put him in the White House. He does well when he listens to me and poorly when he does not."

Attagirl.

Frances Cleveland was the nation's youngest first lady, just 21 when she married President Cleveland. (Reportedly, Frances's mother was a little miffed, having set her eye on the President herself.) First lady Mary Alice McElroy was not President Chester A. Arthur's wife, but his sister. Arthur was a widower whose wife died before his election. By this time, the nation had glommed on to the idea of a first lady. Arthur, an absent husband and father at best, had entrusted the care and education of his daughter, Nellie, to his sister after his wife's death, eventually moving them both to the White House, where Mary stepped into the role of first lady.

Rosalynn Carter, Hillary Clinton and Laura Bush have visited the Ida McKinley house. Michelle Obama, following in the footsteps of both Bush first ladies, Carter, Clinton, and Nancy Reagan, serves as honorary chair of the National First Ladies Library, which oversees the site. Presumably Michelle will pass the role on to the next first lady when her husband's term in office ends.

The museum also has a swell gift shop, chock full of first lady-related this-and-that: first lady coloring books and bookmarks, china patterns of the first ladies, biographies of first ladies for adults and kids (*Eleanor Roosevelt's Life of Soul Searching and Self Discovery* is the title of one), and lots of fussy froufrou apropos to the froufrou home.

In truth, you can learn as much and more about the first ladies by visiting the library's extensive website, which includes a database of biographies. But when you really start thinking about the kinds of women who marry the kinds of men who go on to become President of the United States (and hopefully, the gender inverse soon), the potential for a much larger museum is clear—as long as tourists prove interested. So, go. Let's show we care.

www.firstladies.org

Mount Holyoke College, South Hadley, Massachusetts

WESTERN MASSACHUSETTS IS A BUCOLIC LANDSCAPE. Within the cozy curves of the Berkshire Mountains are tucked lakes and farms and the kind of small towns that inspired Norman Rockwell, who grew up in Stockbridge, Massachusetts (location of the Norman Rockwell Museum).

While you're in the lovely neighborhood, pay homage to all-woman Mount Holyoke College. Because none of the Ivy League schools accepted women, Mount Holyoke was founded in 1837, the first of the so-called Seven Sisters schools. Educator and chemist Mary Lyon founded the school as the Mount Holyoke Female Seminary. The school has a star-studded list of alumnae: Emily Dickinson (more on her in Chapter 59); Julia Philips, the first woman movie producer to win an Oscar; Ella Grasso, the first woman to be elected state governor on her own strengths rather than following her husband; Pulitzer Prize-winning playwright Wendy Wasserstein; and designer Susan Kare, whose work you see every day if you use a Mac—she designed that little smiley face icon.

Not only is the Mount Holyoke campus storybook lovely, with red brick buildings and, yes, some ivy-covered walls, but the entire thing was designated a botanic garden in 1878, under the leadership of botany professor Lydia Shattuck. You stroll under and past hundreds of kinds of trees and shrubs. There are formal and informal gardens, and exotics are nurtured in the Talcott Greenhouse. At the campus art museum more than 15,000 art objects are exhibited on a rotating basis.

www.mtholyoke.edu

❧

MORE PLACES

To pay your respects to some of the state's other impressive women, make a pilgrimage to Mount Auburn Cemetery in Cambridge, Massachusetts.

Here lies abolitionist, pacifist, and suffragette Julia Ward Howell, whose accomplishment include writing the "Battle Hymn of the Republic" and inventing Mother's Day, though she had more lofty ideas in mind than brunch. She wanted a congress of women to gather and promote world peace, "In the name of womanhood and humanity," she wrote in her Mother's Day Proclamation.

Abolitionist Harriet Jacobs is also interred at Mount Auburn. Her book *Incidents in the Life of a Slave Girl* blew the lid off sexual abuse in the lives of slave women.

So is Mary Baker Eddy, who in the late 1800s developed some radical ideas about spirituality and health that she wrote about and named Christian Science. Four years later she founded the Church of Christ, Scientist, and in 1909—when she was 87 years old—she founded the *Christian Science Monitor*. Her life continued colorfully, with fame, ridicule, lawsuits, scandal (at age 67, she adopted a 41-year-old man), and continued poor health (she blamed "malicious animal magnetism") until her death in 1910.

And, oh yeah, a bunch of important guys are buried here too: Henry Wadsworth Longfellow, Buckminster Fuller, Winslow Homer.

www.mountauburn.org

45 *National Historic Sites and Parks Dedicated to Women*

THE NUMBER OF NATIONAL HISTORIC SITES and parks honoring women is a little on the skimpy side, but growing. Slowly, but that's the way things change for women in the USA.

Eleanor Roosevelt National Historic Site in Hyde Park, New York is still the only National Historic Site to honor a first lady. That needs to change, but it's appropriate that Eleanor is leading the way, as she did so tirelessly and passionately throughout her remarkable life and career. At Val-Kill, Mrs. Roosevelt's retreat on the grounds of the family's bucolic home in upstate New York (named for a river that runs through the property), Eleanor could pause for a few days in the splendor of the Hudson Valley, and catch up with close friends and family before plunging into her next trip to the heart of Depression-ravaged America. If you're expecting a dwelling fit for perhaps the most powerful woman of her generation, you'll be let down by the bare-bones cottage, but look closer: it reveals what really mattered to her—people, not pampering.

The Roosevelts' main house is comparatively stately, but if Val-Kill leaves you needing a fix of glitz, take a short drive down the road to the Vanderbilt Estate, a fancy pile of excess that proves, once again, that you can't buy taste.

www.nps.gov/elro/index.htm

Rosie the Riveter World War II Home Front National Historical Park in Richmond, California honors not an individual, but the approximately 18 million women who rolled up their shirtsleeves, put on hard hats or tied their hair up in schmattas and went to work in America's factories. The collective Rosie built the ships and munitions that helped protect and serve their menfolk, who were off putting Hitler in his place. The park, in a port city north of Berkeley, started with the Rosie the Riveter Memorial, at the former location of Kaiser Shipyard No. 2. Richmond's four shipyards built more ships during the war than any other city, and the place was home to 56 different war industries, so there were a lot of Rosies on the job here. The memorial is designed to resemble a ship's hull, and it has a walkway the length of a ship's keel, aligned with the Golden Gate Bridge in the distance.

Images, quotes, and symbolism of the structures honor and tell the story of the tough cookies who not only kept the homefires burning, but also blowtorches. Heading to work each morning was a novel experience for many of the women of America—their first foray into the push-pull of family and job. (All this came to a quick halt when the end of the war ushered in the Donna Reed pearls-at-breakfast mode of womanhood.)

The historical park also incorporates a number of other sites, including a Ford Assembly Plant; some remaining buildings from Shipyard No. 3; the SS Red Oak Victory Ship; and others. Self-drive tour maps are available.

www.nps.gov/rori/index.htm

The Mary McLeod Bethune Council House National Historic Site in Washington, D.C. honors Mary McLeod Bethune, who was born to slaves. In 1904, with a buck-fifty and five students, she founded what eventually became Bethune-Cookman University in Daytona, Florida, which now has more than 3,000 students. Bethune was an advisor to Franklin D. Roosevelt, and she established the National Council of Negro Women. The Mary McLeod Bethune Council House National Historic Site was her last home in D.C. She lived there only about six years before returning to Daytona, but it was also the location of the first headquarters of the NCNW. Tours and educational programs about the history of African-American women are offered at the house, and it holds the National Archives for Black Women's History. You can also visit a memorial to Bethune in Lincoln Park in D.C.

www.nps.gov/mamc/index.htm

The Clara Barton National Historic Site in Glen Echo, Maryland celebrates the former schoolteacher and government clerk who took her prominent place in American history by nursing soldiers in the Civil War and founding the American Red Cross. Ironically, Clara Barton was not actually a nurse.

 The Angel of the Battlefield had to lobby the U.S. Army for permission to carry medical supplies on to the battlefield and tended to the wounded in the front lines of this particularly gruesome war. And although she was a Union supporter, she provided supplies to Confederate hospitals and tended soldiers on both sides.

After the war, Barton worked exhaustively to help locate and account for missing soldiers. She founded the American Red Cross (modeled after the international organization) in 1881 and led it until 1904, expanding its mission from wartime only to assisting in peacetime disasters, such as the Johnstown Flood in 1889.

The national historic site was Barton's home for the last 15 years of her life (she died in 1912), and, until 1904, national headquarters for the Red Cross. On an excellent website virtual tour, the spacious three-story house is described as "home, warehouse-like, hospital-like, hotel-like, sanctuary-like," for this woman whose life was her calling and whose calling was her life. The house may be viewed on tours only, which include her bedroom and Red Cross staff offices, the dining room where she served frugal meals to guests when she absolutely had no choice (she was funny that way), and a guest bedroom supplied with a sewing machine because nobody stayed here without being put to work.

www.nps.gov/clba/index.htm

The Maggie L. Walker National Historic Site in Richmond, Virginia is devoted to the daughter of a former slave/single mother/laundress in post-Civil War Virginia. Maggie Walker grew up to be a mover and a shaker in numerous venues. She was prominent in the administration and growth of the Independent Order of St. Luke, a humanitarian fraternal organization; she founded a newspaper in 1902, *The St. Luke Herald*, to communicate between the order and the public; and a year later, she founded and was president of the St. Luke Penny Savings Bank, making her the first African-American woman to charter a bank in the United States. When that bank merged with two others, to become The Consolidated Bank and Trust Company, she served as chairman of the board. The Consolidated Bank and Trust Company was the

oldest continually operating African-American-run bank in
the USA until acquisitions and mergers sent the name to the
history books.

The historic home, built in 1883, started as a modest row
house on "Quality Row," home to Virginia's professional-class
African-Americans, an area also known as Harlem of the South.
Although she was married at the time, Walker purchased the
home with her own $4,800, and only her name was on the
deed. By 1928, the house was a 28-room mansion. Captured in
the house museum is a portrait of affluent African-American
life, not unlike affluent Caucasian life, but for color. Walker
entertained prominent individuals of the era, including poet
Langston Hughes, and scholars and activists W.E.B. DuBois and
Mary McLeod Bethune.

The Harriet Tubman Underground Railroad National
Monument in Cambridge, Maryland was designated a national
monument in March 2013. The site is still in its nascent stages.
For more on Harriet Tubman, see Chapter 48.

MORE PLACES

Mary McLeod Bethune's home in Daytona, a Heritage Landmark,
was built in 1914 and was her home until her death in 1955. It is
now a museum filled with personal papers, photos and memorabilia. Her grave is on the campus of the university.

www.gcah.org/site/c.ghKJIoPHIoE/b.3522559

Clara Barton's birthplace is a little-visited museum in North Oxford, Massachusetts. that contains lots of artifacts tracing Barton's life from childhood to prominence.

clarabartonbirthplace.org/site

46 Women in Military Service for America Memorial, Washington D.C.

MARGARET CORBIN WAS A SOLDIER IN the Revolutionary war.

On November 16, 1776, she and her husband and about 600 others defended Fort Washington in New York. Her husband John was assisting a gunner, and Margaret had accompanied him as his helpmate. When the gunner was killed, John took over the gun. When John was killed, Margaret took over.

Margaret was the first woman in U.S. history ever to receive a pension from the government for military service.

Loreta Velazquez was a soldier in the Civil War, disguised as a man with the name Harry T. Buford. Sarah Rosetta Wakeman did was the same, under the name Lyons Wakeman.

Women, of course, were crucial to the war effort in World War II, although when the war ended, they got thank you very much, a pat on the head, and were sent back home. Not until 1948 and the Women's Armed Services Integration Act were women allowed to enlist during peacetime, make a career of military service, and receive government benefits. However, the same act also put a cap on the number of women in each of the services, and women could be discharged for no particular reason.

Women, of course, served as nurses (mostly) in the Korean War (you remember *M*A*S*H*) and the Vietnam War. Approximately 7,500 women served in Vietnam before troops were withdrawn in 1975.

By 1990, 40,000 women served in the U.S. armed forces in noncombat roles, although women were taken prisoner, injured, and made the ultimate sacrifice despite the job description. A war zone is a war zone is a war zone.

The Women In Military Service For America Memorial at Arlington National Cemetery, 11 years in development, was dedicated in October 1997, more than 200 years after Margaret Corbin manned the guns for her fallen husband.

You see what I'm saying here?

Really, what took so long?

Well, never mind, it's there now, a curved neoclassical building set into a hillside at the ceremonial entrance of Arlington National Cemetery. The walkway atop the building, which overlooks the cemetery, is lined with glass panels with inspirational and slightly indignant quotes:

From the storm-lashed decks of the Mayflower . . . to the present hour, woman has stood like a rock for the welfare and the glory of the history of the country, and one might well add...unwritten, unrewarded, and almost unrecognized.
—Clara Barton, Founder of the American Red Cross, 1911

The qualities that are most important in all military jobs—things like integrity, moral courage, and determination—have nothing to do with gender.
—Rhonda Cornum, Major, U.S. Army Medical Corps, Operation Desert Storm

Inside, the monument has the feel of a place under development, still finding its voice and style. Which is not to denigrate it, because what's there is deeply affecting, a glimpse into a deep untapped well of stories and history. The nurses who worked in wars zones had a front row view of the terrible toll of war. They provided compassion when the soldiers needed it most. They saved lives, they heard the dying words of young men—hundreds and thousands of young men. And they volunteered for that. They didn"t have to do it.

I'd never given that a lot of thought until I sat and watched, riveted, some of a documentary about Vietnam nurses showing on a video screen in the museum. (You must also visit the Vietnam nurses memorial, see Chapter 11.)

I also learned about Margaret Corbin, the Revolutionary fighter, and the Civil War male impersonators in an introductory video shown in the museum auditorium.

Exhibits about World War II and the Korean and Vietnam wars include uniforms, photographs, and other artifacts of women in the military. Exhibits come up to recent times and include a collection of emails written home by Master Gunnery Sergeant Rosemarie Weber from her station in Baghdad. (I wonder what history and museums like this will do with the sexual violence scandal rocking today's military.)

Pause and take a peek into the guestbook to read messages of admiration and gratitude from visitors. It"ll make you feel good.

www.womensmemorial.org

PLACES TO LEARN MORE

Vietnam Nurses with Dana Delaney is a gripping DVD that's shown at the memorial but also is available elsewhere.

Robert Altman's original movie *M*A*S*H* spawned the wildly successful TV show. There's plenty of nudge-nudge wink-wink sexist humor in both, but at least they acknowledge the presence of women in war.

MORE PLACES

The National World War I Museum at Liberty Memorial in Kansas City, Missouri, is a beautiful museum with lots of information and artifacts related to women's war efforts, from posters extolling sacrifices that women made at home to a beautiful collection of uniforms.

And we can't discuss the U.S. and war without mentioning Pearl Harbor. Everything changed for America when bombs hit Pearl Harbor on Oahu, Hawai'i, shattering a beautiful tropical day and America's illusion of invulnerability. At the USS *Arizona* Memorial, bubbles still rise from the ships below the water, and the final resting ground for many of the more than 1,100 crewmen who died that day. It's impossible not to get choked up.

47 Pioneer Woman Museum and Statue, Ponca City, Oklahoma

THE STATUE IN FRONT OF THE Pioneer Woman Museum is called "Confident" and depicts a woman in a sunbonnet and long dress, with a basket over one arm and a little boy holding her hand. She is stepping bravely forward.

"The kid is talking, of course," said a tired mommy viewing the statue (out of earshot of her energetic toddler).

Yes, well, some things don't change.

But maybe that makes it easier to relate to this woman. Imagine yourself with that chattering child in tow, walking who knows how far to buy sugar, or dry goods to make your own clothes, or medicine for your ailing cow. Imagine living a life in the Oklahoma Territory of never-ending chores, in a rough-hewn house, far from everything familiar and comfortable, and at a time when tension between settlers and Native Americans was high.

The hassles in our lives seem like breaking a nail in comparison. Pioneer women were made from stern stuff.

Interesting that Oklahoma has two of the nation's too-few museums dedicated to women (the other is the Museum of Women Pilots, see Chapter 52). But consider that during the Oklahoma Land Run of 1889, any woman over 21 who was the head of the household could claim 160 acres to do with what she pleased—settle or sell. And, said Oklahoma historian Arrell

Gibson, "It was pioneer women, not the pioneer men, who conquered the frontier."

The Pioneer Woman Museum honors not just only these hardy settlers, but Oklahoma women throughout history who pioneered in any way, from politics to pop music.

The museum is small but crammed with information. Leaf through books in front of each display and learn, for example, what a PITA it was to do laundry ("the weekly affliction") back then, and the day in the life of a pioneer woman—which included getting those kids up and dressed and out. Sound familiar?

Displays and artifacts include a pioneer kitchen with kerosene stove; an 1865 bedstead in which, the label informs us, nine children were born; tools of women's work outside the home, such as a sewing machine and switchboard; the tools of a beauty shop. Even getting a new 'do could be an arduous, all-day affair, and the permanent wave machine looks like the work of Dr. Frankenstein.

Even more interesting than the artifacts are biographies of some of Oklahoma's pioneering women, displayed on panels through the museum. Some of the women were Oklahoma natives, some moved there from elsewhere, some had their greatest successes outside the state, some made their mark in the state. Most are admirable, some are, um, impressive for other reasons. For example, Flora Quick who, acting under the name Tom King, was a horse thief.

But most of the women honored here are, indeed, honorable. Kate Barnard was an activist for prison reform and humane treatment of Native American orphans, among other causes. In 1907, Barnard was the first woman in the United States to be elected to state office—although she probably figured out pretty quickly that she wasn't expected to take it seriously: Her office was a cubbyhole near the men's toilet.

Lucia Loomis Ferguson founded the Planned Parenthood Association of Oklahoma City in 1937 and served as its president until 1953. Clara Shepard Luper organized a sit-in demonstration at a Katz drug store in 1958, leading to the desegregation of Katz stores in three states.

Angie Debo was described as "a knowledgeable and dignified hell-raiser." Debo, a historian, struggled mightily as a woman in male-dominated academia, and there was lots of pushback against her second book, which detailed how the United States hoodwinked Native-American tribes out of land and resources that had been promised to them in treaties. The book was controversial; many of the players were still alive at the time, and her publisher, the University of Oklahoma Press, pulled out of the contract. Years after she finished writing it, the book was finally published by Princeton Press, meeting a chilly reception. Today, however, it is considered a seminal work in the history of Anglo-Indian relations, and Debo is considered one of Oklahoma's premier historians. (Debo's struggles are downplayed on the museum plaque, but these women's stories may inspire you to do a little independent research, as they did me.)

More recently, there was Wilma Mankiller, the widely admired first female chief of the Cherokee Nation, the country's second-largest tribe. Working with a budget that grew from $75 million to $150 million during her tenure, Mankiller invested in education, health care, and community development.

Of course, there are also accomplished women in the arts—S.E. Hinton, author of *The Outsiders;* Reba McEntire; Wanda Jackson; gorgeous prima ballerina (and one-time wife of Balanchine) Maria Tallchief; and Louise Funk Fooke, the

"Betsy Ross of Oklahoma," who won a contest for the design of the Oklahoma state flag. One of the earliest (if not the original, museum administrators are unsure) mock-ups of the flag hangs in the lobby of the museum.

This is a small museum but surprisingly interesting. Well, maybe not so surprisingly. Like the women who marry the kind of man who becomes president (see Chapter 43), the kind of women who settle and succeed in an unforgiving environment—in many senses of the word—are bound to be women worth knowing about.

www.pioneerwomanmuseum.com

48 Harriet Tubman, East Coast

THE STRETCH OF UNPAVED ROAD IN Caroline County, Maryland, along the Choptank River is pretty enough, but undistinguished: flat, tree-lined, with lawns on either side and the river in the distance. But to Kate Clifford Larson, PhD, "It is magnificent. Very spiritual, very beautiful."

This stretch of road is where scholars believe Harriet Tubman ran away for the first time and where she rescued her brothers on Christmas Day, 1854. Today, the road is unchanged from the days Tubman walked it.

Harriet Tubman. We learned about her in elementary school. Short story: Former slave, helped other slaves escape to the North via the Underground Railroad. She seemed almost a mythical figure. We knew she was good, but she was hardly flesh and blood. We learned about her as children and then moved on.

When Larson read about Harriet Tubman with her daughter, a second-grader in 1993, her interest was piqued. "I just thought she was a very cool person," Larson says. She looked for a biography about Tubman written for adults, and found just one, published in the 1940s. "I was stunned." Larson wrote her dissertation on Tubman. Although Tubman couldn't read or write, Larson found a lot had been written about her by others.

"And of course, slaves were considered property, and property was pretty well documented," Larson says.

Today Larson is a consultant for the National Park Service, which has started recognizing Tubman's historic significance. The Harriet Tubman Underground Railroad National Historic Monument was designated in March 2013 in Maryland, where Tubman was born, enslaved, and where much of her activity with the Underground Railroad occurred. The national park is a lot of nothing, but Maryland also has created the 125-mile Harriet Tubman Underground Railroad Byway through Dorchester and Caroline counties and is developing a state park in her honor. Delaware picks up the route at the border for another 95 miles. As of this writing, Auburn, New York, where Tubman lived the last 50 years of her life and is buried, was awaiting designation.

www.nps.gov/hatu/index.htm
www.harriettubmanbyway.org
www.deldot.gov/information/community_programs_and
_services/byways/railroad.shtml

Harriet Tubman is stepping out of the pages of storybooks and into a fully formed historical figure who left footprints along the East Coast.

She was born Araminta "Minty" Ross in 1822 on a farm in Peter's Neck, Dorchester County, Maryland. There's a historical marker at the site of her childhood home near Bucktown, Maryland. The house is different, but, says Larson, "the farm is essentially the same as when Tubman was there, so what you're viewing is what she probably saw when she was a slave there." The site is so moving, she says, "I've seen people actually get down on the ground and grab the soil and put it in their pocket, and cry and pray."

In Bucktown Village, a historic dry goods store, now a museum, was the site of a life-changing injury for Tubman. When an overseer threw an iron weight at an escaping slave, the weight hit Tubman, fracturing her skull and nearly killing her. She suffered seizures, headaches, and sleeping disorders from that injury for the rest of her life.

After her injury, Tubman labored for the Stewart family in the town of Madison, working the fields and on the docks. There she met the rugged black mariners who Larson believes helped her take her first steps towards becoming legendary. Madison today is a tumbledown town on the bay.

Tubman jumped on the Underground Railroad in 1849, making her way to Philadelphia and beginning her storied life of helping other slaves escape. In 1850, she helped her niece Kessiah and Kessiah's two small children escape from the auction block at the Dorchester County Courthouse, where you can view a historical marker. From 1850 to 1860, she conducted somewhere between 11 and 15 escape missions, helping about 70 slaves escape, many of them family and friends.

Tubman's eventful journey through life finally took her to Auburn, New York. In this tranquil, green, and prosperous little town, she settled, purchasing a house from William Seward, former New York governor and senator. (He offered to give it to her, but she insisted on paying.) Her original house was demolished, but the frame house that was the Harriet Tubman Home for the Aged still stands, a National Historic Landmark.

Tubman started the home to help care for soldiers returning from the Civil War, and then started caring for the elderly and indigent. Although internationally famous, she struggled to keep the home going, selling vegetables to raise money for it. In 1903, she deeded the home to the African Methodist Episcopal Zion Church, stipulating that people should be allowed to stay free. The building, which is being slowly renovated through love and donations, is modest and contains a few artifacts—a fan, a butter churn—that belonged to her family.

www.harriethouse.org

Tubman will remain in our national consciousness as the places she passed through start telling her story in greater depth than a second-grade textbook.

"I think there are people throughout history, in our communities, every day, that have some kind of magic to them," Larson says. "I see that in Tubman. Even as a young enslaved woman, people were attracted to her. And I admire someone who was so incredibly ordinary, who came from such horrific childhood circumstances, and yet managed to rise above it and keep challenging the system and moving forward. It's just remarkable to me, and she's worth getting to know and celebrating."

PLACES TO LEARN MORE

Dr. Larson's website, www.harriettubmanbiography.com, is a good starting point. Her dissertation has been published as, *Bound For The Promised Land: Harriet Tubman, Portrait of an American Hero.*

49 Annie Oakley, Greenville, Ohio

IN A WAY, ANNIE OAKLEY'S STORY is timeless and modern: Woman abused in childhood overcomes adversity to find success. And, in a way, the rootin'-tootin' shootin' cowgirl image that has outlived her was just a veneer. Tiny Annie was very feminine, highly successful, and extremely savvy.

The Garst Museum in Greenville, Ohio is home to the National Annie Oakley Center and the best place to acquaint yourself with a woman whose reality might be even more interesting than her legend.

Oakley was born Phoebe Ann Moses to a Quaker farm family in 1860 in Western Ohio. When she was nearly six years old, her father was caught in a blizzard while bringing his crops to a grist mill, 14 miles away. When he arrived home, though still sitting upright, his hands and feet were frozen, and he couldn't speak. He died a few months later, and the family spiraled into poverty.

Annie was sent to the poor farm, then was hired out to a family that treated her so badly that for the rest of her life she referred to them only as "the wolves." When the abuse got unbearable, she ran away, back home to Greenville, Ohio.

After another stint in the poor farm, she returned home again. At 15 years old she taught herself to shoot, to help feed her still-struggling family. She quickly became such a good shot she had quail to spare and sold enough to pay off the $200 mortgage on the family home.

This was not the kind of thing most girls did back in the day. But Annie wasn't like most girls, which might be what Frank Butler found irresistible about her. She was still a teenager when she beat him in a shooting contest, and he was immediately smitten. They were soon married. (So evidently you can get a man with a gun, contrary to a song from the musical about her life, *Annie Get Your Gun.*)

Starting out behind the scenes at Frank's traveling shooting show, Annie eventually took the stage with him. She adopted her paternal grandmother's name, and they toured as Butler and Oakley.

From the very beginning Annie carefully controlled her own image, making all her own costumes and ensuring they were modest, to set her apart from the bawdy broads with whom she shared the bill on the variety show circuit.

Annie's skill with a rifle took her to the heights of celebrity. She joined Buffalo Bill Cody's Wild West Show, which was all the rage during the years when the nation was gripped by the mystique of the increasingly less wild West. She toured America and Europe, performed at Queen Victoria's Golden Jubilee and was one of America's earliest superstars.

When in 1903 a Chicago newspaper incorrectly reported that she had stolen a pair of men's pants to pay for cocaine and was a "destitute" and "pitiful" drug addict, Annie objected—most strongly. She sued the newspaper for libel. In fact, the woman who was arrested had claimed she was Annie Oakley, and the reporter hadn't bothered checking the story out. The libel raced across the country with Annie in hot pursuit. Six years and lawsuits against 55 newspapers later, she spent more than she was awarded but made her point.

The Garst's Annie Oakley collection is in two rooms—one focusing on her personal life and the other her professional life.  Attractive displays mix artifacts with historical background and photographs. Here is a gun Annie owned when she was just six years old, her sewing basket (a recent acquisition for the museum, donated by Annie's great niece), a pair of boots, one of her riding outfits from her later years. (The center would love to acquire one of her hats, says Eileen Litchfield, president of the Annie Oakley Center Foundation, but when one came up for auction recently, it sold for an exorbitant amount.) There are artifacts from her childhood home; posters from her shows; a traveling trunk; coins shot through by her bullets; and a collar and lead belonging to Dave, Frank and Annie's dog, which was part of their act. "He was trained to sit still and she would shoot an apple off his head," says Litchfield. "I always tell children not to try this at home. She was that accurate and he was that well trained. They mourned him like a child when he was hit by a car."

Also displayed are a gold medal and a little loving cup inscribed, "To Miss Annie Oakley, from her old home town friends, Greenville, Ohio July 25, 1900."

"That's one of the few things she kept because it meant so much to her," says Litchfield. "Even though she had traveled all over the world, she had performed for kings and queens, being at home performing for family and friends was the best." After retiring in 1913, Annie had the rest of her medals melted down, using the money to sponsor several girls' education and to donate to a children's health center.

Annie never really slowed down. She and Frank traveled, shooting and hunting, and she advocated physical fitness and firearms for women. "She taught more than 15,000 women to shoot," says Litchfield. (Nonetheless, she did not think women should have the vote.)

Annie died on November 3, 1926, and Frank followed 18 days later. Annie was cremated, and her urn was put in Frank's casket and they were buried together in Brock Cemetery in Greenville. You can visit Annie's grave marker and, like many people do, leave a coin. In case she feels like shooting the middle out.

www.garstmuseum.org

MORE PLACES

The Buffalo Bill Historical Center in Cody, Wyoming (see Chapter 23) also has a small number of Annie Oakley artifacts.

PLACES TO LEARN MORE

You can watch the excellent PBS American Experience about Annie Oakley at www.pbs.org/wgbh/americanexperience/films/oakley.

Of course, there's also the Irving Berlin musical *Annie Get Your Gun*, which was made into a movie in 1950 with Betty Hutton in the title role. It's a highly fictionalized account of her life, but it does include some famous earworms such as *There's No Business Like Show Business* and *You Can't Get a Man With a Gun*.

50 Lizzie Borden, Fall River, Massachusetts

Lizzie Borden took an ax
Gave her mother 40 whacks
When she saw what she had done
She gave her father 41

Whether or not Lizzie Borden actually did do all that whackin'
is still debated by people who like debating that kind of thing.
Actually, it is certain that she didn't do *all* that whacking: the
total number of ax blows inflicted on her parents—by Lizzie or
someone else—is 29. And Abby Borden was Lizzie's stepmother.
But perhaps that's nitpicking.

At any rate, Lizzie Borden, an unmarried 33-year-old woman
who lived in Fall River, Massachusetts with her parents, was
acquitted of the legendary 1892 crime. The decision seems ques-
tionable given the evidence that pointed to her. But some people
considered her too well bred. No blood was found on her—
though there is that little matter of a dress she burned three days
after the murders. No weapon that could be definitively linked to
the crime was found—although the hatchet missing its handle was
mighty suspicious. And much of the prosecutors' case relied on
the fact that nobody could come up with anyone else who might
have whacked Abby and John Borden. Could the maid really have
been that pissed off about being told to wash the windows?

If this is the sort of bloody history that gets your blood moving, you can spend the night in the house where it happened. The Lizzie Borden Bed & Breakfast and Museum has eight guest rooms. You can even stay in the room where Abby Borden was found: "With its beautifully carved Eastlake bed and dresser, the room has been meticulously decorated to transport you back to that fateful morning," the website promises. Which is a little creepy, yes?

If you're not up for staying the night, you also may take a tour of the house; and for Red Hatters, there's a special Tea & Murder tour. Or just pop into the gift shop for T-shirts, hatchet earrings, or maybe a Lizzie Borden bobble head, eh? Then you can visit Lizzie's grave at Oak Grove Cemetery and thank her for giving us something to talk about all these years. If she did it, that is.

www.lizzieborden.com

⁂

PLACES TO LEARN MORE

The Lizzie Andrew Borden Virtual Museum and Library, www. LizzieAndrewBorden.com

MORE PLACES

If you're still in the mood for mayhem, Bonnie Parker is buried in Dallas, Texas, at the Crown Hill Memorial Park. Her grave—marked with a flat stone—is on the west side of the cemetery; it takes a little searching to locate it. Look for a gravestone for Tyner; she's just to the right.

51 Brothel Museum, Skagway, Alaska

THE BROTHEL MUSEUM IS KIND OF goofy—a cruise ship attraction in a tarted-up gold rush town. Young women in saloon girl costumes lead tours of a historic brothel on the second floor of the circa 1898 Red Onion Saloon. It's a quick tour, just a peek into ten little bedrooms filled with antique female frippery, some actual artifacts from the bordello, some not. It's kind of easy to autopilot yourself through the whole thing.

But if you slow down and think about it, you realize the real-life floozies who worked in these little rooms were serious business. They were tough, adventuresome entrepreneurs, making their way with the tools available to them at the time.

Many of the women who turned to dance halls and brothels in the Wild West had run away from their families to seek adventure, or perhaps were fleeing abusive relationships. The prostitutes who came to Alaska in the 1890s had, for the most part, already learned their trade in gold rush towns of the lower 48. They were experienced, and often successful.

The first prostitutes to set up business in Dawson, Alaska, operated out of tents. Business was brisk; men lined up in the street outside the tents of the most popular ladies. With that kind of money rolling in, brothels quickly became more elaborate (and comfortable) affairs, usually attached to dance halls or saloons.

As in modern times, many of these good-time girls didn't have that great a time. Their stories are laced with alcohol, violence, despair, and suicide. But lots of others went on to live comfortable, even respectable lives, either by investing wisely, marrying well, or opening saloons, boarding houses, and hotels.

You have to work a little to make the Brothel Museum more than an entertaining way to kill 15 minutes. But really think about the girls who worked these ten little rooms. They used names like Popcorn Lil, the Oregon Mare, Pea Hull Annie, and Klondike Kate. They used Pear's soap to keep their skin touchably soft and flirted behind feather fans. Their rooms were fussy and feminine (each girl was allowed to pick out her own wallpaper, and fragments remain). But at the same time, they entertained—in the most intimate ways—raw, rough, unshowered men.

Downstairs in the saloon, each of the women was represented by a doll. A man picked his doll and the bartender would lay it on its back as a signal that the girl was busy. When the man came back down—or the girl sent her money to the bartender down the chute designed for that purpose—the bartender sat the doll back up.

If nothing else, the Brothel Museum might make you grateful for all the options women have today. It's easy to tart up the place with fresh-faced young women in cheap satin costumes, but the real women whose stories are represented here were considerably grittier.

www.redonion1898.com

PLACES TO LEARN MORE

I smiled and nodded my way through my tour of the Brothel Museum, but afterward, I stopped into a local bookstore and picked up a book called *Good Time Girls of the Alaska-Yukon Gold Rush,* by Lael Morgan that cast an entirely different light on the experience. Consider reading the book first.

52

Ninety-Nines Museum of Women Pilots, Oklahoma City, Oklahoma

ALHTOUGH AMELIA EARHART IS BY FAR the most famous female pilot in history, she was far from the first. Harriet Quimby was the nation's first licensed woman pilot. She got her license in 1911, but was killed in 1912 when she and her passenger were thrown out of her plane in Boston Harbor. The first African-American female pilot, Bessie Coleman, suffered a similar fate in 1926. The seat belt, patented in 1885, didn't come into common use in airplanes until the 1930s. Hindsight is 20-20.

The Museum of Women Pilots, where I learned about Quimby and Coleman, is a few rooms on the second floor of an obscure building at Will Rogers World Airport in Oklahoma City. It's small and it sure isn't fancy, but plan on taking some time here. There's a lot to see and even more to read; it's a fine collection of artifacts, outfits, photographs, and personal papers of female pilots from Quimby to now.

So much of history is so surprising. Unless you think about it, you wouldn't imagine that clothing for lady pilots could be an issue. In the article "How to Dress for Flying," Matilde Moisant, the nation's second female licensed pilot, declared, "I would not wear the bloomer"—that much-mocked garment of the early feminist movement. She tried a skirt over bloomers, but the skirt caught on her controls, and she had to rethink. Her friend Harriet Quimby wore a flamboyant purple hooded flight suit, and Edith Foltz (first licensed woman pilot in Oregon) patented the Foltz Up dress with a skirt that folded up for flying.

Amelia Earhart is represented here, of course, with artifacts and news clippings (more on her below). But consider, too, Jaqueline Cochran, the first woman to break the sound barrier and, at the time of her death, holder of more records than any pilot, male or female. In 1942, Cochran was appointed Director of Woman's Flying Training for the United States, and the Women's Airforce Service Pilots—WASP—was born.

Jean Parker Rose was one of just about 1,900 women, out of 25,000 applicants, who was admitted to WASP. Rose kept a wonderful archive of her service, including her acceptance letter ($150 a month during instruction, then $250 a month), test papers, pay stubs, and her rabbit's foot. Also a letter from TWA offering her a job after the war: "TWA does not currently assign women as co-pilots, but WASP employees would get first crack at that when they do," the letter reads. It was decades before commercial airlines took that leap: Emily Warner was the first woman hired to pilot a commercial airplane, in 1973.

To fully appreciate these women of the skies, take a seat at the museum's Dreamflyer, a just-for-fun flight simulator. Try taking off and landing from a favorite airport. Pretend you're really flying, and try not to crash. Then imagine doing it in a long dress, without a seat belt.

www.museumofwomenpilots.com

MORE PLACES

But not to neglect Amelia Earhart...

Until the age of twelve, Earhart spent summers in Kansas City with her cash-strapped and unhappy parents and winters with her well-to-do grandparents (grandpa was a judge) in Atchison, Kansas.

That home in Atchison is now the Amelia Earhart Birthplace Museum, a house museum interpreted roughly to the turn of the century, when Earhart lived here. It's furnished with authentic and representative furniture, historical photographs, and a gift shop. Each summer, the museum hosts the Amelia Earhart Festival, a mix of historians, music, theater, and funnel cake.

Though already an experienced pilot, Amelia Earhart's first flight across the Atlantic Ocean, in 1928, was as a passenger. The journey was nevertheless brave. Fourteen people had already died trying since Charles Lindbergh led the way in 1927.

Still, nobody—least of all Earhart herself—expected the fame and adulation showered on her on both sides of the ocean after that flight. She was an American idol the moment she was branded Lady Lindy and sent on that flight by publisher G.P. Putnam, who managed and eventually married her (a contract she entered into with reluctance).

Earhart is one of our first manufactured celebrities, a proto-type superstar. With breezy good looks and the talent and spirit to break ground, her life in photos and newsreels looks like a series of Ralph Lauren ads—she is trim and dashing, standing on the tarmac, smiling, her hair tousling in the wind.

In 1931, Earhart secured her place in history by becoming the first woman to fly solo across the Atlantic. In 1937, trying to fly around the world at the equator, which no pilot had ever done, she disappeared over the Pacific. The mystery of her disappearance has only perpetuated her legend. My favorite theory: She survived the flight and moved to New Jersey to live under an assumed name.

www.ameliaearhartmuseum.org

53 Nina Simone, Tryon, North Carolina

MAKE A PILGRIMAGE TO TINY TRYON, North Carolina (an easy day trip from Asheville) and pay your respects to the birthplace of pianist, singer, songwriter, and civil rights activist Nina Simone.

On February 21, 2010, on what would have been Simone's 77th birthday, a larger-than-life sculpture of Simone sitting at a floating keyboard was unveiled in downtown Tryon, commissioned by the grassroots Eunice Waymon-Nina Simone Memorial Project. As of March 2013, the project was still soliciting donations to finish paying the sculptor. An effort was underway to restore Nina Simon's childhood home—three rooms, 600 square feet—and open it to the public, but that stalled out. Most recently, a company specializing in 19th-century restorations has stepped in to help raise the money to restore the home and help locals find a sustainable way to maintain it.

You also can stop into the Town Hall on Trade Street and pick up a walking tour map of Nina's neighborhood in the East Village of Tryon. It will lead you to the house and historical marker as well as other landmarks of Simone's life in a historic African-American neighborhood.

Simone was born Eunice Waymon in 1933, the sixth of eight children. Her mother was a preacher, and by the time Eunice was three years old, she was playing piano in her mother's church. Her talent was evident, and local benefactors, including the woman whose house Eunice's mother cleaned, paid for her early musical training. These benefactors also later raised money to help Simone take advantage of a scholarship to the Julliard School of Music in New York City; she aspired to be the first famous black concert pianist in the country.

Money woes forced Simone to leave Julliard and move to Philadelphia, where she was denied admittance to the prestigious Curtis School of Music—she later blamed racism. At that point, she gave up classical music, took the name Nina Simone, and concentrated on jazz, standards, and R&B.

Simone's only Top 40 pop hit was "I Loves You Porgy" from the Gershwin opera, *Porgy and Bess,* but she found a place as a voice for the civil rights movement, rising high on the R&B charts with "Young, Gifted, and Black," a perfect anthem with which to make a joyous noise. She also pounded out, "Mississippi Goddam," written in response to the assassination of Medger Evers and the Birmingham church bombing that killed four young girls. In the late '60s, pissed off at America's racial tension and the recording industry, and in hot water with the IRS, Simone became an expatriate, eventually settling in the south of France.

Simone was gifted, but also complex, volatile, and arrogant. She sometimes lashed out at her audiences, and fans speculate about mental illness. The last decades of her life were rife with troubles and very sad. But she performed to the very end. Her last concert in the United States was in 2002; she died the following year.

www.ninasimoneproject.org

❧

PLACES TO LEARN MORE

Princess Noire: The Tumultuous Reign of Nina Simone by Nadine Cohodas traces Simon's life from Tyron to the bitter end. If you want to hear a lot—some readers say too much—about Simone's love affairs, there's *I Put a Spell on You: The Autobiography of Nina Simone.*

See and hear Simone performing at her peak with the DVD *Jazz Icons: Nina Simone Live in '65 & '68.*

54 *Kick-ass Texas Chicks*

DON'T LET THE MANICURES FOOL YOU: Texas women are tempered steel.

Perhaps it's disingenuous for me to include Texas, since I currently call it home. Maybe I'm a little biased? Or maybe not. I've lived here for 30 years, I know what I'm talking about.

Molly Ivins, the late and very lamented Texas political columnist, liked the old saying, "Texas is hell on women and horses." And she liked to point out that until 1918, there was a legal class in Texas that consisted of "idiots, aliens, the insane and women." Texas is certainly among the most macho states in the nation, and women here have had to learn to get their way by any means possible—often those involve womanly wiles. But "...the good news is that all this adversity has certainly made us a bodacious bunch of overcomers," Ivins also wrote.

And that's why Texas has produced such women as Ivins, a tough, witty, hard-drinking writer who wrestled Texas's politicians and always came up the victor, in terms of bulls-eye assessments and laugh value. We also claim Ann Richards, at whose grave you may pay your respects in the Texas State Cemetery in Austin. And you can stop at the University of Texas campus to visit a statue of Barbara Jordan, who served on the Texas senate, the U.S. House of Representatives, and in 1976 was the first African-American woman to give the keynote address to the

Democratic National Convention. (For all of Texas's patriarchal attitudes, women have done pretty well in politics here. In 1995, mayors of the five largest cities in Texas were women. In 2009, Houston elected an openly gay woman as mayor.)

Lady Bird Johnson took on the environment as her cause as first lady and after. With Lady Bird as the woman behind the man, the LBJ administration passed the Wilderness Act of 1964, the Land and Water Conservation Fund, the Wild and Scenic Rivers Program, and more. Lady Bird was a force behind the hike and bike trail around Austin's Town Lake, and every time we drive Texas highways in springtime, we thank her for the fields of wildflowers. You can honor the missus with a visit to the elegantly unmanicured public gardens at the Lady Bird Johnson Wildflower Center in Austin, a research center focused on the nation's native plants. (See Chapter 94.) You can also visit the LBJ Ranch in Johnson City, of course.

www.nps.gov/lyjo/index.htm

The late Mary Kay Ash—she of the cosmetics empire and pink Cadillacs—launched her business at the age of 45 with $5,000 and built it into an international operation. At the free Mary Kay Museum in the lobby of the company's world headquarters in Addison (a Dallas suburb), you can learn her story and see a video of one of her motivational speeches. You can also schedule tours to see her office and the Mary Kay manufacturing plant.

www.marykaymuseum.com

Not long after I moved to Texas, I had the thrill of meeting Hallie Stillwell, who arrived in West Texas in a covered wagon in 1910 and over the course of her long life was a teacher, rancher, horsewoman, sharpshooter, justice of the peace, newspaper columnist, coroner, and all-around beloved Texas icon. When I met her on my first trip to spectacular Big Bend National Park (see Chapter 2), she was sitting in the general store on her ranch in West Texas, where she received admirers with grace and good humor. Hallie died in 1997, just months short of her 100th birthday, but you can visit Hallie's Hall of Fame Museum, about seven miles from the north entrance to the park. Big Bend, by the way, is one of the nation's most spectacular and rugged parks, and here, on this huge, harsh, desert moonscape you can get a sense of what kind of woman it takes to survive and thrive. Could you do it?

stillwellstore.com/hall-of-fame

In Fort Worth, learn about other bodacious overachievers at the National Cowgirl Hall of Fame and Museum. The women inducted into the Hall of Fame are not all Texans, but it took a Texas woman to recognize the part cowgirls play in our national persona. The museum, first called the National Cowgirl Hall of Fame and Western Heritage Center, was established by Margaret C. Formby in 1975 in the Texas panhandle town of Hereford. It moved to its fancy new home in Fort Worth's cultural district in 2002 and has multimedia exhibits about ranching women, rodeo cowgirls, and showbiz cowgirls—Dale Evans to Reba McEntire.

www.cowgirl.net

Dallas also has some of the toughest cream puffs in the state—the Dallas Cowboys Cheerleaders. Yeah, yeah, hot pants and big hair and all those annoying retro prefeminism things. On the other hand, though they don't take the hits on field, they work as hard during football games as any of the bruisers in helmets. Get yourself a ticket for a game at the massive new Cowboys stadium in Arlington and watch. The hair tossing alone is exhausting. And, believe it or not, the cheerleaders earn just $150 per home game and nothing for the hours of grueling rehearsal. They make their money on appearances, calendars, and such.

It took me a while living in Texas to see past the women's polished exterior to the granite beneath, but it's there in qualities I now strive to emulate. I'm still trying.

❦

PLACES TO LEARN MORE

I'll Gather My Geese, by Hallie Stillwell. A remarkable woman's life in her own words.

Molly Ivins Can't Say That, Can She?, by Molly Ivins. A collection of essays by Ivins sheds light not only an original thinker, but on Texas itself.

Molly Ivins: A Rebel Life, by Bill Minutaglio and W. Michael Smith. A biography of the late columnist.

Lady Bird Johnson: An Oral History is transcriptions of a series of interviews with Lady Bird Johnson, recorded over 18 years.

The Yankee Chick's Survival Guide to Texas, by Sophia Dembling. Talk about disingenuous…recommending my own book? Sure, what the heck. I'm proud of it.

55 National Museum of Women in the Arts, Washington, D.C.

I'VE HEARD THE ARGUMENT FROM A number of men that the reason the WNBA is not wildly successful in terms of viewers, money, acclaim—all the things that count for success in American sports—is because even the best female basketball players can't hold a candle to the razzle-dazzle accomplishments of the men. Apparently, dunking is the difference between a thrilling game and a ho-hum one.

I thought of that argument at the National Museum of Women in the Arts. After all, it's well known that male artists dominate in our nation's most important museums. When it comes to artistic celebrity, men have dominated for centuries. But looking at 16th- and 17th-century portraits by painters such as Lavinia Fontana and Marianne Loir, I could  see no difference in the skill displayed or the beauty of the work. If you lined up portraits from this era by men and by women, I can't imagine anyone would be able to discern the difference.

I mention this era in particular because it actually came as a surprise to me that women were painting at that time, including commissions. Painting was, of course, one of the womanly arts that good little ladies developed to keep them busy and make them more desirable, but these weren't just dabblers. They were accomplished professionals working hard, but evidently under the radar.

If you want to escape the crowds at D.C.'s other museums, this is a good place to do it. There were maybe a half-dozen people there, all women, during my visit, though the rest of the city was mobbed.

The small museum is in a lovely building from the turn of the last century, formerly a Masonic Temple. Just a fraction of the museum's collection of 4,000 objects is on display, but the galleries provide all kinds of interesting insights into the challenges of women artists working at a time when men and a restrictive culture really called the shots.

For example, one reason women weren't making a splash in the major artistic salons of the 19th century is that artistic fashions of the time were for large-scale historical vignettes, but women were prohibited from studying the nude figure, and those types of paintings were often pretty fleshy. So women painted still lifes and animals and domestic scenes—all quite lovely, but not the kinds of things that would put them in the celebrity-artist spotlight. (This strikes me as the artistic version of chick lit, considered lesser because it deals with matters particularly relevant to women.)

Call me sexist, but I found myself looking for things that said "woman artist" to me. In "Still Life of Fish and Cat," Flemish artist Clara Peeters captures so perfectly the cat's cockeyed expression of irritation that the fish is on a plate instead of in his mouth, I immediately thought "cat lady." And in one portrait, Marianne Loir "...depicts the soft flesh of middle age under Madame Geoffrini's chin —a detail most fashionable portraitists would have omitted," the paintings interpretive plaque points out, and that speaks to me of a sort of woman-to-woman humanizing, an affection for who women really are rather than idealizing them.

Similarly, Lotte Laserstein's 1930 painting of a bathing woman has none of the soft-focus romantic eroticism we usually see in paintings of this common subject matter. Here, we see a muscular woman getting clean. A tennis coach, as a matter of fact.

Here are paintings by Lee Krasner, who is only just starting to get a fraction of the recognition that her self-destructive husband Jackson Pollock received; some beautiful drypoint sketches by Mary Cassatt (the artist who for many years was first come to mind when we spoke of women in the arts through history); and a sculpture by actor Sarah Bernhardt. I had no idea she was a sculptor too. The exhibits continue up to the present time, and there are galleries dedicated to changing special exhibitions.

The National Museum of Women in the Arts won't demand a large amount of your time but it does demand you consider, if you don't already, the appalling deficit of women represented in the world's great art museums. Sure, photographer Cindy Sherman is considered among the most important artists working today, but there have been a whole lot of talented women producing a whole lot of beautiful art throughout the centuries. Take note here.

www.nmwa.org

56 Dorothy Parker, New York City

WRITER, POET, WIT, AND DRUNK DOROTHY Parker was pure New York and one of the most widely known and beloved of the caustic wisenheimers who gathered at the Algonquin Hotel. We have come to know this daily gathering of opinion makers as the Algonquin Round Table, but they called themselves the Vicious Circle.

Although you're more likely to encounter tourists than critics at the Algonquin these days, the gracious, circa 1902 hotel in the theater district is gleaming and beloved as ever and a favorite pre- or post-theater watering hole. You can even dine at what they call the Round Table, though it's not the "real" round table (some say there was no actual round table, it was metaphorical) and it's oval, so take that into consideration before you plan an evening around it.

The legendary gathering started with a lunchtime roast of theater critic Alexander Woolcott, but the group had so much fun trading jibes and bon mots that it became a daily gathering from 1919 to about 1927. Along with a changing cast, the core group included Parker, Woolcott, humorist Robert Benchley, writer Edna Ferber, and playwright George S. Kaufman.

Members of the Vicious Circle who wrote for newspapers reported the group's brilliance in columns that were distributed nationwide, and this essentially provincial group of New Yorkers logrolled each other to national prominence. Even so, their acerbic wit was not for everyone; while Harpo Marx was a regular, Groucho found the crowd a little too tough. "The admission fee is a viper's tongue and a half-concealed stiletto," he said. However, this bitchy, erudite group inspired one of their own, Harold Ross, to launch *The New Yorker* magazine in 1925, naming Parker to his "board of editors."

You can find a few other sites related to Dorothy Parker's life on the website of the Dorothy Parker Society. Parker's life is not a particularly feel-good story: sites include the Palm Court at the Plaza Hotel where *Vanity Fair* editor Frank Crowinshield took Parker to brunch in order to can her from her job as theater critic, possibly (though not certainly) because Parker had offended the wrong theater powers.

And as funny as Dorothy Parker could be, she also was famously and frequently suicidal (read her poem "Resume"), and possessed by the bottle. She died broke and alone in the Volney Hotel, now just called The Volney, on 74th Street. between Fifth and Madison, in 1967 at the age of 73. Not so funny.

www.dorothyparker.com

MORE PLACES

Hardcore fans can make a pilgrimage to view the historic marker at the site of Parker's birthplace, at 732 Ocean Avenue, Long Branch, New Jersey.

PLACES TO LEARN MORE

The Portable Dorothy Parker includes poetry, essays, short stories, and articles by this great wit. *The Lost Algonquin Round Table* is a compilation of writings by the Vicious Circle, edited by Robert Benchley's grandson Nat, and Kevin Fitzpatrick, founder of the Dorothy Parker Society. Fitzpatrick also wrote *A Journey Into Dorothy Parker's New York.*

Jennifer Jason Leigh portrays Parker in the 1994 film *Mrs. Parker and the Vicious Circle.*

57 Christina's World, Cushing, Maine

Christina's World BY ANDREW WYETH DEPICTS the painter's neighbor Christina Olson, paralyzed from the waist down by polio as a child, lying on the ground in a field looking toward a weathered gray building.

The painting is haunting; the landscape seems to have sprung from a well of emotion. But in fact, the house on the hill is real. The Museum of Modern Art in New York City owns the iconic painting, but the Farnsworth Art Museum in Rockland, Maine, owns the farmhouse, which is ten miles away in the town of Cushing and is open to visitors.

Christina herself touched Wyeth deeply. She was, he said, "limited physically but by no means spiritually." Wyeth painted Christina, her brother, and their house many times between 1939 and 1968; the house appears in about 300 of his paintings. "To me, each window is a different part of Christina's life," he said. Wyeth and his wife were close friends of the Olson family, and he often painted in a third-floor room of the house.

Christina's World, painted over the summer of 1948, was inspired when Wyeth looked out the window of his third-floor studio and saw Christina crawling through the field toward the house. Although the figure is identified as, and represents, Christina, Wyeth's wife, Betsy, was the model for the figure. (Wyeth also repositioned the Olsons's barn in his painting.)

The house is mostly empty—a few pieces of furniture here and there—but for reproductions of Wyeth paintings placed near the views they depict. Across the street from the house is the Wyeth cemetery, which is not owned by the museum, so they particularly ask that you treat it with the respect owed any cemetery.

Oh, and if you decide to put on a pink dress and pose as Christina for a photo—you won't be the first.

www.farsnworthmuseum.org

MORE PLACES

The painting *Christina's World* hangs in the Museum of Modern Art in New York City.

The Farnsworth Art Museum has a collection of about 25 works by Andrew Wyeth as well as by other members of the Wyeth family. Admission to the Olson House is included in the cost of visiting the museum, or you may buy a ticket for the house alone.

58

Orchard House, Concord, Massachusetts

LIKE THOUSANDS OF GIRLS GROWING UP in America, I read *Little Women,* and like many of those thousands of girls, I aspired to be Jo.

So did my girlhood friend Cari Gutkin, who names *Little Women* as her favorite book when she was a girl. "I liked any female protagonist who defied the conventions of what women and girls were supposed to do," she says.

And Elena-Beth Kaye, a computer consultant in Los Angeles, thanks Jo for her happiness. "I've often thought that my internalizing Jo's love of Professor Bauer was part of what prepared me to be open to the love of my own life, who is much older than I am (and a foreign accent, too!)"

"Louisa has always fascinated me because she never gave up despite terrible odds, and she achieved beyond the wildest dreams of most 19th-century men," says historian and writer Andrea Squires. Alcott is an inspiring figure for Squires, who has written a screenplay called *Louisa's War* based on *Hospital Sketches*, Alcott's book about her brief period as a Civil War nurse. "I've always felt close to Louisa," Squires continues. "She was the one who didn't fit in, the oddball, overshadowed by a loving but eccentric father. I felt the same way as a kid."

Louisa May Alcott created her most famous characters from the fabric of her own life. She based Jo on herself. Her sister Elizabeth went by Lizzie, but like Beth, died young from scarlet fever, in a manner far less picturesque than her fictional counterpart. From 1858 to 1877, the family lived at Orchard House, a solid two-story structure tucked among the trees in Concord, Massachusetts. Today Orchard House is a museum, standing nearly as the Alcotts left it.

Louisa was an iconoclast among iconoclasts. Her father, Bronson Alcott, was a forward-thinking writer/philosopher/teacher with unconventional ideas about education that included treating girls with the same intellectual respect boys got. The family friends who came and went from Orchard House included Henry David Thoreau, Ralph Waldo Emerson, Nathaniel Hawthorne, and Margaret Fuller, who wrote an early classic of feminist literature, *Women in the Nineteenth Century*.

Alcott was an idealist, a calling that rarely pays well, and the Alcott family was poor throughout Louisa's childhood. The family had moved 22 times in almost 30 years before finally landing at Orchard House—and this because Louisa's mother Abigail inherited money. For a while, the family lived at nearby Fruitlands, when Bronson tried to found a Utopian society. But that foundered and failed after seven months, and the family returned to Orchard House.

Louisa wrote not only for love, but most decidedly for money, and she did quite well writing lurid pulp fiction anonymously or under pseudonyms. But when her publisher asked for a book for girls, she sat down at the desk Bronson built in her room at Orchard House and wrote *Little Women* (402 pages, longhand), which was published in 1868 and made her famous.

Approximately 80 percent of the furniture in the house today belonged to the Alcott family, and paintings by Louisa's sister May (you might know her as Amy) hang on the walls. In Louisa's airy room, you can see the desk at which she wrote *Little Women*. And remember the March's theatricals? The Alcotts did that too, performing in the dining room while guests watched from the parlor—the room where Anna Alcott, the model for Meg, was married.

You must take a guided tour when you visit Orchard House. Special living history tours, with docents in period costumes, are offered throughout the year, and the museum has a special holiday program— so no griping about how "Christmas won't be Christmas without any presents…"

www.louisamayalcott.org

MORE PLACES

You can also visit Fruitlands, Bronson Alcott's ill-fated Utopian community in nearby Harvard, Massachusetts. With Bronson and British reformer and journalist Charles Lane at the fore, the Alcotts and several other people moved to Fruitlands in June of 1843. By January 1844, the place had fallen into near chaos, with far more philosophizing than farming, and Abigail Alcott put her foot down to Bronson and told him it was Fruitlands or his family. He chose family.

The farmhouse and the surrounding 210 acres of forest and meadow were restored and turned into a museum in 1914. There, you may visit the farmhouse where the Alcotts lived, including Louisa's attic room. A gallery of American art on the property includes a collection of Hudson River School landscapes and a large collection of 19th-century vernacular portraits (and some paintings and drawings by May Alcott), a museum about the Shakers, and a Native American collection.

www.fruitlands.org

PLACES TO LEARN MORE

If you've already read *Little Women* (or maybe even if you haven't), try *Behind a Mask: The Unknown Thrillers of Louisa May Alcott* and meet the other side of Alcott.

Louisa May Alcott: the Woman Behind Little Women by Harriet Reisen has also been made into a fine documentary for the PBS series American Masters. The book is widely available, you may buy a DVD of the documentary at www.alcottfilm.com

59 *Massachusetts Women of the Arts*

POSSIBLY THE ONLY THING THAT TEXAS and Massachusetts have in common is a history of producing remarkable women, although while Texas women are physically rough and tumble, the women of Massachusetts flex cognitive and creative muscles.

Emily Dickinson lived nearly all her life in Concord, about 25 miles from Boston. The Homestead started as a two-story brick Federal-style home, but was added on to in a  hodgepodge of ways. It was built by Dickinson's grandfather, who was one of the founders of Amherst College. Emily was born on the Homestead in 1830 and lived there at the time of her death in 1886. Her prodigious output of poems—about 1,800, most written between 1858 and 1865—were written there, though none were published during her lifetime, except anonymously, and scholars aren't sure if those were published with her knowledge.

The Homestead was designated a National Historic Landmark in 1965 and purchased by Amherst College. In 2003, it opened as a museum along with adjacent home, The Evergreens, where Emily's brother, Austin, and his family lived.

The Evergreens, which was a social and cultural center for the town during the Dickinsons' time there, was preserved as it was during Emily's day and is completely furnished with the Dickinsons' furniture. Not so The Homestead, which is sparsely furnished with period pieces while the museum tries to track down the family's belongings and sort out which of The Evergreen's furnishings belong in The Homestead. However, the house has been repainted as it was in Emily's day, and the landscape is being restored (Emily was an avid gardener). The museum also is trying to restore the Dickinsons' library, and a list of the books being sought is posted on the museum's very informative website.

www.emilydickinsonmuseum.org

The meticulous formality of the gardens at The Mount in Lenox are a reflection of author Edith Wharton's firm opinions. My favorite author, hands-down, Wharton was successful, outspoken, highbrow, well-traveled, and wealthy. Wharton was the first woman to win a Pulitzer Prize in fiction; the first woman to receive an honorary Doctorate of Letters from Yale University; and the first woman granted full membership in the American Academy of Arts and Letters.

The Mount, Wharton's summer estate, centers on an exquisitely proportioned white confection of a house on a hill, set against a verdant backdrop. Built in 1902, it was designed by Wharton according to what her pal Henry James called her "almost too impeccable taste," which she explained in her 1897 book *The Decoration of Houses*. Originally 113 acres, The Mount is down to 49.5 acres now. The gardens have been restored to Wharton's design: she concluded that formal gardens should be divided into rooms after studying dozens of villas and gardens in Italy for her book *Italian Villas and Their Gardens*. The Mount's grounds include a walled garden, rock garden, flower gardens, and many thousands of meticulously chosen and placed trees and shrubs.

Wharton's taste is timeless enough to have attracted photographer Annie Liebovitz and *Vogue* magazine creative director for a shoot in 2012, in which they recreated photographs taken at The Mount in Wharton's day. (Ironically, though real-life writers were intermingled with professional models for these high-concept photographs, none of those writers were female. Oops.)

Restoration of the house itself is ongoing. Guided tours are offered, and The Mount frequently hosts programs about design, writing and other appropriate topics.

www.edithwharton.org.

Though a poet herself, Isabella Stewart Gardner is better known as a patron of the arts (ah, those were the days). She helped ensure that the artists of her day—dancers and musicians, writers, and painters—were seen and appreciated. She was well-born and known as a passionate consumer of life and a hostess who surrounded herself with some of the brightest creators of her day: John Singer Sargent, Julia Ward Howe, Henry James, James McNeill Whistler. She was also a bit of scandal, refusing to act the part of demure Victorian lady. She drove fast, smoked cigarettes, and was an avid sports fan, especially of the Red Sox and Harvard football. She had two diamonds mounted on springs and wore them like antennae.

Gardner's passions included collecting art, from Titian and Michelangelo to her buddies Whistler and Sargent. Her collecting was curtailed in her later years because the day's "squillionaires," as she called them—J.P. Morgan, Henry Frick, and the like—could outspend her. She decided to share her collection in a Boston museum that entirely reflects her vision. It opened in 1903 with a big fancypants bash. First called Fenway Court, the building housing the collection is fashioned after a 15th-century Venetian palace, with galleries wrapped around a lush courtyard. (Gardener traveled the world and her favorite place was Venice.)

Now called the Isabella Gardner Museum, this is a highly personal collection of more than 25,000 artworks, from Japanese screens to Matisse paintings. And like Gardner did in her lifetime, the museum hosts a variety of arts, music, and educational programs. A new wing, designed by Italian architect Renzo Piano, opened in 2012.

www.gardnermuseum.org

❧

PLACES TO LEARN MORE

Hermione Lee's biography of Edith Wharton (called *Edith Wharton*) is exhaustive and exhausting. I adore Edith Wharton but pooped out partway through and returned to Wharton's novels.

My Wars Are Laid Away in Books: The Life of Emily Dickinson by Alfred Habegger is a well-regarded biography of Emily Dickinson.

Not At All What One is Used To: The Life and Times of Isabella Gardner by Marian Janssen is the most recent biography of Gardner.

60 *Georgia's Lady Scribes*

FLANNERY O'CONNOR MANAGED TO TAKE A prominent place in the canon of American literature with a mere two novels and 32 short stories (as well as some essays and commentary). O'Connor's writing was quintessentially Southern Gothic, with characters often described as "grotesque"—although, she once wrote, "I have found that anything that comes out of the South is going to be called grotesque by the Northern reader, unless it is grotesque, in which case it is going to be called realistic."

O'Connor lived in Savannah (see Chapter 88) until she was 13 and you can visit her childhood home, overlooking quiet Lafayette Square. The three-story building was divided into apartments in the 1970s, but was purchased by a nonprofit foundation in 1989. The bottom two floors have been restored to the time the O'Connor family lived here, from 1925 to 1938.

Sunlight filters into the pretty little house, which contains an eclectic collection of artifacts. Here is baby Mary's baby buggy, family photographs, books, some original furniture, a doll that O'Connor probably ignored, family photographs, books. The front window looks out on the square, little changed since O'Connor's childhood.

Mary Flannery O'Connor dropped the "Mary" because, my tour guide Toby Aldrich explained, "She said, 'Who would buy the books of a Catholic washerwoman?'" And O'Connor was a

195

character from the get-go. "At about four or five years old, she was an adult," Aldrich said. From the age of four, she swore off dolls. By around age six, she was calling her parents by their first names.

From windows in the back of the house, you can see the garden where the family kept chickens and where five-year-old Flannery taught a couple to walk backwards, as documented by a skeptical British news organization. This was, she said later, "the most exciting thing that ever happened to me."

www.flanneryoconnorhome.org

MORE PLACES

The O'Conner family moved from Savannah to Atlanta in 1938 and then to a family home, called Andalusia, a dairy farm in the piney red-clay hills of Milledgeville, Georgia. From here O'Conner went off to study at the famed Iowa Writer's Workshop, and she lived in New York City for a time. But when she started exhibiting symptoms of systemic lupus erythematosus, the disease the killed her father, she returned to Andalusia, where she wrote her enduring works. (Although she started her first novel, *Wise Blood*, at the Yaddo artists' colony in New York.)

Andalusia is an inviting 544-acre estate of home, farm, forest, walking trails, ponds, informal gardens, barn and sundry buildings, and a peafowl aviary (occupied, but none of the peafowl here are descendants from the flock O'Connor nurtured and immortalized in the essay, "King of the Birds"). The land and buildings have a long history before O'Connor, but most visitors come to pay tribute to the author.

The main house dates to circa 1850, a white Plantation-style two-story home with a red roof and the obligatory wide-screened porch for those sultry summer evenings. Inside, you may see the refrigerator O'Connor bought for her mother, Regina, after selling TV rights to her story, "The Life You Save May Be Your Own." O'Connor's bedroom includes a desk and typewriter where she wrote for three hours each day, and the crutches she needed to get around as her disease progressed.

O'Connor lived at Andalusia for 13 years, until her death in 1964. She is buried at Memory Hill Cemetery in Milledgeville.

www.andalusiafarm.org

PLACE TO LEARN MORE

If you're making one of these pilgrimages, you presumably have read O'Connor's fiction. But her collected letters, in *The Habit of Being*, may provide insight into the mind that created the dark tales.

Another famous female Southern writer was even less prolific, publishing just one book. Margaret Mitchell was a rebel, a beauty, a tomboy, a feminist, a flirt, and author of one of the world's most popular books and beloved movies (*Gone With the Wind*), winner of a Pulitzer Prize, and philanthropist. Other than all that, she had a kind of rocky life. Her skirt caught on fire when she was three. Later, she broke an ankle in a riding accident (the horse fell on her), causing her a life of problems. When she was 17, her fiancée was killed in action shortly before World War I ended. Her mother died shortly after, while Margaret was en route home to be by her side.

Even the apartment in which she wrote her famous book has had a hard time. The Margaret Mitchell House has burned twice. But the three-story brick Tudor Revival building stands today and is listed on the National Register of Historic Places. Margaret's apartment, which she called "the Dump," has been more or less restored, and her little desk by the window recreated. The home has a collection of GWTW movie memorabilia, a research center, and a literary center.

Gone With the Wind was the only novel Margaret wrote, and she did it in the little apartment on Peachtree Street. She got rich and famous and gave generously to philanthropic causes, including anonymously donating money to educating African-American doctors and helping fund the first hospital for African-Americans in Atlanta. Then, in 1949, she was hit by a drunk driver while crossing Peachtree Street; she died a few days later.

www.margaretmitchellhouse.com

MORE PLACES

If you're more interested in the characters than the writer herself, The Road to Tara Museum in Jonesboro, Georgia and Scarlett O'Hardy's Gone With the Wind Museum in Jefferson, Texas both have large collections of GWTW memorabilia, real and reproductions.

Original costumes and other authentic memorabilia from the movie are part of the enormous David O'Selznick collection at the Harry Ransom Center at the University of Texas in Austin. Although not part of the center's permanent displays, lots can be viewed in an online exhibit.

www.hrc.utexas.edu/exhibitions/web/gwtw
www.exploregeorgia.org/listing/3880-road-to-tara-museum
www.scarlettohardy.com

PLACE TO LEARN MORE

You've already read *Gone With the Wind* and seen the movie. PBS has an excellent American Masters documentary about Mitchell at video.pbs.org/video/2218395311.

Eudora Welty traveled the world and won international acclaim, but she always returned to her family home in Jackson, Mississippi. Her parents built the three-story Tudor-revival house in 1925, when she was 16, and she lived there when she died in 2001, at age 92.

Welty was, of course, among the grande dames of letters in her lifetime, and so she knew her home was likely to be of interest to readers through the ages. She gave it to the state of Mississippi, stressing that it should represent a family's love of literature and the arts and not be all about her. Unlike many other writers' house museums, this home is intact as it was when Welty lived and worked there.

The Welty family was close, and warmth and a sense of ease seem to permeate the sunny home. Furniture is sturdy and comfortable, surfaces are stacked with books, and bookshelves everywhere are stuffed with more. Welty's desk and typewriter are by big bedroom windows overlooking trees and lawn. With such a place to work, it is no wonder she approached each day's writing with joy.

Welty was famously a gardener—it was a pleasure she and her mother shared—and the gardens have been restored to their most glorious era.

eudorawelty.org

61 Georgia O'Keeffe, Santa Fe, New Mexico

ALTHOUGH GEORGIA O'KEEFFE WAS BORN IN Wisconsin, studied in Chicago, taught in Virginia, South Carolina, and Texas, and lived in New York, once she started making regular pilgrimages to New Mexico in 1929, she took the striking red-rock landscape as her muse and became forever associated with it. Her modernist paintings capture the essence of the landscape with spare lines and rich color.

The woman herself was private, curmudgeonly, prolific, and famous in her lifetime thanks, in part, to photographer Alfred Stieglitz, who exhibited her work at his avant-garde gallery in New York, provided financial support to allow her to paint, and finally married her. She was also generous; when she moved to little Abiquiu, New Mexico, she funded village improvement projects.

O'Keeffe once told a friend that she loved New Mexico, "almost as passionately as I can love a person." After years spending summers in New Mexico and winters in New York with her husband, O'Keeffe bought property in New Mexico in 1940. She moved there permanently in 1949, after Stieglitz's death. Today, Taos, Santa Fe, and their immediate surrounds are known to many as O'Keeffe Country.

The Georgia O'Keeffe Museum in Santa Fe (see Chapter 16) opened in 1997, and its collections have been growing steadily since, to nearly 3,000 of O'Keeffe's paintings, drawings, and sculptures. The collection also includes thousands of photographs of O'Keeffe, her friends, her houses, her pets (she was partial to Chows), and places represented in her work. The museum rotates exhibits of her artworks, and exhibits works by her contemporaries and current artists. A research center and archives contain letters, books, and personal items, and the museum owns O'Keeffe's New Mexico homes as well.

www.okeeffemuseum.org

O'Keeffe's first extended stays in New Mexico were at what was then Mabel Dodge Luhan's home in Taos. These were the sex, drugs, and rock and roll years, in a manner of speaking. Luhan was a wealthy socialite and benefactor of the arts who was widowed young and moved to Taos, where she married a full-blooded Taos Pueblo man (more on the Taos Pueblo, Chapter 96) and built this home, where she entertained such friends as D.H. Lawrence, Carl Jung, Willa Cather (see Chapter 62), Martha Graham, Ansel Adams, Steiglitz, O'Keeffe and other creative, volatile luminaries. Attendant intrigues, arguments, and affairs ensued. Today, the Mabel Dodge Luhan House is an inn and conference center and continues the Luhan legacy with a calendar of arts workshops. Bring your own drama. Eventually, though, O'Keeffe stepped away from the social whirl of Taos and Santa Fe to find peace and solitude with her work at the Ghost Ranch.

www.mabeldodgeluhan.com

The Ghost Ranch was a successful dude ranch owned by Arthur Pack when O'Keeffe first steered her Model A up a rugged dirt road in 1934. "I knew the moment I got up here that this is where I would live," she once said.

O'Keeffe first lived among the ranch guests but kept aloof; guests learned not to speak to her unless she spoke first. In 1940, she bought the Packs' home, miles from the ranch center, where she looked out on the mountain Cerro Pedernal, which she painted over and over again. "God told me that if I painted it enough, I could have it," she said. As strong as the association between O'Keeffe and the Ghost Ranch is, she owned only about 8 acres of the 21,000-acre property.

You may not visit O'Keeffe's Ghost Ranch home; it is owned by the museum and strictly off limits. But you can visit the ranch (which is owned although no longer used much by the Presbyterian church) and experience that rich liquid light and the sprawling landscape of rosy mesas, mountains, and buttes that so moved the artist—especially if you take the Georgia O'Keeffe and the Ghost Ranch Landscape Tour, which visits sites O'Keeffe painted. You may day trip to hike the ranch's trails (a hike to Chimney Rock affords a grand view, including O'Keeffe's home); sign up for one of the weeklong spiritual or artistic workshops scheduled throughout the year; or simply rent a room and stay.

www.ghostranch.org

O'Keeffe's second home, in the town of Abiquiu, was an 18th-century adobe ruin when she bought it in 1945, but she and her friend Maria Chabot spent three years restoring it, and O'Keeffe then divided her time between there and the ranch. The Georgia O'Keeffe Museum owns the home and studio and keeps a tight control on visits and visitors. You'll need reservations for the one-hour tour (and will be required to leave all cameras, cell phones, and note pads in the car), but the serene beauty of the spare, elegant home with picture windows framing perfectly composed views, decorated with collected rocks, O'Keefe sculptures, and Charles Eames and Isamu Noguchi furniture, makes acceding to the museum's will worthwhile.

www.okeeffemuseum.org

❧

PLACES TO LEARN MORE

Georgia O'Keeffe: A Life, by Roxana Robinson, is the first biography to be written with the cooperation of her family and has a feminist perspective.

Georgia O'Keeffe in New Mexico, by Marsha Bellavance-Johnson, is a guidebook to the places that mattered to O'Keeffe.

Ghost Ranch by Lesley Poling-Kempes traces the long history of this exquisite hunk of America.

62 *Willa Cather,*
Red Cloud, Nebraska

THE STREETS OF RED CLOUD ARE quiet on a late afternoon during my mid-October visit. Dogs bark as I stroll past, and drivers give friendly waves. The cottonwoods are vivid yellow against a clear blue sky, modest frame houses sport autumn displays of pumpkins and scarecrows and American flags. It's all-American with an air of Norman Rockwell about it, and it's author Willa Cather's country, the corner of Nebraska that provided her with enough fodder to pen a canon of fiction that places her among America's greatest.

Born in Virginia in 1873, Cather moved to the Red Cloud area when she was about ten years old. She was not impressed.

"This country was mostly wild pasture and as naked as the back of your hand," she said later. But, she continued, "...by the end of the first autumn, that shaggy grass country had gripped me with a passion I have never been able to shake."

About 10,000 visitors and scholars pass through Red Cloud each year because the people and places in *O Pioneers* (which turned 100 in 2013), *The Song of the Lark, My Antonia,* and other novels and short stories can be easily traced back to these streets, these houses, the long-gone souls who once occupied them, and the prairie surrounding them.

Cather's father first tried farming on the prairie, but struggled. In 1883, he moved his growing family to Red Cloud, where he opened a land office. Willa lived in Red Cloud until 1890, when she left for college in Lincoln, Nebraska. After that, she lived in Philadelphia and then New York, though she returned to Red Cloud often to visit her family. The town adores its famous daughter and has dedicated itself to her memory.

One of the benefits of becoming famous in your lifetime is that people figure out pretty early that they should hang onto stuff for posterity. The entire town of Red Cloud is a living museum of Cather's life. You can even stay in Willa Cather's Second Home. She never lived here full-time, but her family bought the house in 1903 and owned it until 1944, and Cather stayed here often. Since then the house has been various things, including a hospital, but the Willa Cather Foundation, trustees of Cather's legacy, opened it as an inn in 2011.

You can view the exteriors of Cather's childhood home and other relevant buildings any time, but to get inside you have to sign up for a tour at the foundation headquarters in the old opera house downtown, which is where the tour starts.

The Cathers rented a trim little house on North Cedar Street. Willa's little attic room is preserved behind Plexiglas because visitors kept making souvenirs of the original wallpaper, which Willa (or as she preferred to be called for many young years, William) bought with money she earned working for the local pharmacist. In this attic nest, young Willa, like Thea in *The Song of the Lark*, found retreat, herself, and her voice as an artist.

The Harling House, named for the family that hired Antonia as a house maid and softened her rough edges, is also based on truth. The Miners, who lived in this house, hired Anna Pavelka, the model for the heroine of *My Antonia*. You can visit Cather-related churches and family graves, and you can drive out of town to visit Anna/Antonia's grave and her last home, a worn white farmhouse surrounded by prairie. Around the side, doors leading down to the root cellar are exactly as described in one of *My Antonia*'s sweetest scenes, when Antonia's flock of towheaded children burst from underground into the sunlight.

Finish your tour at the Willa Cather Memorial Prairie, 610 acres of virgin prairie grassland, unchanged from Cather's day.

www.willacather.org

❧

PLACES TO LEARN MORE

Red Cloud hosts an annual conference for Willa Cather scholars each spring.

The Road is All, a PBS American Masters biography of Cather, is available on DVD.

63
Little House on the Prairie, De Smet, South Dakota

MENTION LAURA INGALLS WILDER'S *Little House on the Prairie* books
and many women go all misty and sentimental.

"My sister and I each had long dresses and bonnets and used
to act out scenes all the time—I was Laura, she was Mary," says
Patti McCracken, a journalist who grew up in Virginia and now
lives in Europe. "And when one of us was sick, the other would
read from the Little House books."

"I wanted to be her. I thought she had such a cool life," says
Erin Correale, a New Yorker and new mom. "It seemed like a
real adventure to me. I can remember loving the idea of living
in all the different houses she lived in. I grew up in two different
apartments, and she lived everywhere and saw so much."

And, she says, "They worked, they really worked. I didn't get
a sense in my own life that I was ever going to work that hard to
survive. And I loved the idea that once the sun goes down, you
really have to sit with each other and talk, quilt, make things."

Amazing how the life of a little girl way out in the prairie
would so deeply touch women whose paths have probably never
crossed with a gopher.

But their fantasies can come true at the the Ingalls
Homestead—Laura's Living Prairie in De Smet, South Dakota.
The Ingalls Homestead is the piece of prairie where Pa actually
set his claim in 1880, and it was the setting for *By the Shores of*

Silver Lake and *The Long Winter*. Laura lived on the homestead for five years, until her marriage to Almanzo Wilder in 1885; her family lived there for three more years until they moved to a house Pa built them in town.

Today the homestead includes a reconstruction of the little house and hay-roof barn, a dugout home like the Ingalls's Minnesota home, an original claim shack from 1878, a prairie  schoolhouse, and all that glorious prairie, where you may camp or spend the night in a covered wagon—sitting together and talking when the sun goes down.

Kids adore this place because the rule here is that there is nothing they may not touch, climb on, play with. They can visit with horses, cows, chickens, and other farm animals, ride a covered wagon, don pinafores, bonnets, and straw hats for a lesson in the schoolroom, try their hand at the hard work of washing clothes with a washboard and ringer. They can grind wheat, make corn husk dolls. The kindly staff makes sure that kids not only get hands-on experiences, but also think about what Laura's life was really like. This is a theme park only in the most literal sense of the word—it also has sincerity and authenticity that transcend self-consciousness. And you can't fake that big, big prairie. Here, kids may run free as Laura did, and women can revisit the fantasies of their girlhood.

MORE PLACES

Rocky Ridge Farm, near Mansfield, Missouri, is where Laura and Almanzo lived when she wrote all the Little House books.

Here, you can see Pa's fiddle, and Laura's living room is preserved as it was when she died at age 90, in 1957. Laura and Almanzo are buried in Mansfield Cemetery.

Walnut Grove, Minnesota is home to the Laura Ingalls Wilder Museum, which is housed in historic buildings and includes memorabilia from visits of stars of the TV show. Here you may also visit the site of the original dugout house, although all that is left of it is a deep depression, and Plum Creek, setting for *On the Banks of Plum Creek*.

The circa 1970s Little House TV series, with Michael Landon as Pa, is available on DVD and has its fans, but book loyalists don't necessarily embrace it. "I remember being offended by the TV series," Erin recalls. "It was a little too polished."

64 Rock and Roll Hall of Fame, Cleveland, Ohio

THE TICKET TAKER AT THE ROCK and Roll Hall of Fame and Museum was grizzled, bearded and denim-clad and wore one button (among many others) that says, "I might be old, but I saw all the good bands."

Right on, right on, man. Me too. And this museum made me proud of my grizzled baby-boom cohort.

The first female artist I saw represented in the museum was Madonna, who is almost exactly my age. Her image was one of a series of panels of much-larger-than-life photos; she hung alongside the likes of John Lennon, Robert Johnson, Ray Charles. I had mixed feelings about this. I'm a Madonna fan, but at the same time, I wonder if she represents my gender's greatest contribution to rock and roll.

But no time to fret about that. An entire enormous museum stretched before me and, although my husband and I didn't realize it at the time, it was going to be a long day.

I could have spent hours at the very first exhibit alone, a timeline of the precursors to and very early forms of rock and roll, with listening stations. Put on the headphones and listen to Billie Holiday, Bessie Smith, Dinah Washington, the Jacksons—Mahalia and Wanda—and Ruth Brown, who was so integral to establishing Atlantic records, the company was sometimes called "the house that Ruth built." I greedily listened to half a song of this and half a song of that before I gave up and gave myself over to the understanding that I would be able to absorb only the smallest fraction of what is available here.

The museum has a wealth of everything—so much muchness, so much history, so many artifacts, so much fashion, and all parsed in various ways, starting with the roots of rock (gospel, blues, R&B, country/folk/bluegrass), moving into the sounds that came out of various cities—Memphis to Seattle, LA to London. Here's a little heavy metal. There's some Jimi Hendrix. We have the sounds of the Midwest and the sounds of Cleveland.

There's an exhibit about the forces that have rallied against rock and roll over the years. "The first amendment should not apply to rock and roll," opined a councilman from San Antonio, Texas in 1985. Yeah, phooey on that. Rock and roll is here to stay, dude.

We detoured into a theater to be charmed by Dick Clark in a film compilation from *American Bandstand*—Cyndi Lauper and Pat Benatar and Irene Cara and, Dick himself, of course, interacting adorably with stars and teenagers. Our progress was slowed by a documentary of Elvis on tour in 1972, showing on a large screen in a room dedicated to The King. We had to pause again to listen to some one-hit wonders in yet more listening booths and were mesmerized again by a documentary that traces, through commentary and archival footage, each of The Beatles's 13 albums.

Here are some of Stevie Nicks' flowing stage outfits, Roy Orbison's glasses, and a telegram from Malcolm McLaren to Sid Vicious's mom about funeral arrangements. There's a bunch of Jimi Hendrix's very groovy clothes, Janis Joplin's psychedelic Porsche convertible, John Lennon's gray collarless suit, a dress belonging to Wanda Jackson and no, that's not her hot pink jumpsuit next to it. That belonged to Little Richard. There is a duffel bag stuffed with hotel room keys collected by Timothy Schmit while touring with The Eagles. There are Alice Cooper's leopard-print platform boots, one of Bob Mackie's feathery 1969 gowns for The Supremes, and some impossibly tiny Rolling Stones stage wear. Keith Richards' jacket—the one he wore at Altamont—would fit a nine-year-old girl. Who knew such big talent could be so small? But Mick Jagger is no bigger, nor is Roger Daltry of The Who. Useless information, of course, but the kind of thing that only really hits home when you see things like that right up close.

We spent six hours at the Rock and Roll Hall of Fame and Museum, and even so, by the end we were speeding past exhibits, watching only snippets of films, barely absorbing the wall of Hall-of-Fame inductees' signatures. And by the time we got to the gift shop, we were whipped—although I was sorely tempted by a large boxed set of *Soul Train* DVDs, I managed to get out with nothing more than tired feet and a new respect for my generation. (Sure, many have followed, but we started it.)

www.rockhall.com

65 Country Music Hall of Fame and Museum, Nashville, Tennessee

I'M A FAN OF NASHVILLE IN general. It's urban pretty, skyscrapers tucked among rolling Tennessee hills. It's an industry town, and you can hear its gears cranking. Music spills out of every club, and any picker who makes it onto any stage in Nashville must have serious chops, because there's a lot of competition. Even the waitress singing under her breath sounds good. Plus, she's bringing you pulled pork sandwiches.

Whatever you think about country music going into the Country Music Hall of Fame, you're going to come out the other side respecting its depth, drama, color, and prominent position in American popular culture. The museum is layer upon layer of things to look at, watch, read, and hear. There are videos and listening stations, gleaming guitars and sparkly costumes, handwritten lyrics, posters and programs, and so much more. And it's getting bigger. Taylor Swift donated $4 million for a new education center. The museum more than doubled its space in early 2014; perhaps we'll see more exhibits celebrating women's contributions to country music.

Women are well represented among the exhibits, but the Hall of Fame, on the first floor, is pretty guy-centric. Early country, like early rock and roll, was male dominated, to be sure. The Hall of Fame was established in 1961, and as of 2012, only 18 of 118 members were women. The first women inducted, in 1971, were cousins Sara and Maybelle Carter, as two-thirds of The Carter Family, along with Sara's husband, A. P. Carter. Patsy Cline made it in 1973; Minnie Pearl in 1975; and Kitty Wells in 1976. More recent inductees include Emmylou Harris in 2008 and Barbara "You Can Eat Crackers in My Bed" Mandrell in 2009. (I'm a Barbara fan, and if you are too, you can tour her former Nashville mansion, Fontanel. Mandrell retired in 1997, and she has been mostly flying under the radar since.)

The thing about male-dominated industries is that the women who *do* get ahead in them must be plenty sassy, which makes them a lot of fun. Consider hard-headed woman Wanda Jackson (as of 2013 not yet inducted), cheerily bodacious Dolly Parton (1999), and spunky Loretta Lynn (1988) whose songs include "The Pill," which she recorded in 1975. *That's* sassy. (A few years earlier she'd had a hit with "One's on the Way." Clearly Loretta had a point she wanted to make.)

More women are scattered among the permanent exhibits at the museum. I hit up my Nashville-based friend Nancy Kruh, who volunteers with the museum, to suggest cool women to look for. She recommends first looking for the 1929 video of The Blue Ridgers with Cordelia Mayberry performing "Oh! Susanna," featuring Cordelia on the harmonica. "Cordelia is adorable—pert and perky and wearing kind of a flapper shift," Nancy says. And, she says, the pièce de résistance is, "Cordelia's harmonica interpretation of a freight train. It's adorably kitschy, definitely a performance worthy of *America's Got Talent*."

Look for Kitty Wells's mahogany guitar; Dolly Parton's original handwritten lyrics for "Jolene"; Maybelle Carter's Gibson L-5 (purchased for $275 in 1928, and the finest guitar she could find); the Judds' Academy of Country Music and CMA awards, as well as a couple of their five Grammys; and guitars belonging to Emmylou Harris and Loretta Lynn, who wrote "Don't Come Home A'Drinkin' (With Lovin' on Your Mind)" on the Gibson J-50 on display. Be sure to watch the videos of songwriters talking about songwriting. The best advice Dolly Parton ever got? "Try not to ramble. Two verses and a chorus." That's a pro speaking.

And there are dresses of course—there always are when we talk about women in history. Look for a form-fitting cocktail dress belonging to Patsy Cline (and, very affecting, a cigarette lighter belonging to her that was found in the wreckage of the plane crash that killed her in 1963). There's one of Minnie Pearl's dresses (her trademark hat comes and goes because it's so fragile), and Tanya Tucker's uber-1970s puffy-sleeved dress. There's an itty-bitty glittery Bob Mackie costume belonging to Dottie West. (I love her 1980 hit "A Lesson in Leavin'," which was covered by Jo Dee Messina in 1998.) There's a shimmering gold gown belonging to Tammy Wynette; the low-cut crimson sequined gown that Reba McEntire wore to the 1993 CMA awards; and the off-white chiffon Taylor Swift wore to the 2009 CMA awards. Oh, and a T-shirt belonging to tough chick Miranda Lambert.

Taylor Swift is a long way from Cordelia Mayberry making like a choo-choo on her harmonica. Women have definitely arrived in country music. Many special exhibits in recent years have honored women, including Tammy Wynette, Patsy Cline, and Brenda Lee.

And be sure to stop into the museum's most excellent gift shop to find lots of music made by very cool chicks, past and present. And in Nashville, it's the music that matters most.

www.countrymusichalloffame.org

American Jazz Museum, Kansas City, Missouri

JAZZ IS AN ALL-AMERICAN ART FORM. Though it draws a little of this and a little of that from here and there, it was born and matured in America. (At which point a lot of it packed up and moved to  Europe, where it is more deeply appreciated. Jazz has been sadly marginalized from mainstream music here in the USA.)

Kansas City is where the structured sounds of the big bands evolved into complicated, cerebral bebop. Kansas City was a sizzling town through the 1930s, in part because Tom Pendergast, a shady political boss, let the liquor flow despite Prohibition. Under those circumstances, as you might imagine, clubs and dance halls flourished; at one point there were 50 jazz clubs on 12th street, and 18th and Vine was the center of the city's African-American community and music. Count Basie played with a Kansas City-based band for years before setting up his own, Charlie Parker was a Kansas City native, and all the jazz greats played Kansas City. The jam session was born here, and music at after-hours clubs went on until the very wee hours.

The American Jazz Museum is located in what is now called the 18th and Vine Jazz District. It's a compact museum, just 10,000 square feet, but thorough, informative, engrossing and lively.

As with any museum focused on music, the listening stations are irresistible and necessitate scheduling plenty of time here.

My "quick spin" through (I was on a schedule) took more than an hour, and I had to keep tearing myself away from things.

The main permanent exhibit tells the story of jazz by focusing on four of the greats: Duke Ellington, Charlie Parker, Ella Fitzgerald, and Louis Armstrong, although many other players—famous and nearly forgotten—are touched upon. Music, posters, album covers, artifacts (Parker's sax, Armstrong's trumpet, a sequined gown worn by Ella) and fabulous vintage photos detail the history of jazz. There's also the interactive 18th and Vine Recording Studio where you can learn about and experiment with melody, harmony, and rhythm. I loved the collection of jazzy album covers—I think I recognize a couple from my parents' record collection.

And just when I thought I was ready to leave, I came upon the room where highlights of the John H. Baker Jazz Film Collection play on video monitors; the museum is in the process of digitizing the large collection, where I could have stayed all day watching "soundies"—short clips of jazz performances from the 1920s and 1930s. The museum also keeps jazz alive in its own nightclub, the Blue Room, which has live music four nights a week.

www.americanjazzmuseum.org

❧

PLACES TO LEARN MORE

Jazz by Ben Blumenthal covers the subject succinctly and informatively, for a newbies introduction.

Ken Burns's 10-part documentary about jazz covers the topic pretty thoroughly and includes Kansas City, of course (episode 6).

67 Motown Museum, Detroit, Michigan

MOTOWN RECORDS WAS RIGHT THERE IN the heart of the Detroit 'hood, a magnet to local kids with ambitions. They'd climb the five stairs to the front door. The receptionist (Martha Vandella, at one time) would make them wait for Mr. Gordy in the chairs facing her desk in the small, shabby reception area. Then, the hopeful kids off the street would take their shot singing for Berry Gordy. If he was impressed, they'd be signed up and sent down a sort of star-making assembly line. And I mean that in the most admiring way. Gordy took in raw talent, and he and his team polished them up into stars, producing some of the most iconic music of the 20th century.

And it all happened right in this little blue frame house, now the Motown Museum, that sits on a wide, busy (by Detroit standards—which is to say, not very busy, see Chapter 14) avenue in the inner city.

Today, people in this neighborhood live among burned-out houses and trash-strewn lots, and it can be hard to tell which houses are occupied and which are abandoned. But in the 1950s and 1960s, when Detroit was a boomtown, the kids growing up in these houses included Aretha Franklin, Diana Ross, the Four Tops, the Temptations. And they all found their way to Motown, founded by Berry Gordy when he was just 29 years old; the average age of employees at Motown was 23.

Once a young artist was signed to Motown, Gordy set his team to work. Maurice King was voice coach. Cholly Atkins choreographed their songs.

"Remember the Temptations walk?" my lovely young guide asked our group, demonstrating the step, chug, step that yes, of course, we all know. "And the Pips?" she continued, doing the arm roll up and the arm roll down that the Pips did because, she confided, they couldn't get the hang of the Temptations walk.

But that wasn't all; Gordy was creating stars, not just performers, and Motown artists learned about grooming, deportment, and how to dress (the girl group outfits were called "uniforms") from Maxine Powell. When you went through Motown, you came out the total package.

With vision, a carefully maintained image, and Berry Gordy's exacting presence at the helm, Motown became "Hitsville USA" and broke ground, helping black artists cross over to white audiences.

The building, including re-created offices and more, is the most interesting artifact, but displays also include Michael Jackson's hat and sequin glove; beaucoup gold and platinum records; and albums on the many labels on which Motown released records (because disc jockeys could not play more than three songs from one label in a single hour).

You pass engineers' booths, where the floors are worn through with the restless feet of people sitting at the board, the dining room table where millions of dollars of product were packed and shipped, an orange couch where Marvin Gaye would sometimes crash after a long recording session. The tour ends in Studio A, where all the songs that have burned themselves deep into our collective amygdala were recorded. "Whatever your favorite song is, it was probably recorded in this room," said our guide.

Studio A is, of course, just a room. Kind of dark, acoustic tiles; musical instruments (including a grand piano that Sir Paul McCartney had restored because he was saddened by its condition); and just the slightest whiff, if you use your imagination, of musician funk from back in the day, when Motown hummed 24/7.

After the label moved to Los Angeles in 1972 (and things were never the same again), Gordy's sister and senior vice president of the company, Esther Gordy, stayed behind to manage the Detroit office. Enough people stopped in wanting a look at the famous building that in 1985, she turned it into a museum.

After autos, Motown is Detroit's most important contribution to American culture, and it's a doozy. Is it even possible to listen to a certain kind of hit radio and *not* hear something that came out of this little frame house? The city of Detroit doesn't have money to put into the Motown museum, and it runs on a shoestring, so we can only hope it hangs on. It deserves a permanent place in our pop culture landscape.

www.motownmuseum.org

※

PLACES TO LEARN MORE

Of course you should brush up on all the Motown hits before you visit the museum, and there are lots of books about Motown, though nothing definitive.

For some silly fun (well, it's not all fun—lots of tragedy too) *The Temptations*, a TV biopic, is a guilty pleasure, or look for *The Jacksons: An American Dream*.

The movie *Dreamgirls* isn't actually about Motown, but it's a sort of, almost, a roman à clef about the Supremes. Kind of.

Or, look for the documentary *Standing in the Shadows of Motown*, about the musicians playing behind all those great singers.

And check out the documentary *20 Feet from Stardom*, the untold story of backup singers.

68 Stax Museum of American Soul Music, Memphis, Tennessee

NOT THAT THE STAX MUSEUM OF American Soul Music needs a female storyline to make this top-100 list, but it has one anyway.

The museum is in the former location of Stax Records, one of the seminal record labels in American soul music through the 1960s and 1970s. The new building is a homage to the old, which was torn down in the 1980s, and the museum traces the history of soul music, but with special emphasis on the Stax story.

Stax was born when Estelle Axton put a second mortgage on her home to launch the studio with her brother Jim Stewart (STewart + AXton=Stax). The label went on to produce a canon of smoking soul music—Otis Redding, Isaac Hayes, Sam & Dave, Al Green, Wilson Pickett, the Staples Singers, backed by the sizzling house band, Booker T and the MGs. *Mustang Sally, Sitting on the Dock of the Bay, Mr. Big Stuff, Soul Man,* the *Theme from Shaft* and many more soul classics came out of the ragtag studio in a converted theater on McLemore Avenue.

The Stax Museum exhibits follow the rise and influence of Stax and soul in general. Your immersion starts with an introductory video of interviews and old performance clips that prepares you for what is ahead—after you're all hopped up on Booker T & the MGs, Isaac Hayes, and Aretha Franklin, you file from the theater to an absorbing hours-long education in an irresistible American art form.

The museum is a long and winding road through the history of soul music, starting with the rebuilt, rough-hewn Hooper Chapel AME Church where, on a small screen, flickers a loop of clips of black congregations bearing witness in song, and little old church ladies singing praise on the street.

Deeper in, display cases are packed with artifacts: Tina Turner's yellow beaded dress, which practically dances even without her in it, and Ike's guitar; Booker T and the MGs's touring trunks; Isaac Hayes's towering platform boots and crazy yellow suit with his face stitched on the back of the jacket. (Not here is the chain shirt that seems to amuse a young Jesse Jackson, Jr. in a clip from the 1972 Wattstax Concert.) Not to mention Hayes's gold-plated, shag-carpeted, baby blue 1972 Cadillac El Dorado. "Don't touch my ride," says a sign by the car, with a drawing of a glowering Isaac Hayes driving home the point.

My husband and I spent hours working our way through the museum, not only because of the copious reading material, but also because video loops of performances and interviews throughout demand your attention. I had to stop and watch James Brown at his most pompadoured, then Jackie Wilson, Ray Charles, Ben E. King...and that was just the first room.

I also watched Estelle Axton and others talk about how the studio was a completely integrated family in the racially divided South. "We never looked at color, we looked at people," said Axton, who was white. (And, whose accomplishments in her later years included producing *Disco Duck.*)

The interracial Stax Records gang couldn't hang out together many places, but the African-American owned Lorraine Motel wasn't too far away, and they congregated there; Wilson Pickett and guitarist Steve Cropper wrote *In the Midnight Hour* there.

But when Martin Luther King, Jr. was gunned down on the balcony of the Lorraine (now the site of the National Civil Rights Museum, see Chapter 38), the temperature of the nation and the city changed.

"If Martin Luther King had not been shot in Memphis, Tennessee, Stax Records would still be operating today," Booker T. Jones said.

At least the music, and now the memory, lives on.

www.staxmuseum.com

PLACE TO LEARN MORE

Wattstax is a documentary, made at the time, about a 1972 music festival in Los Angeles. You can pick up a copy in the museum's small but most excellent gift shop.

MORE PLACES

While you're in Memphis and in a music mood, you will, of course, want to visit Sun Studio, too, where Elvis, Johnny Cash, Carl Perkins, Jerry Lee Lewis and others cut career-making records. Sun is a whole different experience. It's small, a little rickety, low-tech (as a museum) and still a working studio, so it still has some eau de musicians about it. In a good way.

www.sunstudio.com

69 Buddy Holly Center, Lubbock, Texas

FEW OF ROCK AND ROLL'S GREATEST stars don't list Buddy Holly as an influence. In a few short years—he was 23 years old when he died in a plane crash in 1959—Holly innovated in sound, songwriting, and recording technique.

A film about Holly's life and contribution to music recording history is a good introduction to all he accomplished in his short life. The museum has a good collection of artifacts, from elementary school papers to a pair of terrifying-looking early contact lenses that he wore once but found unbearable.

Of course, his big black glasses were his trademark, and you may view the pair he was wearing the night the music died (you did know that was the reference in *American Pie*, of course). After everything was recovered from the Iowa field in which his plane crashed, killing him along with Ritchie Valens and the Big Bopper, Holly's glasses sat forgotten in a sheriff's desk drawer until the 1980s.

 Oh, and don't forget to have your picture taken as Buddy Holly's nose at the giant glasses outside.

www.buddyhollycenter.org

꒰꒷

MORE PLACES

With a little research, you can find places to pay your respects to
your favorite recording artists. In Port Arthur, Texas, you can
visit a plaque in front of the childhood home of Janis Joplin,
and the Museum of the Gulf Coast has an exhibit about her. At
the Joshua Tree Inn in California, you can spend the night in
the room where Gram Parsons died. Selena's family has opened
a museum to the slain Tejano star in her hometown of Corpus
Christi, Texas. Visiting the one-room Roy Orbison Museum
will require a pilgrimage to Wink, Texas, and in New York City's
Central Park, you can visit Strawberry Fields. It's right across
the street from the Dakota, where John Lennon and Yoko Ono
lived, and outside of which he was murdered.

III

Participate

70 Becoming an Outdoorswoman

I WAS A DISMAL FAILURE IN the Land Navigation class, getting hopelessly lost somewhere around the tennis courts, but I learned some good stuff in Camping Basics and Outdoor First Aid (pack your first-aid kit at the *top* of your backpack so you don't have to rummage around when you need it). The Dutch Oven Cooking class inspired me to buy a cast-iron Dutch oven as soon as I got home.

All in all, I had a grand time at the Becoming an Outdoorswoman weekend workshop I attended in Brownwood, Texas. Becoming an Outdoorswoman (BOW) started at the University of Wisconsin-Stevens Point in 1991 and has since spread coast-to-coast (and into Canada and New Zealand). BOW workshops are sponsored by various parksy, outdoorsy agencies; the one I attended was a program of Texas Parks and Wildlife. Although classes offered vary from state to state, the goals and spirit are the same everywhere.

BOW workshops teach outdoors skills to women like me, who don't know a tent stake from a flank steak, as well as to women who know a little bit but want to gain confidence, and to women who just like the camaraderie of being with outdoorsy women doing outdoorsy things.

Accommodations for these very affordable weekend-long workshops are likely to be spartan, at church camps, park cabins;

mine was at a 4-H camp. Women who had attended other BOW workshops told me that our accommodations—cinderblock dorms with communal bathrooms—were better than some. You will likely have to share sleeping quarters and/or bathrooms, and you might have to bring your own bed linens and towels, but everything else, from tents to compasses to meals, will be provided.

Women at these weekends are all ages and all skill levels. I met a couple of women who had already attended eleven BOW weekends together, mostly because they liked doing outdoors things more than their husbands did, and this made it easy. I met a Cub Scout leader looking to brush up on her first aid skills. I met an empty nester wanting to learn about equipment she could handle alone, since her camping companions had grown up and moved out.

We were a congenial group, and although my buddy in the Land Navigation class gave up and abandoned me to my blunders, the instructor was nothing but kind and compassionate about my broken sense of direction. So I was bruised but not beaten.

You can find BOW workshops for any environment; classes cater to local interests. There's clamming and crabbing in Delaware; snowshoeing in Colorado; game cleaning in Indiana; muzzle loading in Nebraska; bog slogging in North Dakota; and "Get the Poop on Wildlife" in New Mexico—tracking animals by their scat, because you never know when that might come in handy.

www.uwsp.edu/cnr/bow/map.aspx

71 Gauley River, West Virginia

THE NEW RIVER GORGE STEEL ARCH bridge is a graceful span high above a gentle river that cuts through the lush Appalachian Mountains in West Virginia. Passing beneath the delicate bridge was one of the highlights of my first rafting trip, taken in preparation for the next day, when I would venture out onto the nearby Gauley River.

The Gauley was anything but gentle. We prepared to launch by the Summerville Dam, which was open, water roaring forth mightily to prepare for winter runoff. It was "Gauley season," and this crashing wall of water makes the already raging Upper Gauley River even more raucous, attracting thrill-seeking white-water rafters from around the world, with rapids ranging from Class III to V+.

If whitewater class designations are meaningless to you, here's the definition, from the International Scale of River Difficulty, of Class V rapids:

Extremely long, obstructed, or very violent rapids which expose a paddler to added risk. Drops may contain large, unavoidable waves and holes or steep, congested chutes with complex, demanding routes. Rapids may continue for long distances between pools, demanding a high level of fitness. What eddies exist may be small, turbulent, or difficult to reach. At the high end of the scale, several of these factors may be combined. Scouting is recommended but may be difficult. Swims are dangerous, and rescue is often difficult even for experts.

The New River trip had given me a taste of riding a gentle rapid, but this was something else altogether. I went with an outfitter and had an expert guide, but there is no going along for the ride in this. You suit up in a helmet and life vest, and you paddle.

It was a shrieking thrill ride, terrifying and invigorating. The rapids themselves were a blur of bouncing, screaming, faces full of water, moments of sheer terror and amazing demonstrations of the laws of physics, ending with relieved, triumphant laughter.

Following directions bellowed by our guide, my group of mostly novice rafters successfully breezed through rapids named Fuzzy Box of Kittens and Heaven Help You, rode through Roller Coaster and Pure Screaming Hell, and screamed through Screaming S Curve, Shipwreck Rock, and Sweet's Falls. It was an exhilarating ride with no swims (which is what they call going overboard.) Vivid autumn foliage along the route (and there are stretches calm enough to take it in) was a definite bonus.

There are stellar rivers for whitewater rafting all over the country, and the Gauley River is among the best, certainly best in the East. West Virginia is economically depressed but topographically blessed with steep mountains (where they haven't had their tops blown off for mining), deep gorges, winding rivers, and sweet-smelling forests of maples, birch, elders, oaks...the list is long, the beauty runs deep.

www.visitwv.com

The website gauleyriverrapids.com has videos of all the Gauley rapids.

❧

MORE PLACES

Some of the nation's of the other top-rated rides:

Riding the Colorado River through the Grand Canyon (see Chapter 6) is an American classic experience that I plan to have someday. I've heard it described as a time machine; the point is less the rollicking rapids than the descent through eons of geology. If you are a knowledgeable rafter and want to plan an independent rafting trip, start planning early. A weighted lottery (giving preference to people who have not been down the river recently) is held annually for the following year's permits. Read the FAQ about the lottery on the park website. Or, forget going independently and join an outfitter for a single or multiday trip. With an outfitter, no experience is necessary. Just put on your helmet and hang on for the ride.

www.nps.gov/grca/index.htm

An 84-mile stretch of the Rogue River in southwestern Oregon has been designated a National Wild and Scenic River. I've hiked through piney woods along the river's edge there and can definitely vouch for both descriptors. The river itself is considerably gentler than the Gauley, with most rapids only about Class III, and there are campsites and lodges along the way.

www.traveloregon.com

With more miles of whitewater rivers than any other state in the lower 48, Idaho is rafter's paradise, and that includes Hell's Canyon—the nation's deepest river gorge—on the Snake River.

The Snake and the Salmon rivers are the most popular (the Middle Fork of the Salmon is the most popular of the state's long rafting trips). The rapids top out at Class IV, but the scenery is extreme—beautiful, wild, and wildlife rich.

www.visitidaho.org

 And in Alaska (and Canada's Yukon), the Tatshenshini River has been called America's wildest river, not for quality of the rapids (the adventure website GORP calls them "controlled rollicking"), but for the spectacular, unsullied wilderness through which it tumbles. The Tat runs 180 miles from put-in to take-out, and there's nothing but scenery and wildlife—no towns, bridges, or roads—between. And it's a migratory corridor for bears and moose.

www.travelalaska.com

72 Ride a Wild Wave

DESPITE THE DIMINUTIVES BUILT INTO HER name, let's not forget that Gidget (a combination of girl and midget) was a chick who accepted no limits. Let the other girls worry about stuffing wild bikinis. She wanted to catch a wave. Let her be your role model.

Surf Diva has schools in Los Angeles and San Diego. Run by twin sisters Isabelle "Izzy" and Caroline "Coco" Tihanyi, it caters to women, though men may take private lessons or join designated coed parties. No boyz are allowed in the weekend or weeklong clinics.

Izzy is a competitive surfer who has been surfing since she was eight years old. She and Coco opened the school in 1996. Surf Diva has special packages for bachelorette parties (dare you to book the Bridezilla Package for your best friend's wedding).

www.surfdiva.com

Nancy Emerson was surfing the big waves when few other women were, and now she has her own surf school on Maui in Hawai'i. Her two-hour lessons or multi-day clinics (two to five hours of surfing a day) are not for women only, but they are good for beginners through experienced surfers. Oh, and Nancy was a stunt double for the *New Gidget Show* in the 1980s.

www.mauisurfclinics.com

Also in Hawai'i, on Oahu, you can get an extra thrill and take lessons from firefighters at Hawai'ian Fire Surf School. The instructors are known for being big buff boys—although when Philadelphia-based writer Cathleen McCarthy took lessons, the teacher who got her started was differently buff: a woman. And, says Cathleen. "Guess what? You don't have to jump up on your board like some gnarly 20-year-old in order to ride a wave! It helps if you can, but I stood up pretty tentatively and still managed to get up on the board my first time out—and ride several waves thereafter, mostly for a few thrilling seconds, but eventually for a couple of nice, long glides. I probably didn't look like Gidget out there but it was really fun."

www.Hawaiianfire.com

A steady wind blows through the Columbia River Gorge in Oregon, making it an ideal spot for windsurfing—a sport increasingly popular with women as equipment gets lighter and trimmer. Big Winds in Hood River, Oregon has women's clinics for intermediate and advanced windsurfers. If that's not you, start with the three-lesson beginner program.

www.bigwinds.com

73

Take to the Seas (and Rivers and Lakes)

AMERICA IS A GRAND LAND, BUT there's a lot of glorious ocean out there, too. You could get out on someone else's boat to have an ocean experience, or you could take matters into your own hands.

My friend Gigi McFarlane learned to sail years ago and hasn't been the same since. She and her husband, Mike, are mad for sailing; we call them Cap'n Gigi and Matey Mike, although those roles aren't set in stone. Mike *does* get to be in charge sometimes.

Gigi learned to sail at a women's clinic, and though the company she learned with is no longer in business, she says the place wasn't as important as the bonding she had with other women, as well as the lessons particularly geared to women's needs. For example, she says, for what a man would do by brute force, a woman might need tools. "There are ways to position your body to take advantage of your strength," Gigi says, adding that the experience was "a true highlight in my life." Now Cap'n Gigi and Matey Mike (and friends) take a major sailing trip every couple of years and at least a little jaunt annually. You can, too, to get a different view of America.

Womanship has one of the all-time great slogans: *Nobody yells—everybody learns.* And if you've ever tried to take lessons in anything from a man in your life, there's a very good chance you know exactly what that slogan is talking about. This sailing school based in Annapolis, Maryland (home to the United States Naval Academy, but don't let that intimidate you) is for women only. Women teach women sailing skills, from rank beginners to apprehensive sailors to advanced sailors. Womanship has day classes and live-aboard multi-day advanced skills sessions.

www.womanship.com.

Whitewater kayaking is not for the timid, and unlike whitewater rafting (see Chapter 71), you can't depend on your guide to keep you on course. So if you are inclined to wear your vessel through fast waters (kayaks fit pretty closely), you'd best study up first. Girls at Play in North Carolina gives girls-only kayak lessons under the tutelage of champion kayaker and registered yoga instructor Anna Levesque and her staff. Anna also offers custom private and small-group kayak and yoga lessons for both men and women. Girls at Play has weekend and weeklong women's clinics at the Nantahala Outdoor Center, near Bryson City, south of Great Smoky Mountains National Park and regularly takes the show on the road for clinics and retreats.

www.watergirlsatplay.com

On the other hand, no experience is necessary to get into a sea kayak and have good, safe fun. Sea kayaks are longer, more stable, and less tippy than whitewater kayaks, and they are used on flat water. Sea kayaking is offered just about anyplace there's water in the USA, but I'm going to point you towards Washington state's tranquil and just-remote-enough San Juan Islands, where you can go looking for orcas and bald eagles, explore cliffs and caves, watch sea birds, and really experience the islands in the most ideal fashion. Any reputable outfitter can get you suited up, trained, and on the water in no time.

www.visitsanjuans.com

74 Ski America

I LOVE SNOW AND MOUNTAINS AND hot toddies and crackling fires and all the things that go along with a ski vacation. But I hate heights and speed, and my one attempt at cross-country skiing was a lesson in humiliation, so I turned to Claire Walter, a travel, food, and skiing writer who lives in Boulder, Colorado, to advise me on good places for an all-American ski vacation. Or snowboarding or snowshoeing or cross-country skiing, since, Claire says, most ski resorts groom trails for all of the above these days.

If you want lessons, you can get those at most resorts, too. The Professional Ski Instructors of America have standardized their teaching structure, so one resort's lessons will be about the same as the next. If you're a beginner, Claire suggests looking for a resort where the classes are small and/or go off-season.

Ski resorts are very different from one another, so all sorts of things come into consideration when choosing where to go, from cost to convenience to the challenge of the mountains. Claire weighed in with informed opinions about different resort experiences.

Skiing in New England is one kind of experience. "Vermont and New Hampshire and Maine all have the quintessential New England charm," Claire says. "The mountains are gentle and very pretty—it's all very Currier and Ives—and they are at a much lower elevation than the Rocky Mountains, which can be a plus for people inclined towards altitude sickness."

In Vermont, Stowe Mountain Resort is a classic. "It's one of the earliest Vermont resorts," Claire says. "Many champions grew up in the town of Stowe, and it's a real destination for families."

www.stowe.com

For a soulful ski experience, Claire chooses Taos Ski Valley. "Taos is a really fascinating mix of Anglo artsy, Hispanic, Native American," she says. "And it's one of the few remaining major ski resorts in this country that is family owned and family run."

Resort founder Ernie Blake came to the U.S. from Switzerland, where everyone skied, and he excelled. He and his family emigrated to America in 1938 to escape the growing anti-Semitism in Europe, arriving around the early days of skiing here. Blake worked as mountain manager for a couple of Rocky Mountains resorts, but knew he wanted to open his own resort. A private pilot, he scoped out likely places while commuting between a couple of jobs. That's how he spotted the  perfect bowl. He moved his Brooklyn-born wife and their small children from Santa Fe to a tiny trailer there. "They started skiing with cans of paint and marked the runs," Claire says. "The original runs are the most challenging in the country."

www.taosskivalley.com

The nation's most glamorous resort is probably Aspen. "It's old and classic and iconic, and you get a lot for your costly ski ticket," Claire says. Your ticket allows you to ski on four very different mountains: Aspen (if you're in the know, you call it Ajax), Buttermilk, Aspen Highlands, and Snowmass. "Each of these would be a worthy resort in its own right," Claire says.

Aspen is a charming old mining town and, "at this point 'rich' is the dominant gene. It's very social in high season, full of beautiful people in beautiful clothes." Rich is an all-the-time thing, but around Christmas is when you're most likely to see famous, too. "It's like a fantasy vacation," Claire says.

www.aspensnowmass.com

Claire also gives a shout-out to Sun Valley in Idaho. "It's another absolutely iconic resort." Sun Valley, sometimes called the American Shangri-La, was built as a destination by Union Pacific Railroad chairman Averell Harriman, who wanted a grand resort that people would reach via his railroad. In its early heyday, the resort attracted the likes of Clark Gable, Claudette Colbert, and Bing Crosby. The Sun Valley Lodge still has a sort of movie-star glamour to it.

"Sun Valley has long, long runs, beautiful scenery," Claire says. It has two mountains: gentle little Dollar Mountain, and Bald Mountain, aka Baldy. And for trivia fans, the country's first chairlift (and possibly the world's) was installed on Proctor Mountain, two miles east of Baldy, in 1936.

If you ski Sun Valley, you'll probably hang out in Ketchum, an educated kind of place that treasures its Hemingway legacy; the writer owned a house in the area. He also shot himself here and is buried here, but never mind that.

www.visitsunvalley.com

And finally, I cajoled out of Claire the U.S. resort where, all other things being equal, she would choose to take a ski vacation. That would be Jackson Hole, Wyoming.

"I love Jackson," she says. "It's beautiful, on the edge of Grand Teton National Park. The Tetons are a gorgeous range, the town of Jackson is laid back and very Western in the winter, there's incredible terrain there, a lot of steeps but an increasing number of intermediate and beginner runs. Where it once had a reputation for 'you better be really good,' there's now an entire range of abilities. And there's a real mystique to Wyoming."

www.jacksonhole.com

75 *The Iditarod, Alaska*

O.K., MOST OF US WILL NEVER actually run the race, but attending the Iditarod certainly requires determination even if you're not taking a dog team; you have to decide to go to Alaska in the wintertime, after all.

I've never been to the Iditarod, an annual 1,150 mile dogsled race through the Alaskan wilderness, from Anchorage to Nome. I have ridden a dog sled, though, and loved it. I didn't feel sorry for the dogs—putting me on one side of a heated ongoing argument between mushers and animal rights activists. So let's just get this out of the way: I believe the dogs like pulling sleds. They're captive beasts anyway, might as well give them something to do. Riding was fun. The dogs are yippy and excited, then they get poised and focused, then they take off, butts a-bobbing.

The Iditarod was a life highlight for travel writer Jenna Schnuer. "I went up to write a few articles about the Iditarod and was just completely blown away by the intensity of the relationship between the mushers and the dogs," she says. "I'm not sure I know any humans who trust each other as much as the mushers trust their teams, and vice versa. It's a beautiful thing to witness. And from what I've seen, mushers have to be fools to treat their dogs poorly. The mushers' lives, quite literally, depend on these animals. Out on the trail, for the most part, the mushers watch the teams and the lead dogs watch the trail. It's usually the dogs who warn the mushers off danger. Also, there is no excitement level more evident than a dog team watching their musher approach. Take the excitement of a kid waiting for Christmas morning and multiply it by, oh, a hundred."

In the Iditarod, men and women compete against each other; there's no women's race and men's race. "I also love that age is respected in the race," Jenna says. "As much as you need some degree of swagger and confidence to say, *yeah, I think I'll go race 1,000 miles through Alaska*, it's more important to really know yourself, to understand your limits, and to trust your skills. Life experience serves mushers well."

And of course, one of the best things about the Iditarod is that it's in Alaska, which is someplace everyone should go because it's awesome. And I use that in the literal sense of the word, not in the teenaged slang sense. Alaska is grand beyond grand—all those enormous spaces, wildlife living wild, the otherness of it, the far awayness, the fjords and icebergs and bald eagles and iconoclasts. Visiting Alaska from the mainland requires effort, but the payoff is big. In all ways. The state is big. The scenery is big. The glaciers are big. The experience is big. Go for the Iditarod, stay to see more. (For example, Chapter 10.)

Companies offer Iditarod tours that start in Anchorage, along with the race, and then check in (via airplane) at sites along the route, but that's pretty hardcore. If that's more than you need, go to the ceremonial start in Anchorage. "It's a big festival of a day, and starts go on for hours and hours," Jenna says. Alternatively, you can park yourself in Nome to welcome the racers who make it all the way, sometime between ten and 17 days after they started out.

Various accommodations allow close proximity to the action. The Millenium Alaskan Hotel Anchorage is the official race headquarters. Lots of mushers stay here for the ceremonial start, and race results are tracked here. Rainy Pass Lodge is located on the trail 125 miles northwest of Anchorage and offers packages for the race. Winterlake Lodge is 198 miles northwest of Anchorage and the only upscale lodge on the route. It's also a checkpoint for racers. Co-owner/chef Kirsten Dixon feeds the mushers as they pass through, so you'll get a chance to meet them (and hang with their dogs). The lodge also offers a four-day mushing school, if you'd like to give it a shot yourself. And the Nome Nugget Inn Hotel is the prime spot for watching the end of the race—book way in advance.

www.nomenuggetinnhotel.com
www.iditarod.com

76 The Cloisters, New York City

UP NEAR THE NORTHERN TIP OF Manhattan Island, Fort Tryon Park feels a million miles away from Times Square. (It is, in fact, a mere nine miles.) Sit on a bench and watch the Hudson River ambling by. Appreciate the wooded cliffs of Palisades State Park on the other side—John D. Rockefeller purchased and protected them to preserve this very view from Fort Tryon Park, which he gave New York City as a gift.

The lovely 67-acre park, built in 1917, is a manicured ramble of gardens, walkways, woods, lawns, and playgrounds designed by Frederick Law Olmsted, Jr., son of the architect whose elegant accomplishments include Central and Prospect parks, and the Biltmore Estate in Asheville, North Carolina.

Rockefeller is also responsible for the crown jewel of the park: The Cloisters, a faux monastery housing a museum of medieval art. In 1924, Rockefeller coughed up the dough for the Metropolitan Museum of Art to buy a collection of medieval art and the building housing it from collector and sculptor George Grey Barnard; Rockefeller also donated a large portion of his own medieval art collection. Barnard's original building is now gone, and John D. also paid for the building that rose in its place, designed by Charles Collens, architect of the imposing Riverside Church on 120th and Riverside Drive.

The Cloisters is a cool, dark, and hushed interpretation of medieval architecture—it incorporates arches, apses, and a slew of medieval elements into its design, making it a stroll through several of the Roman Catholic Church's most affluent eras.

My blood pressure drops immediately upon entering the Fuentiduena Chapel, right off the main hall, a 12th-century Spanish chapel with Romanesque barrel-vault ceiling, frescoes, and a larger-than-life crucifix suspended from the ceiling.

The Gothic Chapel also is peaceful in a pleasantly spooky way, as Gothic architecture is wont to be. Under arched ceilings and illuminated by light filtering through stained glass windows, tomb effigies lie in eternal rest. The famous and exquisitely detailed Hunt of the Unicorn Tapestries, perhaps the museum's most famous treasures, recount Christ's death and resurrection in allegory.

Light and dark, cool and warm, spacious and closed, the museum invites rambling. The cloister gardens are planted with herbs, flowers, and fruit trees, and the terrace overlooks the Hudson.

My last visit to the Cloisters concluded with a Mr. Softee ice cream cone, with sprinkles, purchased from a truck parked right outside the park entrance. Thus fortified, I was ready to plunge back into the bustle of the city.

www.metmuseum.org/visit/visit-the-cloisters

77 *Goddess Sites*

TO START LOOKING FOR AMERICA'S GODDESS sites, you first must understand what they are.

"Simply put, it's a site that recognizes and reveres a feminine face of god," says Karen Tate, author of *Sacred Places of Goddess: 108 Destinations*. "A feminine face of god was honored 70,000 years ago, before a male god ever entered the picture. This isn't some subjective, looloo, touchy-feely sort of assessment or characterization of these sites being goddess sites. It's not just the idea that some people believe that there's a female face in the heavens. It's also beliefs that go with it. It's about partnership, negotiation, about wisdom, about women reclaiming their sexuality, their sacred blood, women's empowerment, about creating a caring culture."

And this isn't just abstract ideas of goddess worship. Many goddess sites are contemporary and vibrant with living traditions. "People are actively practicing reverence for the goddess," Karen emphasizes. "They see what's happening to the planet, they see what's happening to average Americans. There's backlash to patriarchal religion. It's the idea of the divine archetypal mother, and they need their mother. Everything is out of control and out of balance. It's not about doing away with the male idea of god, it's about bringing the feminine and the masculine back in balance."

Some goddess-worship sites are quite literal. For example, the
Goddess Temple of Orange County in Irvine, California where

their thealogy (no, that's not a spelling error, it's
from Thea, a Greek goddess of "sight, light and
the brilliance of gems") honors "Mother Nature,
Mother Earth and Her cycles."

The California coast is strung with goddess
sites; you could use Karen's book for a West
Coast pilgrimage. You can stop at the Kali
Temple in Laguna Beach, where Indian and Western traditions combine in worship of the Mother Kali, from whom all
are said to be born; visit the Temple of Isis and the ocelots who
live at Isis Oasis Sanctuary in Geyserville; pay respects at the
shrine to Our Lady of Guadalupe at Our Lady of the Angels
church in Los Angeles (look for the shrine on the north plaza
wall); climb to the top floor of the Thien Hau Temple in San
Francisco's Chinatown to see a shrine to Thien Hau, the goddess of Heaven. And for semi-traditionalists, Her Church in
San Francisco is a Lutheran church, with curves. "The whole
church has feminine imagery in it," says Karen. "Throughout
the church, there are no male gods."

But goddess sites also are anywhere a goddess is represented.
The Statue of Liberty (see Chapter 20) is a goddess.

The Vieux Carré in New Orleans (Chapter 13) is a goddess
site. "It's the essence of New Orleans, the whole energy, so many
cultures living peacefully together. It's in all the flora and fauna
of the bayous and wetlands," Karen says. Goddess is also in Our
Lady of Guadalupe Church on Rampart Street, which is the
oldest surviving church structure in the city. And the goddesses
of the African Yoruba pantheon are represented by the city's
hoodoo and voodoo women.

Nashville, Tennessee has a statue of Athena that many revere as a goddess site. She stands inside a reproduction of the Parthenon, built for the Tennessee Centennial Exposition. "Goddess advocates go there quietly, and they'll maybe lay flowers at her feet," Karen says.

And of course, Native American religions are rich with feminine power. For the Navajo, the earth itself is female, the sky male. Canyon de Chelly National Monument, on Navajo land in northeastern Arizona, has Spider Rock, an 800-foot-high sandstone spire. Navajo believe the taller of the spires is home to one of their most important and powerful deities, Spider Woman, who taught the Dineh ("the people") how to weave.

Gobernador Knob in northwest New Mexico is one of the most sacred landforms in Navajo beliefs. It is the heart of Navajo Country and the birthplace of Changing Woman, who represents (to oversimplify) the cycle of birth, death, and rebirth of the seasons. The Zuni Salt Lake, 50 miles south of the Zuni pueblo in New Mexico, is the home of that tribe's Salt Woman. The spring-fed lake has a pillar of salt rising from the middle. According to Zuni legend, she used to live among them, but got angry at them and moved away. Members of the Zuni as well as the Acoma, Navajo, Apache and other tribes make pilgrimages to the lake to collect salt used in various ceremonies. According to legend, the trails leading to the lake are umbilical cords.

Hawai'i's Pele, goddess of fire, is said to live in Halemaumau Crater in Hawai'i Volcanoes National Park, but more on that in Chapter 9.

❧

PLACES TO LEARN MORE

For more sites, pick up *Sacred Places of Goddess: 108 Destinations* by Karen Tate.

The Great Cosmic Mother: Rediscovering the Religion of the Earth by Monica Sjoo and Barbara Mor is a young adult book providing a good grounding in women's historic role in religion and culture. Merlin Stone's *When God Was a Woman* came out in 1976, and readers are still finding it eye-opening.

78

Lily Dale, New York

Is this heaven?

No, it's Lily Dale.

The denizens of Lily Dale aren't your lost loved ones—but they can get in touch.

Lily Dale is a community of Spiritualists who believe that we are not bodies with spirits, but spirits who live in bodies. When we die, our spirit just moves on to someplace else. And the (mostly) women of Lily Dale have access to those spirits who have moved to the next life.

Lily Dale is a community of mediums in upstate New York, about an hour south of Buffalo. It's an intimate enclave of Victorian homes tucked in the leafy shade of centuries-old maple, hemlock, and oak trees on the shores of Cassadaga Lake.

Lily Dale was created as and remains mostly a summer camp. Fewer than 300 people live in Lily Dale all year. In summertime the population grows slightly, and mediums, carefully vetted by the Lily Dale Assembly, the camp's governing board, hang out their shingles for the approximately 20,000 tourists a year who pay to enter the gated community. There, they can attend healing and group message sessions, or commune, via the medium of their choice, with lost loved ones in private sessions. (Yes, I know. Healthy skepticism and all that. But questioning beliefs is not the purpose of this book. I shall leave this for you to do when you visit Lily Dale.)

Upstate New York has a long history of attracting freethinkers and iconoclasts. The first Shakers settlement in America was established here in 1776. John Humphrey Noyes established his free-loving Utopian community, Oneida, here in 1848—while the women's suffrage movement (see Chapter 40) was taking shape nearby. (Oneida, the tableware manufacturer, was started as a source of income for the Utopian experiment.)

Actually, 1848 was a big year for the region. Spiritualism also got its start then, when a family in Hydesville, New York heard knocking that seemed to be coming from their basement. Their young daughter then purported to be able to communicate with the spirit by knocking back, and the whole thing snowballed. In 1871, Spiritualists started having summer meetings by the shores of Cassadaga Lake, eventually forming the Lily Dale Assembly. The village grew from there.

It is an unabashed wonderland for suspended disbelief, where stone angels peep from the shrubbery, crystals hang in windows, and several times a day, visitors gather at Inspiration Stump for public demonstrations by mediums. In order to sell their services in Lily Dale, mediums must be certified by the Lily Dale Assembly and board of directors.

"During the height of the summer season," wrote Christine Wicker in *Lily Dale: The True Story of the Town that Talks to the Dead,* "...it resembles nothing so much as a sorority sleepover for aging sisters. They laze about in the hotel parlor and fan themselves in white rockers that line the veranda. They sweep down the streets in flowing dresses." (All that fanning might be because there is no air conditioning in Lily Dale. The Maplewood Hotel, the only hotel within the gates, dates to 1880 and has no a/c, no television, no telephone or elevators. Same with the Leolyn Hotel, outside the gates.)

Lily Dale tends to attract people in pain and nursing wounds who come in hope of hearing something consoling or enlightening, something to help them gain closure and move forward. Whether you believe in messages from beyond the grave, you have to admit that if such things bring comfort, we can afford to be generous. Who are we to judge faith?

www.lilydaleassembly.com

PLACES TO LEARN MORE

Lily Dale: The True Story of the Town That Speaks to the Dead by Christine Wicker is a journalist's memoir of the years she spent getting to know Lily Dale.

No One Dies in Lily Dale, an HBO documentary about the town, is available on DVD.

79 Kripalu, Stockbridge, Massachusetts

I SUBSCRIBE TO KRIPALU'S MAGAZINE TO dream about my first visit there. My friend Lisbeth Levine has been there several times and waxes rhapsodic.

The first time she and her friend Helen Brown drove to the Kripalu Center for Yoga & Health in the Berkshires of Western Massachusetts, even their GPS couldn't locate the entrance road to this holistic retreat in Stockbridge.

"You truly feel like you're off the grid at Kripalu," says Lisbeth, a freelance writer who has spent several weekends there with Helen. "It's a chance to unplug from your wired daily life, connect with a different part of yourself and try things that are outside of your regular comfort zone—like kale soup for breakfast or kirtan chanting."

This is not your run-of-the-mill girlfriends' getaway, given that the strongest beverage in the dining hall is green tea, dessert is only served on Saturday evenings, and the accommodations lean toward spartan. Sure you can luxuriate in a massage, but don't confuse Kripalu with a spa. Plush, it is not.

The accommodations are clean, if spare, and range from dormitory rooms with shared bathrooms in the institutional-looking main building (it was built as a Jesuit seminary in the 1950s) to private rooms in the LEED-certified Annex.

The bucolic setting is spectacular. Kripalu's 350-acre hilltop setting is situated in a region that's long been a favored retreat of the wealthy (read about Edith Wharton's summer estate in Chapter 59) and is just down the road from Tanglewood, the summer home of the Boston Symphony Orchestra. The main buildings offer restful panoramas and opportunities for both active and meditative pursuits, from kayaking and hiking to walking the labyrinth. (More on labyrinths, Chapter 81.)

Three meals a day are served buffet-style and emphasize whole foods using local ingredients whenever possible. "I expected it to be all brown rice and black beans and taste monochromatic," says Helen, a fundraising professional. "But it's absolutely wonderful—healthy food cooked very creatively." As well as plenty of variety for meat-eaters, vegetarians, and vegans, and a separate "Buddha Bar" is all Ayurvedic, stocked with vegan, gluten-free legumes, whole grains, vegetables and condiments.

Breakfast in the main dining room is eaten in silence so you start the day mindfully. Some people love this. "I didn't have to socialize, and that's a gift sometimes," says Ilene Zeiger, a psychologist in Chicago. Others—not so much. Lisbeth and Helen tried the silent treatment, but after learning about a small "talking" breakfast room across the hall, opted for that instead.

The center opened in 1983 and now attracts 30,000 guests per year. Visitors can sign on for a structured program, many of which are led by well-known authorities in the field, or choose from a mix-and-match menu. Your days may include yoga (no experience necessary) and movement classes, workshops, guided outdoor activities, meditation sessions, and spa services in the Healing

Arts center that range from facials to Ayurvedic sinus treatments. The main building also houses saunas and clothing-optional whirlpools.

And for a lot of people, a big part of Kripalu's appeal is the other people there—guests, teachers, and staff. "The community is so warm and enthusiastic and helpful and full of knowledge," says Zeiger.

To reap the most benefits, stay open to new experiences while you're there. Lisbeth, a confirmed night owl, shocked herself by making it to a 6:30 a.m. yoga class. Ilene found that she "loved every workshop" she attended—"even the ones I thought would be boring."

www.kripalu.org

80 *Perfect Bookstores*

A TRUE BOOKSTORE JUNKIE PREFERS THE independent bookstore to garish, overly bright big-box chain stores. The big boxes are designed for hunt-and-kill shopping, the independents offer a few minutes—or hours—of escape. You step in, time stands still. The light feels different when you're standing in the stacks, breathing in that dry, bookish (and in second-hand bookstores, sometimes musty) air. If there are comfy chairs, even better. And maybe a cat. Yes, a cat is good.

There aren't a lot of independent bookstores left in the U.S., which means that the survivors are not likely to be your ordinary bookstores; they are destinations for a certain kind of traveler.

The Tattered Cover is the pulse of Denver's literary community. "It has great signings and author talks, a massive travel section, old creaky wood floors, comfortable places for browsing, a nice central location; I love the Tattered Cover," says travel writer Cynthia Barnes. "And it's walking distance to My Brother's Bar." (My Brother's Bar? The oldest bar in Denver and a hangout for the Beat writers; Neal Cassady's brother worked there. Look for the bar without a sign out front.)

www.tatteredcover.com.

Speaking of the Beats, City Lights in San Francisco, founded and still owned by Beat poet, publisher, painter, and self-described "voice of the people" Lawrence Ferlinghetti, has three floors of books and things and an anti-establishment vibe.

City Lights has been in the same location since 1953; it became part of the national consciousness in 1956 when Ferlinghetti published Allen Ginsberg's then-shocking, still-powerful poem "Howl," for which he was arrested (for distributing obscene content) and then acquitted. City Lights started out selling only paperbacks, and especially banned books. Today, along with the usual suspects from the big publishing houses, you'll also find hard-to-find books from small presses.

www.citylights.com.

Iowa is among our most literate and educated states, and Iowa City is home to the famous University of Iowa's Writers' Workshop (notable alumni include Raymond Carver, Jane Smiley, Tracy Kidder, Curtis Sittenfeld...the list is long). So, of course, Iowa City has a great independent bookstore: Prairie Lights. Founded in 1978, Prairie Lights is now three stories of books and a café located in a space that once hosted readings by luminaries such as Carl Sandburg and Langston Hughes. Leading writers still come here to read. While you're there, ask the staff to recommend some Midwestern literature. It's out there, but often overlooked.

www.prairielights.com.

A few more quick hits: A Room of One's Own in Madison, Wisconsin is a feminist bookstore, and its children's section has only non-sexist books. In New York City, The Strand is a longtime institution and boasts "18 miles of books"—new, used, and rare. It has a kissing cousin in Powell's City of Books in Portland, Oregon. http://www.powells.com/locations/powells-city-of-books. In Washington D.C. you have Politics and Prose; John K. King in Detroit deals in used and rare books and is among the nation's largest bookstores; Larry McMurtry owns Booked Up in Archer City, Texas; Book Passage in Marin County just north of San Francisco is a mainstay of the Bay Area's thriving literary community with author events (sometimes more than one) every day and a full calendar of conferences and classes. And for ambience in particular, a shout-out to Baldwin's Book Barn in West Chester, Pennsylvania, which is five stories of books in an old dairy barn, built in 1822. "It's lovely," says Sarah Schlichter, editor of IndependentTraveler. com. "Like any good barn, it has cats."

81 *Enter the Labyrinth*

THE LABYRINTH OF MY HEART IS at the Ghost Ranch in Abiquiu, New Mexico (see Chapter 61). Fifty feet in diameter and facing a large red rock, it is surrounded by fragrant desert plants. In two days at the Ghost Ranch, I walked the labyrinth three times, and spent lots more time just sitting alongside it, breathing and soaking in the scenery.

It's hard to say what, exactly, is so soothing and mind-opening about walking a labyrinth. In part, it's because for the duration of the walk, no decisions are required; your path is laid out for you, and you only need follow it. In part it's because the destination is clear. Although the path meanders, it inevitably takes you deep into the center of the experience, both literally and metaphorically.

Though the words labyrinth and maze are sometimes used interchangeably, they are different in a very important way: While a maze is designed to get you lost, a labyrinth is designed to help you find something, be it yourself, insight, peace...whatever it is you need at the moment. And there are no dead ends in a labyrinth. Every step takes you towards your goal, the center. And, perhaps, your center.

Before you take the first step, it's a good idea to pause at the entrance and determine what you're walking for. Then, breathe and walk and breathe. Of course, the mind is funny. It might accommodate your intention, or it might take its own twists and turns to end up someplace surprising by the time you reach the labyrinth's heart.

I am irresistibly drawn to labyrinths, and they are surprisingly easy to find once you start looking for them. Many churches of all denominations have them; I know of two in my Dallas neighborhood, one built by a Unitarian church, one by a Methodist. I was surprised to find one in Lion's Park in Cheyenne, Wyoming, and equally surprised to read that there's one in Frank Day Park in Lewistown, Montana. (I've visited friends in Lewistown a couple of times, and it never struck me as a labyrinth kind of place.) The Boone County Master Gardeners' labyrinth in Harrison, Arkansas is surrounded by daffodils and hyacinths that bloom in the spring; Tonkawak, Oklahoma has a heart-shaped labyrinth; the Charles M. Schulz Museum in Santa Rosa, California has a Snoopy-shaped labyrinth; and in Teaneck, New Jersey, a group of volunteers took a former garbage dump and lined it with rubble to create the The Lenape Turtle Peace Labyrinth. Some bed and breakfasts and inns have them (the Hannah Marie Country Inn in Spencer, Iowa, for example, and the Lookout Point Lakeside Inn in Hot Springs, Arkansas), and of course, lots of spas and retreat centers have them.

I do have my labyrinth preferences. Firstly, outdoors. I want to smell the air, feel a breeze, and see changing light. (Although I have to say, the labyrinth inside San Francisco's Grace Cathedral looks pretty inviting. The cathedral also has an outdoor labyrinth and labyrinth-related events.) I prefer gravel or earth to paving stones because I like the sound of my footsteps crunching. Although I am not expert enough to discern among the subtle differences in the types of labyrinths, I have

most often walked a medieval type, often called a Chartres labyrinth after the one outside Chartres Cathedral in France. It is
essentially a series of concentric circles. I prefer a large labyrinth
because it takes some time to settle my monkey mind.

I'd also rather be alone. To me, walking a labyrinth feels
very private. You probably won't catch me walking the labyrinth
outside the Museum of International Folk Art in Santa Fe. I'm
happy it's there, but it's too public for me.

No, the Ghost Ranch is more my style. And yes, I had a rev-
elation or two. I got right to the heart of myself. But those are
personal. You'll have to walk to your own epiphanies.

❦

PLACES TO LEARN MORE

The Labyrinth Society and Veriditas, another labyrinth-centric
organization, teamed up to create the Labyrinth Locator, at
www.labyrinthlocator.com. And if you need a particular reason
to give a labyrinth a try, May 1 is World Labyrinth Day. People
will be walking in circles all over the place.

82 Best Friends Animal Sanctuary, Kanab, Utah

LOVING ALL CREATURES GREAT AND SMALL is good for heart and soul, and nestled up against the spectacular red rocks of Zion National Park is a place to shower love on outcasts who need it, to everyone's benefit.

Best Friends Animal Sanctuary is the nation's largest animal sanctuary, where even unwanted and unlovable pets may live out their lives while others are cleaned up and socialized to hopefully be sent to new "forever homes." The assortment of animals—about 2,000 on any given day—includes dogs and  cats, of course, but also birds, bunnies, horses, pigs, and wild animals from bobcats to turtles that are released back to the wild whenever possible. And Best Friends welcomes volunteers for a week, a day, a few hours—whatever you can spare. Volunteers do everything from poop scooping to dog walking and cat petting, to whatever the animals need that day.

The sanctuary, founded in 1986, is part of the Best Friends Animal Society, which was formed in the 1970s by a group of animal-loving idealists from England. The friends started by rescuing animals whose time was running out at regular shelters, rehabilitating them, and finding them homes. That's essentially still the organization's main mission, though the scale has grown. After Hurricane Katrina, Best Friends staff and volunteers saved 6,000 dogs and cats. Best Friends went to Haiti after the earthquake there to help residents care for their pets; they performed surgeries, dewormed, spayed and neutered. Among the other Best Friends Animal Society's missions is putting an end to kill shelters. A lofty, maybe impossible, goal, but noble.

Until then, though, it rescues as many animals as it can and brings them to live on 33,000 exquisite acres in Angel Canyon—a critter paradise within day-trip distance of Zion, Lake Powell, and the north rim of the Grand Canyon (which many people consider its best side—see Chapter 6).

If I were a homeless quadruped, I'd want to land at Best Friends. The views are great, and the living is easy. Animals don't live in cages; dogs are grouped in packs and live congenially in large runs; cats have indoor-outdoor accommodations in which to roam, nap, hide, and be as aloof as they please; horse pastures are on prime real estate.

And here among the red cliffs, canyons, and pines, feral animals are domesticated, sickly animals are nursed, elderly animals are pampered, ill-mannered animals are trained, and ornery animals are respected. Leaving the sanctuary without a new pet takes a will of steel, but animals that aren't adopted get to live out their lives at Best Friends, eventually ending up in the hilltop cemetery, Angels Rest. (Donors may also bury pets here.)

Even if you don't take home a warm and fuzzy new pet, you're guaranteed to leave Best Friends with a warm and fuzzy feeling.

www.bestfriends.org

༻ઌ

PLACES TO LEARN MORE

For the backstory, pick up *Best Friends: The True Story of the World's Most Beloved Animal Sanctuary* by Samantha Glen.

The National Geographic series, *Dogtown*, about dog rescue at Best Friends, is available on DVD.

83 Miraval, Tucson, Arizona

MIRAVAL, AN ALL-INCLUSIVE RESORT SPA BY the Santa Catalina Mountains, is expensive. Let's just get that out of the way. It's not the kind of place every woman can go, and I know that. I haven't. Someday. I hope.

So I talked to my friend Jean Fain, psychotherapist, author of *The Self-Compassion Diet,* and self-proclaimed "spa hopper" who has been there, and she confirmed that yes, indeed, I do want to go.

Jean was skeptical at first. Everything she'd heard about Miraval made it sound "too wonderful." And yeah, pretty much everything you read or see about the place includes some form of "life-changing" in the description, which sounds a little hyperbolic. Oprah Winfrey raved about it, has said it's her favorite spa.

That's a lot to live up to. But Jean went with her sister and came home a believer, calling it, "a truly fabulous vacation in every way." She even learned stuff she didn't know about nutrition, which, considering she is an expert on eating, is saying something.

What's so great about it?

For one thing, Jean says, the beds. "I have never slept in such a comfortable, luxurious bed in my entire life." The room, she says, was stunning—"like a little apartment with perfect feng shui."

And the food! "Ten times better than any spa I've ever been to," Jean says (and, as a travel and health writer, she's been to about 20). "It's top-notch cuisines as beautifully presented as at any restaurant, but more healthful. And they have a bar, which most spas do not have."

Otherwise it does have a lot of what other spas have, but with a different vibe. "There's a little more spiritual tilt to the activities, and the people reflect that," says Jean. "They're a lot less competitive and warmer—other guests and the staff."

Miraval's focus is healthfulness, mindfulness, and personal growth. Daily schedules are packed with activities and classes: horseback riding to hiking; "aerial yoga" to mountain biking; cardio drumming to spinning, abs and glutes and other familiar fitness classes. There are personal growth activities, some of which involve climbing up to high places and jumping. ("I don't get it," Jean says.) There's golf and photography. And you can arrange a personal consultation with a staff of experts in everything from diet to astrology to trauma, and participate in seminars on topics such as stress reduction and getting through grief. And Miraval has a changing schedule of focused workshops and retreats with guest experts.

Actually, it would take far too long to detail everything this place offers; every day is packed with possibilities, and it would be very easy to overschedule yourself and leave the spa more stressed than when you arrive.

"The compassionate thing to do for yourself on this vacation is not to overdo it," Jean says. "These vacations can be like a boot camp with good food if you overdo it."

So Jean hiked. She had massages. She took yoga classes. She went to a seminar where a woman read people's energy and told

them what to do with their lives. She walked the meditation labyrinth (see Chapter 81). She sat quietly and read. And somehow,
it added up to something more than a usual spa getaway for her.
"Everything made sense there in a way that I had never antici-
pated," she says. "It was the best vacation of my life. It's the only
spa I would go back to. It feels just perfect."

So, there you have it. More hyperbole. I choose to believe it.

www.miravalresorts.com

84 Monument Valley Navajo Tribal Park, Four Corners Region

THE NATIVE AMERICAN BELIEF SYSTEM CENTERS on nature, and the magnificent, eerie landscape of Monument Valley can evoke spiritual feelings in even the most earthbound of travelers. (That would be me.)

After my first visit to Monument Valley and the Four Corners region, several decades ago, the place nagged at me. The haunting landscape where Arizona, New Mexico, Utah, and Colorado meet is sacred territory for the Navajo people (the Dineh, or "the people"). The massive sandstone buttes jutting hundreds of feet up from the desert floor have sacred stories tied to them. They loom stately and stoic, prehistoric, implacable. Their moods change with the light, their size seems to change with perspective; I couldn't tell how large the Mittens were until I saw horses grazing at the base of one. The Mittens, the Totem Pole, the Three Sisters, Elephant Butte—those are the names we have come to know them by.

This landscape touched me deeply, and I imagined, on that first visit, coming to understand how the Native Americans feel about this land.

Which is just silly. Not possible. But I keep trying.

Navajo territory originally spread over much of the American Southwest, but the inexorable tide of Manifest Destiny forced them to accept Four Corners as their reservation. "As far as the

Anglos were concerned, there was really not much going on out there, just lots of sand and rocks," says Robert S. McPherson, author of *Sacred Land, Sacred View,* a book about the Four Corners region.

The Navajo feel differently, and so do I.

You may view the valley from a lookout point or take a 17-mile scenic drive. To explore any deeper, you must hire a Navajo guide. But don't expect your guide to spill his culture for your sightseeing pleasure. The significance of this landscape is not right there for the tourists' taking. He will point out where John Wayne sat on his horse in *The Searchers* (for a small fee, a local will recreate the pose for photographs); he might point out rocks that look like Snoopy, Jay Leno, Jesus Christ. It's all very tourist-friendly and fun, but hardly as spiritual as the landscape feels.

"The Navajo have names for all those rocks, but my gut impression, if we're talking generally, is that many guides may not know the names," McPherson says. And even if they do, he says, "They look at this knowledge as a cultural resource. They're looking at the preservation of the information as something that should be handled very carefully."

And the Navajos keep their stories close. "The story is a very tangible power," says McPherson. "They're not treated lightly, they are not given away freely, they are treated with respect. Some stories, for example, may be told only in certain seasons."

The valley's stories will be forever shrouded from me. So I just let myself feel the landscape rather than try to put words to it, letting the rocks speak for themselves. And I think about Mother Nature: powerful, strong, and profound.

www.navajonationparks.org

⁂

PLACES TO LEARN MORE

Robert S. McPherson, who teaches Native American history and culture at the College of Eastern Utah, provides wonderful insights into the significance of the Four Corners region in his book, *Sacred Land, Sacred View*.

Monument Valley makes an appearance in a number of classic Westerns, including *My Darling Clementine, The Searchers, Stagecoach, How The West Was Won, The Legend of the Lone Ranger*, and others. A stunt for the Clint Eastwood film *The Eiger Sanction* was filmed on a formation called Totem Pole Rock, but, I learned from a local, many Navajo people blamed a subsequent drought on this desecration, and nobody has been allowed to climb it since.

IV

X (Chromosome) Rated

85 Chick Flick Locations

YOU KNOW THE ONES. THEY'RE THE movies you turn to when you're home with the flu, the cheesy classics that you watch for the umpteenth time on lazy, rainy evenings. They're the comfort food of the film world: chick flicks. But they're also good for more than curling up on the couch with. Their real-life locations have become modern pilgrimage sites.

Some chick-flick landmarks have their own pre-celluloid claims to fame, entering our artistic vernacular. The Empire State Building observation deck, for example, where Cary Grant's Nickie Ferrante waited in vain for Deborah Kerr's Terry McKay to meet him in *An Affair to Remember*. Extensive lines and elaborate security measures may have dampened the romance some, but you can still take the long ride to the top and gaze forlornly into the Manhattan night. Or, cheer yourself up and remember Meg Ryan and Tom Hanks recreating the same scene, but happier, in *Sleepless in Seattle*.

Katz's Delicatessen was a New York City landmark long before Meg Ryan faked an orgasm at a small table in the middle of the room; still, despite its century-plus of history, the deli is probably best known for hosting that classic *When Harry Met Sally* scene. The famous table is marked with a sign that reads "Where Harry

Met Sally... Hope you have what she had!," and there are a few photos of Billy Crystal and Meg Ryan on the cluttered walls, but otherwise, business at the deli goes on as usual.

katzsdelicatessen.com

"Come on, ladies, God wouldn't have given you maracas if he didn't want you to shake them!" *Dirty Dancing*'s action was officially set in the Catskills, but really Johnny and Baby were doing the mambo in Mountain Lake, Virginia, where the Mountain Lake Lodge (which is still operational today) stood in for Kellerman's during filming. The entire movie wasn't filmed here—alas, the outdoor stairs where Baby practiced her moves are on private property in North Carolina—but the distinctive stone lodge should bring your favorite moments flooding back.

www.mtnlakelodge.com

Just outside of Birmingham, Alabama, at the Irondale Café, you'll find the world's most famous fried green tomatoes. The diner, which has been going strong since 1928, is the real-life inspiration for the Whistle Stop Café, home to Idgie and Ruth in 1991's *Fried Green Tomatoes*. But it's no longer the sleepy small-town café you saw in the movie: These days, the Irondale serves up hundreds of slices of its famous tomatoes every day.

www.irondalecafe.com

Way out West, head to Utah's Dead Horse Point State Park, next door to Canyonlands National Park outside of Moab, to have your own *Thelma and Louise* moment. (Wait, no, don't do that.

Just go look.) In the movie, we're led to believe that the crucial final showdown takes place at the Grand Canyon, but it was really shot here, in a dusty corner of the fractured Utah landscape.

stateparks.utah.gov/park/dead-horse-point-state-park

OTHER PLACES

Pretty Woman—Beverly Wilshire hotel in Beverly Hills, California; shops along Rodeo Drive.

Sweet Home Alabama—Coon Dog Cemetery, northwestern Alabama.

Twilight—Forks, Washington; Bella Italia restaurant in Port Angeles, Washington.

86 *Tiffany & Company, New York City*

AH, THAT LITTLE BLUE BOX. IT'S instantly recognizable, and it attracts the magpie in us all, for within is bound to be something shiny and lovely and indulgent.

 Yes, we are strong women, nobody's fools, we can buy our own diamonds, thankyouverymuch. But who among us is entirely immune to the draw of a beautiful gem or elegant bauble?

Tiffany now has stores all over the world, but none has the cachet of the original location in New York City. Don't be shy. Open the door and walk on in. It doesn't cost anything to look. At the very least, stand outside with a Danish and coffee, and covet, like Audrey Hepburn/ Holly Golightly in *Breakfast at Tiffany's*, the 1961 movie that added to the mystique wafting about the already legendary company. (More movies, see Chapter 85.)

Tiffany was founded by Charles Lewis Tiffany in 1837. The original store, at 259 Broadway, sold a variety of fancy goods, and the first day's sales, on September 18, 1837, totaled a whopping $4.98. (Maybe $100 or so today.) The company had several locations before moving, in 1940, to its current elegant, understated building on Fifth Avenue and 57th Street.

Not only did Tiffany publish the first mail-order catalog in the United States, it also set the standard for silver, instituting the 925/1000 parts pure silver standard that the United States later adopted. And if you are wearing a diamond engagement ring, there's a pretty good chance your diamond is in the "Tiffany Setting" the company introduced in 1886: a six-prong setting that raises the diamond off the band and into the light to let it sparkle. It remains among the most popular settings for engagement rings.

On the ground floor of the store, you can see the enormous Tiffany Diamond the company acquired in 1878. One of the largest yellow diamonds in the world, it was more than 280 carats when Tiffany purchased it. It was cut down to a little more than 128 carats and sparkles with 90 facets. Audrey Hepburn wore it, set in a necklace designed by Jean Schlumberger, for publicity photos for *Breakfast at Tiffany's*.

Renowned for his Art Nouveau glass and design, Charles's son Louis Comfort Tiffany became the store's first design director in 1902 and took over the company at his father's death in 1902. Brand-name designers who followed the younger Tiffany include Schlumberger, whose trademark was witty animals and designs inspired by nature; Elsa Peretti, whose organically shaped silver was a particular rage in the 1970s (she also designed the bottle for Halston perfume, the must-wear scent for disco divas in the day); Paloma Picasso, who drew on graffiti for inspiration; and now Frank Gehry, of crazy-shaped buildings fame.

Oh, and that distinctive blue box? Tiffany blue was chosen as the store's trademark color shortly after it first opened, in 1837. It's been representing the company—and making mouths water—ever since.

www.tiffany.com

PLACES TO LEARN MORE

You won't really learn anything about the store by watching *Breakfast at Tiffany's*, but rent it anyway. It's a lovely portrait of New York, and anything starring Audrey Hepburn is worth your time, yes? (Although we can't help but cringe at Mickey Rooney playing Hepburn's Japanese neighbor.)

87 Metropolitan Museum of Art Costume Collection, New York City

THE METROPOLITAN MUSEUM OF ART IN New York City calls the 35,000 items in the collection of its Costume Institute "works"—as in artworks, which they are. From the heavy *how-did-they-wear that?* panniers and bustles of the 18th and 19th centuries to the tailoring of Chanel and the draping of Dior, each piece in the collection is a historical artifact and a work of art.

The collection was started in 1937 by Irene Lewisohn, who founded the legendary Neighborhood Playhouse theater school (Joanne Woodward, Robert Duvall, and Diane Keaton are among its many prominent alumni). It merged with the Met in the 1940s, and in 1959 got its own curator and set down roots to become one of the world's premier costume collections as well as the venerable institution's contribution to celebrity culture.

Diana Vreeland is credited with shaking the dust out of the collection and seeing its potential in the 1970s and 1980s with exhibits focused on Balenciaga, Hollywood design, and Russian costume. These thematic exhibits have since become the template for museum costume collection exhibits everywhere.

With the support of New York's fashion industry, the costume collection has established a glamorous high profile within the high-profile museum. Its annual fund-raising gala, co-chaired by *Vogue* magazine's Anna Wintour since 1995 (with a couple of years off) has become one of New York City's most dazzling events. Jacqueline Onassis her fashionable self was among past co-chairs of the gala, and in 2010, Oprah Winfrey co-chaired with Wintour. The star-studded party, which usually launches the collection's spring show, attracts fashion luminaries, movies stars, socialites, and supermodels (the theme of a 2009 exhibit was titled "The Model as Muse").

Day to day, the increasingly theatrical and high-tech shows attract huge (often oppressive) crowds by merging fashion-as-art with fashion-as-pop-culture, drawing both readers of *Vogue* and *People* magazines. (Not that the two readers are mutually exclusive.) In 2004's "Dangerous Liaisons: Fashion and Furniture in the Eighteenth Century," mannequins dressed in elaborate eighteenth-century finery struck saucy, slightly racy poses in French period rooms to explore "the dressed body's spatial negotiation of the eighteenth-century interior as a choreography of seduction and erotic play," according to the museum's description of the exhibit. "AngloMania: Tradition and Transgression in British Fashion" looked at British fashion from 1976 to 2006, from the punk rock of Malcolm McLaren and Vivienne Westwood through the equally bold John Galliano and Alexander McQueen.

In 2009, the Brooklyn Museum transferred its costume collection to the Met, creating the ponderously named Brooklyn Museum Costume Collection at The Metropolitan Museum of Art. Thus combined, this is now the world's largest and most comprehensive costume collection. The first show after the merger highlighted the Brooklyn Museum collection and focused on American women's style, from the Gibson Girl to today.

If the costume exhibit is too crowded on your visit to the Met (it's happened to me), you can also explore fashion as it is represented in the other museum galleries, either joining a Fashion in Art tour (it's free with admission, check museum website for dates and times), or rent "Costume: The Art of Dress" audio tour narrated by Sarah Jessica Parker.

www.metmuseum.org

88 *Savannah, Georgia*

SAVANNAH IS A SASSY SOUTHERN BELLE of a city—feminine and genteel, sensual and a little bit eccentric. Savannah also is a tourism machine. Tourists are everywhere, doing the shopping death march on River Street, listening to tour guide shtick on sightseeing trolleys that buzz the town day and night (Savannah prides itself on being heavily haunted, and nighttime ghost tours are a perennial favorite), shuffling through historic homes. Not that there's anything wrong with any of that. Trolley tours offer a good overview of the city's pretty historic district, and the historic homes are filled with fascinating tales.

Savannah was founded in 1733 by James Oglethorpe, who established Georgia as the 13th American colony (named for King George), and Savannah as its first city.

Oglethorpe's plan was to build a Utopian society, but people just wouldn't get with the program. Settlers squabbled about who had better land; and rum, lawyers, and Catholics were forbidden, which created hard feelings for various reasons. And even though outlawing slavery was an admirable ideal, it turned out to be an economic liability in those days, when neighboring states were prospering on this free labor.

Savannah (and Georgia) was a military buffer protecting South Carolina—particularly the vulnerable plantations around the well-established city of Charleston—from the Spanish, who were in Florida and would have gladly kept moving north. One of the bloodiest battles of the Revolutionary War was fought in Savannah. In the last gasps of the Civil War, Sherman ended his destructive March to the Sea here, sparing the city and presenting it to Abraham Lincoln as a Christmas present. During Reconstruction, Savannah developed a strong African-American community of freed slaves.

Savannah is considered America's first planned city. Oglethorpe laid it out in grids of streets and squares; at one time there were 24 shady squares; 22 are left, though not all in their original state. Historic preservation kicked in here in the 1950s, and the city has aged with elegance. (Well, mostly. There is one circa 1972 federal building that locals call "the bathroom building," pointed out guide Jonathan Stalcup of Architectural Tours of Savanna.)

You will, of course, want to visit the Juliette Gordon Low Birthplace, where the founder of the Girl Scouts was born on Halloween night of 1860. The house was saved from destruction by Girl Scouts, who raised $60,000 in three years through their "Dimes for Daisy" initiative. (Daisy was Low's nickname.) The first National Historic Landmark in the city, it's still owned by the Girl Scouts of the USA and is staffed by grown-up Girl Scouts. Set up as it was in 1886, the house has much of the family's furniture, including artwork by Daisy. But the stories are the best part of the tour; my witty and gossipy guide spoke of Daisy like an old friend.

Daisy dated William Mackay Low behind her father's back (Dad thought he was a spoiled brat) and then married him, but was divorcing him when he died at age 45. The cad left the bulk of his estate to his mistress, and Daisy, who was childless, felt her life was a failure. Then she met Sir Robert Baden-Powell, founder of the Boy Scouts and Girl Guides, and was inspired to her life's work. "We might not have our organization if she'd had a happy marriage and children," my guide speculated. Daisy and her cousin Nina Pape founded the Girl Scouts in 1912 and published the first handbook a year later. Daisy died of breast cancer and was buried in her uniform in 1927.

Savannah has a Girl Scout Museum, too, located in the building that was the organization's first headquarters.. Here, your visit starts with an old, silent recruitment film in which Girl Scouts do all sorts of impressive things: swim 50 yards fully dressed to deliver an important message; find a crime scene and alert authorities via Morse code; and help a soldier's overburdened wife and children by cooking, cleaning and babysitting. (In fact, during World War II, Girls Scouts operated day care centers to help.) The rest of the museum is a colorful collection of artifacts, including uniforms from the beginning to the 1990s, all the variations of pins (the most important display, my guide said solemnly), handbooks, and much more.

Oh, and look for a photo, used in the very first handbook, of Girl Scouts carrying a boy in a stretcher. The museum recently learned from one of those girls—now elderly, of course—that the boy in the stretcher is Savannah native Johnny Mercer, who grew up to write lyrics to such classics as "You Must Have Been a Beautiful Baby," "That Old Black Magic" and "Moon River."

www.gshg.org/Things-to-Do/Visit-First-Headquarters/Pages /default.aspx

One of Savannah's most famous women is kind of a sad tale. The Waving Girl statue by the harbor is Florence Martus, who lived from 1868 to 1943. A lonely young lady, she took to waving to passing ships, a tradition she maintained for 44 years. Legend has it she was waiting for a sailor who loved her and left her. The statue is the first memorial to a woman in any public park in Georgia.

Once you've done all the obligatory touring and learning and shopping, step away from the gift shops and tour guides to just meander the pretty streets and linger in the squares, where sunlight filters through the Spanish moss that spills languidly from the limbs of live oaks. (Quirky fact I learned on my trolley tour: the closest relative to Spanish moss is the pineapple.)

Like any woman, sultry Savannah is complicated, multifaceted, mysterious, and not easy to know. She flirts with the senses. Reveals herself slowly. I visited once, but once is not enough. She requires a second date. Probably a third and a fourth, too. You need to take your time with Savannah to get past her superficial beauty, because she has lots more going for her.

www.savannahvisit.com

꙳

PLACE TO LEARN MORE

Midnight in the Garden of Good and Evil by John Berendt, published in 1994, put Savannah solidly on the modern tourist map with its true-ish story of murder, mystery, and drag queens. Alas, the movie, released in 1997, is kind of a stinker.

MORE PLACES

Readers who love Charleston, South Carolina are now getting huffy because Charleston, which is older, larger, and as gracious as Savannah, is not the focus of this chapter. I understand. This is about as close to an arbitrary decision as I will admit to in this book. Savannah long called to me for reasons I couldn't tell you. It was just one of those places, and that seemed a good enough reason to choose it for this chapter. But Charleston has everything Savannah has and more of it, and it is also on my life list.

www.charlestoncvb.com

89 *Antiquing*

ANTIQUING IS NOT JUST SHOPPING; IT'S a noun that has been verbi-
fied into an absorbing pastime all its own, around which many a
vacation has been planned.

Antiquing may strike at any time; just about any place you
visit will have at least one antique store/flea market/junk shop...
maybe even a yard sale (see Chapter 24 to learn about the world's
largest yard sale). But if you're going to be serious about it, there
are a few places you need to see.

The nation's largest outdoor antiques fairs are the Brimfield
Antiques and Collectibles Shows in central Massachusetts. These
shows are each six days long (Tuesday through Sunday), in May,
July, and September.

The Brimfield shows started in 1959 with 67 dealers who
opened their car trunks, spread their wares on blankets, and
created a monster. Today the shows attract about 5,000 dealers
and spread out on 21 fields over about a mile.

Brimfield has a complicated schedule of fields and dealers
opening and closing, coming and going throughout the week
(some fields charge admission, some don't), and experienced
shoppers get out early (as in daybreak) and shop as fast as they
can. If you find something you want here, buy it right away. No

time to think it over—put it down, and someone standing right behind you might snap it up.

www.brimfield.com

I'm a fan of Heidi Chapman's kooky little shop, the Cloverleaf Boutique, in Ardmore, Oklahoma (with an outpost in Oklahoma City). I absolutely had to check it out when I saw the giant ice cream cone out front. This, I later learned, was the mother of all impulse purchases, made at the Round Top Antiques Fair in Central Texas.

For Heidi, Round Top is a never-miss event. "It's my most favorite thing I do in my life," she told me. "I stay the entire time; it's like going to camp. I have made so many great friends there since I have been going—many I feel I've known all of my life. They're kindred spirits."

Nobody knows exactly how big the twice-yearly (spring and fall) fair is, but in its nearly 50 years it has expanded from just a weekend in Round Top (population, about 79) to two weeks of antiques fairs in small towns from Austin to Houston, including Marburger, Warrenton, Carmine, and Shelby. And that's just the official action—lots of smaller shows hitch a ride on the main event's fame. (As in Brimfield, some shows charge admission.) With all that, you can—as Heidi does—stretch the trip into a full two weeks of rummaging around in old stuff.

roundtoptexasantiques.com

Those are the two big kahunas for antiquing, but lots of spots all over the U.S. have their points. The Old King's Highway from Sandwich to Orleans on Cape Cod is a Regional Historic

District and meanders through pretty, and antiqued-up, villages. Antiquing is easy to do in Savannah (Chapter 88) and New Orleans (Chapter 13). Of course, any good antiquer/junker knows that small town antiques/junk/secondhand/thrift stores are always potential treasure troves.

90 *Teatime*

O.K., MAYBE AFTERNOON TEA ISN'T REALLY an American thing. We're more about the coffee break. But afternoon high tea is an English tradition we have happily adopted for special, frou-frou occasions. We like to dress up, perch on gilded chairs, sip tea, nibble sandwiches with the crusts cut off, and feel like Eliza Doolittle visiting a different kind of life.

The mother of American high teas is at the Plaza Hotel in New York City, but many of the country's most historic hotels also do tea, and it's one way to soak in the historic vibes for a lot less than a night's stay would cost.

The Plaza Hotel has been standing stately by the southeast corner of New York's Central Park since 1907. Here's the plan: a long stroll up Fifth Avenue during the holiday season, window shopping and joining the avenue's hustle and bustle. You finish up at the opulent windows of Bergdorf Goodman (or maybe at the iconic cube Apple store across the street), and then cross Army Plaza. You walk past the fountain, say a friendly hello to the doorman, and step into the hotel and the airy, elegant, rococo Palm Court. There, you settle into gilded chairs (large enough to be comfortable, no perching necessary). Yes, the Palm Court has palm trees, also marble columns and a stained glass skylight. Your tea (the menu has about a dozen blends to choose among) is accompanied by such nibbly things as truffled quail egg salad, warm seasonal scones, or, if you happen to be in an Eloise mood, peanut butter and jelly sandwiches and pink Jell-O.

I probably don't need to tell you that the Plaza Hotel is all kinds of historic. It's a National Historic Landmark that has been touched by celebrity both fictional (*Eloise, The Great Gatsby, The Way We Were, Breakfast at Tiffany's, Plaza Suite,* and dozens more) and real—Mark Twain to P Diddy, who celebrated his 40th birthday there.

www.theplaza.com

All other teas are, it must be admitted, kind of also-rans, but no less pleasant. I am particularly fond of the circa 1929 Arizona Biltmore, a resort in Phoenix designed by a (heavily influenced) protégé of Frank Lloyd Wright. Tea is served in the lobby, one of the loveliest spaces in the resort, with big windows, warm wood, and deep sofas under a gold leaf ceiling. In Memphis, after you visit Graceland, The Peabody is where you go for the finger sandwiches and scones tradition, and if you time your tea right, you can catch the famous march of the ducks in the lobby at 5 p.m. In Chicago, The Drake, which opened in 1920, serves tea in its own Palm Court. At Denver's Brown Palace, a sturdy railroad hotel, tea is brewed in water pumped from an artesian well 720 feet beneath the lobby floor. And in San Francisco's Fairmont Hotel, tea service has moved around over the decades, but finally landed back in the Laurel Court, in the grand lobby, where it was first served 100 years ago.

91 Napa Valley, California

LESLIE BRENNER, A FOOD AND WINE writer, gets a little misty-eyed when she talks about Napa Valley. "Napa has always been intertwined with the touchstones of my life," she says.

Although the first commercial winery was established in 1861, the event credited with putting Napa wines into the big leagues was the Paris Tasting of 1976, when a California Cabernet Sauvignon and a Chardonnay received top honors against those snooty Euro wines. That was around the time Leslie was attending college at nearby Stanford University and making frequent trips to the area. "It felt very exciting in those days," she says.

In 1995, when the Napa wine industry was mature and had grown to hundreds of wineries, Leslie and her husband eloped and were married at the Napa County Courthouse. And while she was pregnant with her son and working as a food writer in Los Angeles, she was invited to participate in Cakebread Cellars' annual American Harvest Workshop, an autumn event that brings together chefs and serious foodies and, um, winos? (kidding) for cooking, touring and tasting. Leslie even had the opportunity to participate in actually harvesting grapes.

"It's definitely not as romantic as people think," she says. "It's meticulous, physically difficult manual labor—it's not like a Lucy-style romp."

Still, she says, harvest, which is late summer or early autumn, is a particularly lovely time to visit Napa. "The valley is so beautiful that time of year," Leslie says. "A lot of the vines turn colors you would associate with autumn leaves. Being in the valley at that time of year is totally romantic and wonderful."

Studded with elegant inns and chef-driven restaurants, the verdant valley invites leisurely exploration. To get off the beaten track—which is Highway 29, on the west side of the valley—Leslie suggests instead taking the Silverado Trail, on the east. Or you could plan a trip around women winemakers; you'll find them at Cakebread Cellars, Beringer Vineyards, Beaulieu Vineyard, Nickel & Nickel, Domaine Carneros, Corison Winery, and many others.

If you're serious about your wine, you can even participate in the harvest. At Schweiger Vineyards' annual "Old Fashioned Harvest Stomp," you can get your Lucy on and do the grape-stomping thing, along with picking, tasting, and dining. And Schramsberg Vineyards, which produces sparkling wine, has a multi-day "Fall Harvest Camp" that also provides hands-on experience with the harvest.

While it's just about impossible to get a bad meal in the region's restaurants, one of Leslie's fondest memories of Napa was when she and her husband and friends rented a cottage. They visited wineries, tasting and buying, shopped for fresh and artisan foods at the Oxbow Public Market and the adjacent farmers market (Tuesday and Saturday mornings) in Napa, and cooked up their own feasts.

Of course, for a food and wine expert, Napa is kind of a no-brainer. But even so, the valley is more than that for Leslie. "It speaks to my soul," she says.

☙

PLACES TO LEARN MORE

The website visitnapavalley.com provides loads of information about Napa. For information on the nearby and also lovely wine-making region, Sonoma Valley, see sonomavalley.com. For general information on visiting California, go to visitcalifornia.com.

MORE PLACES

In the years since Napa and Sonoma have established their winemaking chops, vineyards have sprouted all over the United States. You could pair history and wine in Upstate New York, a region that has its own formidable reputation for wine. Texas, too, is developing a respectable industry.

92 *Tenement Museum, New York City*

RUTH ABRAM WAS DISCOURAGED IN HER search for a location for the museum she imagined.

The well-connected daughter of prominent civil rights advocate Morris Abram, Ruth wanted to create a museum in an original tenement that would interpret the immigrant experience in New York City at the turn of the century. But all the buildings she could find had been altered to meet modern building codes.

In 1988, Abram and her partner in the endeavor, Anita Jacobson, decided to rent a storefront to start establishing the museum while they continued seeking a permanent home. That's why they were looking at a storefront at 97 Orchard Street. And when Ruth needed to use the bathroom and was directed to a hallway in the building, she opened the door on exactly what they were looking for.

The four-story building she entered, built in 1863, abandoned and untouched since 1935, breathes the stories of the 7,000 immigrants who called it home. They whisper to you as you climb the narrow staircase, touching the banister that every one of them touched at some point. The tenements of New York were a way station; immigrants moved in, got their legs under them, and moved on to all that America promised. Abram and

Jacobsen bought the building for $750,000 and founded what is becoming a major historical museum and research institute.

You must take a guided tour to visit the museum, and the tours are based on stories about families who lived here. You can visit a Jewish turn-of-the-century garment shop wedged into a tiny flat; the homes of two families who survived crushing economic downturns—a German-Jewish family that went through the Panic of 1873 and an Italian-Catholic family that lived through the Depression; or the home of an Irish-Catholic family mourning the loss of a child in 1869.

As the daughter and granddaughter of garment workers, I chose the "Piecing it Together" tour, about the Jewish garment shop. We started in a 325-square-foot unrestored apartment, in which 13 people lived at one point, our guide told us. In one place, they found 20 layers of wallpaper on the wall; in the middle of the room a case holds some eloquent artifacts found during building renovations: a Rokeach jar full of kasha, a spool and pattern tracer, a coupon written in Italian, a circa 1870s beer stein, and more.

Then we moved on to a small one-bedroom apartment interpreted to 1897, where the Levine family operated a small garment factory—a miniature sweatshop, in essence—making dresses that sold for $75 to $100 apiece, which was no chump change in 1897. "He makes the rent in a week and then some," my guide said. "I don't know any New Yorkers who make their rent in a  week." The house is crowded with sewing machines, dressmaker's forms, and the family's furniture. "Mother is trying to function while the big dangerous iron is steaming in her kitchen, dad is doing the stitching by the window, girls are doing the dainty work."

This sort of family-run business was just a flash in the history of the garment industry in New York City. In 1903, the Williamsburg Bridge opened, linking the Lower East Side with Williamsburg, Brooklyn. "It was like a pressure cooker releasing people," said my guide. Jewish immigrants moved from the crowded tenement by the thousands, while at the same time standardization of clothing sizes and increasing industrialization changed the garment industry. By 1910, the home-based sweatshop was gone.

I saw the telltale sign of a modern-day sweatshop on a fascinating neighborhood walking tour, also offered by the Tenement Museum. Our guide pointed out what looked like a pipe sticking out a window: a sweatshop vent. The walking tour— it was called Immigrant Soles—taught me things I never knew about my motherland. Why did it never occur to me that Canal Street was named for an actual canal?

This excellent museum merits more than one visit, and I hope to sample all the tours eventually. In November 2011, the museum opened the Sadie Samuelson Levy Visitor and Education Center in an adjacent building, and in October 2012, added the "Shop Life" exhibit, recreating a German saloon and adding stories of various shopkeepers.

The museum has an outstanding gift shop with a huge selection of books about the Lower East Side, New York City, immigration and more, as well as all sorts of other tsotchkes and chazzerai. And once you've fallen in love with 97 Orchard Street, as you will, you will want to go to the museum website to peruse the database of photos of people who lived there over the years.

www.tenement.org

PLACES TO LEARN MORE

How the Other Half Lives: Studies Among the Tenements of New York is a book of photos and commentary by Jacob A. Riis. Published in 1890, it exposed the squalor of the tenements and ushered in a period of reform.

93 Newport, Rhode Island

I FIRST VISITED NEWPORT MANY YEARS ago with a couple of friends. Here was the drill: We would tour a Gilded Age mansion, then go outside and throw ourselves on to the impossibly green manicured lawn overlooking Narragansett Bay and wail, "Why, oh why, can't we live like this? Where is the justice in the world? Woe is us!" Or something to that effect. Then we would move on to the next mansion and repeat the process.

These fantastic summer homes were built by New Yorkers with money and social standing at the turn of the last century, and the ostentation is breathtaking. Not everyone considered what they represented lovely. Mark Twain coined the term Gilded Age as a dig—after all, he didn't call it golden. It was just gold on the outside, but what went on inside in these early days of the industrial revolution was not so shiny. It was also pre-personal income tax, which was instated in 1913 and marked the beginning of the end for the Gilded Age.

So maybe nobody lives quite the life of a turn-of-the-(last)-century railroad/coal/banking mogul anymore. (Or maybe they do, I don't run in those circles.) But thank goodness The Preservation Society of Newport County has been able to preserve these monuments to conspicuous consumption and open them to the public. Where else might we see panels decorated with platinum—real platinum—as in the morning room at The

Breakers, the mansion built by railroad millionaire (billionaire by today's standards) Cornelius Vanderbilt II. The Breakers has 70 rooms, including 33 for the domestic staff and 20 bathrooms with hot and cold running rain or salt water; Baccarat crystal chandeliers, alabaster columns, and the most advanced technology for the time, including modern plumbing, central heating, and electricity.

Here, too, you will see the room of daughter Gertrude Vanderbilt, who married Harry Payne Whitney and went on to found the Whitney Museum of American Art (see Chapter 12). Gertrude's room (among others) was decorated by Ogden Codman, who was recommended to the family by the era's most stringent doyenne of good taste, author Edith Wharton (see Chapter 59).

The running of a household required an army of 40 servants, and although the serving staff had its own strict hierarchy, the ladies of these houses were responsible for keeping things humming along—from planning menus to making sure guests and family members all had carriages available to them as they needed.

And just being ladylike in that time and place was a lot of work, requiring a great deal of dressing and undressing and dressing again for an active social life—morning dresses to yachting outfits, tea gowns to ball gowns. The houses were, in a way, jewel boxes to show off their ladies; for instance, steps of the grand staircase of the Breakers were shallow, so that women might appear to glide down the stairs as they made their entrance.

Of course, while the ladies and gentlemen of the house had one experience of Newport, servants had a completely different experience. (One, let's face it, that probably would have been closer to my fate had I lived in that time; most of the servants were recent immigrants to the United States, as were my grandparents.)

The audio tour of the Breakers touches on some of the experiences of the household staff, such as female servants, who were to remain unseen and had special doors and corridors from which to access bedrooms. The only servants who could be visible were male butlers and footmen, and the latter at the Breakers had to be at least six feet tall to appear properly elegant in their livery.

Another mansion, The Elms, which was owned by coal magnate Edward Julius Berwind, offers a tour entirely focused on life for servants behind the scenes—from the weeks of work required before the family arrived for the summer (including scrubbing all the marble floors), to schlepping up four flights of stairs to their shared living quarters after long hours of work.

Marble House was built by another branch of Vanderbilts, Cornelius's grandson William K. Vanderbilt and his wife, cotton heiress Alva Erskine Smith. The mister turned ownership of this most opulent of summer cottages over to his wife when it was completed in 1892; the couple divorced in 1895, and Alva, who remarried, became an ardent suffragette. In 1909, she opened Marble House as a fundraiser for that movement, charging $5 for people to hear speakers (among the guests of honor was Julia Ward Howe, see Chapter 59), and the paparazzi were there— "Some of the women...discovered that they were being snapped. They turned their backs, but in many cases too làte," *The New York Times* reported.

It is this event that I commemorate every time I drink out of the Votes for Women mug—a reproduction of the service used that day—I bought in Newport. It's the closest I'll come to living that life, I guess.

www.newportmansions.org

⚘

PLACES TO LEARN MORE

Scenes from the 1974 film *The Great Gatsby* were filmed at the
Marble House and Rosecliff (built by silver heiress Theresa Fair
Oelrich). Newport also makes appearances in *27 Dresses, True Lies,
Amistad* as well as movies based on the mansions' heyday, such as
The Buccaneers, based on an unfinished novel by Edith Wharton
(more on her in Chapter 59), and *The Bostonians*, from a novel by
her buddy, Henry James.

Mark Twain's *The Gilded Age* satires the moguls and politicians
of the day. Edith Wharton's *The Custom of the Country* and *House of
Mirth* offer a glimpse into the lives of people who lived in, or on
the fringes of, this sort of society.

94 *Where Gardens Grow*

 AMERICA IS, OF COURSE, DOTTED WITH spectacular gardens, but I'm going to shine the grow light on Georgia first. I'm not sure what it is about Georgia and gardens, but within an hour of Atlanta alone are several interesting plots. You could base yourself in that city and gorge on gardens for days.

Callaway Gardens in Pine Mountain is the big kahuna: 13,000 acres of gardens, lakes, woodland trails, a butterfly garden, birds of prey show, lodge, spa, golf, and more in the southern foothills of the Appalachian Mountains. Founded in 1952 by Cason and Virginia Hand Callaway, it was originally named the Ida Cason Gardens, after Cason's mother.

"When I was a little girl growing up in Columbus, people called it Ida Cason's," Georgia native Linda Erbele told me. "We'd say, 'You goin' to Ida Cason's this weekend?'" (Imagine that said in a sweet Georgia lilt.)

Though Callaway Gardens has something to see year-round, springtime is a big time, when some 700 species of azalea burst into colorful bloom.

www.callawaygardens.com

Dunaway Gardens, in nearby Newnan, has a particularly won-
derful story behind it. The floral and rock garden was planted by
Arkansas vaudevillian Hetty Jane Dunaway and was both a garden
and theatrical training ground with a 1,000-seat amphitheater.
Walt Disney frequented the place, and Sarah Ophelia Colley
Cannon, who was theatrical director for seven years, created her
Minnie Pearl character here.

But the 25-acres of gardens fell into neglect after Dunaway's
death in 1961, wisteria and ivy grew to choke the property, and
the place looked like just a tangled wilderness when Jennifer Rae
Bingham bought it on a whim—and without realizing the treasures that lay beneath the overgrowth. When her family started
digging the garden out, they found they'd bought more than just
a pretty piece of land. They found patios and walkways, walls and
ponds, pools and waterfalls. Bit by bit, they have been restoring
the gardens to their former informal splendor. The garden
reopened to the public in 2003 and is now on the National
Register of Historic Places.

www.dunawaygardens.com

Then there's the quirky gardens at Hills & Dales Estate in
LaGrange. Although the mansion was built in 1916 by textile
magnate Fuller and Ida Callaway (the Callaways are big players in this region), the formal gardens were planted in about
1841 by Sarah Ferrell. Sara was 24 when she started, and she
tended those gardens until her death in 1903. Among other
things, Sarah sang praises by planting boxwood hedges spelling
out GOD and forming other phrases and symbols. (Perhaps
that's why when Union troops marched through LaGrange in
1846, they spared the gardens.) Fuller Callaway Jr. and his wife

Alice moved into the mansion in 1936, and Alice, although at first overwhelmed, tended those gardens for 62 years, until her death in 1998. Today, the gardens are maintained by the Fuller E. Callaway Foundation. You may tour both mansion and gardens, but the latter is the better, though the mansion is kind of cute—big but decorated like granny's house, complete with family photos scattered about.

www.hillsanddales.org

O.K., so maybe you're not heading for Georgia. You can smell the roses (and daffodils and camellias and orchids and so on and so on) all over the USA.

The oldest botanical garden in the United States is the Missouri Botanical Garden in St. Louis. Locals still call it "Shaw's garden," even though nobody around today actually knew Henry Shaw, who founded the 79-acre garden in 1859. Among its attractions are a Japanese garden, greenhouse-grown camellia collection, Victorian district, and the "Climatron" (sounds a little dirty)—a geodesic dome housing a tropical rain forest of more than 2,800 plants.

www.missouribotanicalgarden.org

Once you've finished milling around the Mall of America (see Chapter 31), you can detox at the Eloise Butler Wildflower Garden and Bird Sanctuary in Minneapolis, within the Theodore Wirth Regional Park. Opened in 1907, it is said to be the oldest public wildflower garden in the nation. The ashes of botanist and teacher Eloise Butler, who led the charge to save this slice of natural Minneapolis, were scattered here after her death in 1933.

www.minneapolisparks.org/default.asp?PageID=1355

On the other hand, the Coastal Maine Botanical Gardens Botanical Gardens are fairly new; they opened in 2007. The groomed and naturalized gardens are set on 128 acres in Boothbay Harbor, and include the edible Burpee Kitchen Garden, a children's garden, a walking trail/native plant garden along the tidal Black River, a pond, a Garden of the Five Senses (it includes a labyrinth, see Chapter 81) and more.

www.mainegardens.org

The Lady Bird Johnson Wildflower Center in Austin, Texas preserves and researches native plants. Wander the butterfly garden, a Central Texas meadow, a country stream with water-loving plants. Theme gardens display the infinite possibilities for Texas native plants, where you can smell the sage baking in the sun and walk short trails through various native landscapes.

www.wildflower.org

Green Topiary Garden in Portsmouth, Rhode Island is just plain fun. The estate overlooking Narragansett Bay was the summer home of cotton executive Thomas E. Brayton in the 1870s, but it was property superintendent Joseph Carreiro (from 1905 to 1945) and then his son-in-law, George Mendonca, who created the topiary menagerie that gives the place its name. The oldest topiary garden in the country includes 80 pieces—there's an elephant and a giraffe, bears and bunnies all fashioned from English boxwood, California privet, and yew.

www.newportmansions.org/explore/green-animals-topiary-garden

The International Rose Test Garden in Portland, Oregon (aka "The Rose City") grows more than 500 varieties of roses—the scent alone could make a girl swoon. It was founded in 1917, and during World War I, rose breeders from around Europe sent new hybrids to the gardens for testing and to protect them from the bombing. Today it is the oldest continually operating rose test garden in the country, and it's still testing new hybrids; it also has a whole garden of miniatures.

www.rosegardenstore.org

This barely scratches the surface of America's collection of marvelous gardens. Longwood Gardens in Pennsylvania is more than 1,000 acres and is known for its Fireworks and Fountains shows scheduled throughout spring and summer. During Virginia's Historic Garden Week each April, hundreds of exceptional private as well as public gardens are open for tours. The Brooklyn Botanic Garden in New York City celebrated its centennial in 2010 and (among many others) includes a fragrance garden for the visually impaired. The Boston Public Garden dates to 1837. The Swan Boats that paddle around its lagoon are a beloved tradition. There are Desert Botanical Gardens in Phoenix, Arizona, and in Coral Gables, Florida, the Fairchild Botanical Garden displays and conserves tropical plants. And in California, there's the San Francisco Botanical Garden, in Golden Gate Park; the Asian gardens at Hakone Estate and Gardens in Saratoga; the gardens around Filoli, a historic country estate in Woodside; and the garden by the sea—the Mendocino Coast Botanical Gardens.

95 *Antebellum Vacation*

FOR THE MOMENT, IF YOU WILL permit me, let's lay aside the painful implications of the Southern plantation. Yes, they carry a lot of baggage, and I don't mean to trivialize this. But history is implacable, and if there's one happy ending out of a painful chapter in American history, it's the remaining plantation homes that dot the South. These plantations not only showcased landowners' wealth and power, they also provided a graceful backdrop for Southern women's particular charms.

Stripped of the ugly side of their history, these are now just graceful manses, many of which welcome guests to stay, dine, or tour. Most of these antebellum homes share a similar style, symmetrical Classic Revival, Greek Revival or Federal style architecture, pillared entries, shady porches, sprawling grounds, gardens, and guest rooms filled with antiques (or reproductions). These mansions and their sweeping grounds are particularly popular for weddings.

Here's a small sample of plantations that welcome overnight guests.

In 1817, the Natchez, Mississippi postmaster built Monmouth Plantation and named it for the county in New Jersey he had previously called home. And from there, things got interesting. The plantation's rich history went on to include one of the largest slaveholding families in the state; looting and occupation by Union soldiers; slaves fleeing to enlist in the Union army; spunky Southern women clinging to the home as best they could, a la Scarlett and Miss Melly; abandonment and decline; and finally, in the late 1970s, rescue, restoration, and rebirth as a luxury hotel. And that's just the short version.

www.monmouthplantation.com

Washington Plantation, originally the Chandler-Irvin House, was the seat of a 3,000-acre cotton plantation in Washington, Georgia, which was in one of the most affluent cotton counties in the state. The town of Washington has more than 100 antebellum homes, so a stay in one of Washington Plantation's five guest rooms could facilitate a full-immersion antebellum getaway.

www.washingtonplantation.com

The Cottage Plantation in St. Francisville was the first in Louisiana to be converted to a B&B, and it still has all of its outbuildings, including slave quarters, schoolhouse, carriage barn, and more. It is pretty much an intact plantation, circa the early 1800s. Andrew Jackson stayed at The Cottage on his way to Natchez after protecting Louisiana from invading British forces in the Battle of New Orleans (St. Francisville is about 100 miles from New Orleans). Visitors may stay in the six guest rooms, or you may just tour the property.

www.cottageplantation.com

Also in St. Francisville, The Myrtles Plantation, built in about 1796, is advertised as one of the most haunted houses in America. It was built by General David Bradford, also known as "Whiskey Dave" for his part in the Whiskey Rebellion of the 1790s. (Dude was not down with the high tax the feds had levied on whiskey.) It's changed hands many times over the years, but now is on the National Register of Historic Places and is a bed and breakfast with 11 rooms, a restaurant, and at least 12 ghosts. So they say.

www.myrtlesplantation.com

Madewood Plantation House, in Napoleonville, Louisiana, was built in the 1840s as a sugar plantation. It has been in the Marshall family since the 1960s, when the current owner's mother visited the perishing mansion, which was up for sale, and impulsively tossed out a lowball bid. And Bob's your uncle. Today, the mansion is not terribly strict about its own vintage; other historic buildings have been moved to the property—one, a 20th century plantation house, has been converted into an opera house (no kidding), where operas are staged about once a year.

www.madewood.com

96 Taos Pueblo, Taos, New Mexico

SUN AND SHADOW ON THE RED multistory adobe buildings of the Taos Pueblo make it living art, with emphasis on living. Continuously occupied for more than 1,000 years, the Taos Pueblo, about 70 miles from Santa Fe, is a National Historic Landmark, a UNESCO World Heritage Site, and still home to members of the tribe today. It is past, present, and future. It is a home and a source of income to its residents, both through admission fees and shops selling handmade art and crafts. This commerce is nothing new; the Taos Pueblo has been a trading center since long before Europeans moved in. It's just that today, they trade not only with other tribes—you will find art by members of other Pueblo tribes and Navajo artists—but with tourists.

The pueblo sits on 95,000 acres on the Rio Pueblo, still the primary source of drinking water for its residents. The main structures were built between A.D. 1000 and 1450 and are little changed since at least 1540, when the Spanish arrived.

Study up on the etiquette and restrictions of making art here yourself; you can't just photograph and sketch willy-nilly. On my first visit, I lifted my camera to my eye and was very politely informed of the rules by a young man who happened to be passing. (You will also pay a fee for each camera you bring in with you, including cell phone cameras.) And although you are welcome to observe celebrations that take place throughout the year, you must do so with the same respect you might take to church, and no photography is permitted.

And for all the rich history swirling around this pueblo, it also is home to many people living in the here and now. Sure, pop into any of the shops, but make sure that where you're popping is indeed a shop. It would be terribly rude to just stick your big tourist head into somebody's living room. If you would like to meet members of the community and learn while you look, you can take a 20- to 30-minute walking tour with a resident. But you won't learn everything about everything. Some things about their culture and religion Native Americans keep to themselves. Can't blame 'em. America's indigenous people have lost an awful lot already. That they open to tourists this precious living artifact at all, even with an entry fee, is incredibly generous.

www.taospueblo.com

97 Navajo National Monument, Arizona

I STUMBLED ON THE NAVAJO NATIONAL Monument by accident decades ago, during one of my earliest meandering road trips. I didn't know it was there, followed some signs on a whim, took a little walk, and came to one of the most intensely moving sights I had ever seen.

From a lookout at the edge of a wide green canyon I saw Betatakin Ruins, 370 feet across, 450 feet high, notched into the red sandstone. And I could make out, even from a distance, ancient dwellings built in the rock—windows and ruins of walls. These were home to 13th-century Pueblo people, who settled here to take advantage of springs that flowed from the porous rocks. They farmed the land at the edge of the alcove, enjoyed morning sun in winter and shade in summer, and were protected from the elements by the sheltering rocks. Why they left this inviting spot, nobody knows.

Between me and the alcove was the fragrant canyon. It smelled of juniper and sunshine. Hawks wheeled above the tree-tops, below the lookout point. I was only just getting to know the Southwest, only just starting to love it. And as I gazed at this evocative archaeological treasure, I suddenly got it. And I had the urge to tear off my clothes, stick a feather in my hair, and disappear forever into the canyon. I would gather edible roots and berries (because I would know a lot about stuff like that) during the day, and in the evening, I would return home to the dwelling in the rock, build a fire, and watch night fall over the fragrant canyon.

I didn't do that, of course. I didn't even take one of the tours into the cliff dwelling because I'd stumbled on this splendor late in the day—too late for tours, and I had to get back on the road for some reason or another.

Maybe someday I'll go back and hike into the canyon, tour the cave dwelling. Or maybe not. This serendipitous experience is so perfectly preserved as magical in my memory, I hate to do anything to sully it. So you'll have to go and tell me about it.

www.nps.gov/nava/index.htm

98 *Hearst Castle, San Simeon, California*

HEARST CASTLE SITS PERCHED HIGH ON a hill overlooking the Pacific, a monument to money and ego given free rein, a spectacle of conspicuous consumption with 165 rooms and more than 100 acres of lush landscaped grounds, including three guest houses, and opulent mosaic and marble indoor and outdoor swimming pools lined by colonnades and overlooked by statuary.

The land on which Hearst Castle sits was in William Randolph Hearst's family for many decades, but it was called Camp Hill and used for camping retreats. The media magnate inherited the property from his mother in 1919 and decided to change the whole tone of the place. He hired architect Julia Morgan, a favorite of his late mother's. Morgan had a degree in civil engineering from UC-Berkeley and was the first woman to graduate with a degree in architecture from the Ecole Nationale et Speciale des Beaux-Arts.

Unmarried and intensely focused on her work, Morgan took an interest in the lives of working-class women via the numerous YWCA buildings she designed. Still, Hearst Castle remains her most famous commission.

Inspired by the castles of Europe he saw in his privileged youth, Hearst's vision for his home grew ever grander as they built. Hearst Castle is as much compound as mansion, with influences ranging from Medieval Europe to ancient Rome.

The indoor Roman Pool is fashioned after a Roman bath; Hearst loved and collected art and antiquities with mythological figures and scenes. Some of the medieval architectural touches were created by modern-day craftsmen, others—such as the 14th-century ceiling in Hearst's bedroom, called "the Gothic Suite"—are authentic. Although the exteriors of the buildings are Mediterranean Revival, the interiors are Gothic, a little gloomy and kind of overbearing.

The castle was host to all the leading stars and politicians of Hearst's day, including Winston Churchill, Charles Lindbergh, Howard Hughes, Charlie Chaplin, Bing Crosby, Joan Crawford, Norma Shearer, and Cary Grant. Not to mention, with the unhappy forbearance of Hearst's wife Millicent, actress Marion Davies, whom Hearst met in about 1918 and who was his main squeeze until his death in 1951. Davies was one of the era's most famous stars, and she threw lavish parties at the Hearst castle. When Hearst Corporation hit hard times in the late 1930s, she was able to write her honey a check for a million dollars to help keep it afloat. (Millicent, meanwhile, remained Mrs. Randolph Hearst and was an established society hostess, activist, and philanthropist in New York who outlived her husband-in-name-only by a couple of decades.)

Today the mansion is part of the California State Parks system, and five different tours are offered covering different aspects of the castle. (Make reservations well in advance.) The grounds and gardens also are open for self-tours in the late afternoon, after regular tour hours. These tours do not allow you to enter the buildings, though docents are available to answer questions and keep you on the right paths.

www.hearstcastle.org

꙰

PLACES TO LEARN MORE

Orson Wells's 1941 masterpiece, *Citizen Kane*, is essentially the life of William Randolph Hearst, although Wells insisted it was a composite portrait. Still, there had to be some reason that no Hearst newspaper reviewed the movie until the mid-1970s. (By the way, though critics loved it, the film was a box-office disaster when it was released.)

99 *Pike Place Market, Seattle*

THESE DAYS EVERY BEND-IN-THE-ROAD TOWN HAS a farmer's market, but the Pike Place Market is the big kahuna and the oldest in continuous operation. It's a monster of an indoor market comprising nine acres and more than 200 businesses selling mostly but not only locally produced food. But that's not all— there are gift shops and toy stores and wine merchants and clothes and leather goods and antiques. It's enough to make a shopaholic hyperventilate and a foodie celebrate.

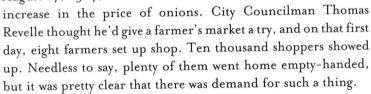

"It's a foodie heaven, that whole place, between the produce and the fish and the bakeries and the confectioner and the wine shops," said my friend Lara Mayeux, a psychology professor and foodie.

The Pike Place Market was born on August 17, 1907, in reaction to a tenfold increase in the price of onions. City Councilman Thomas Revelle thought he'd give a farmer's market a try, and on that first day, eight farmers set up shop. Ten thousand shoppers showed up. Needless to say, plenty of them went home empty-handed, but it was pretty clear that there was demand for such a thing.

Anyone who goes home empty-handed from the market today just isn't trying. Lara and her friend bought everything they would need for that night's dinner—wine, baguette, chocolate ("The caramels at The Chocolate Market were the best I've ever had," she said) and a (very expensive) salmon, which they first watched fly at the fish market where your future dinner is famously hurled between fishmongers.

If you're a fan of the movie *Sleepless in Seattle* you can dine at The Athenian Inn, which was featured in the movie (for more chick flick movie locations, see Chapter 85). "It was slightly touristy but tasty and affordable and has a great view if you sit upstairs," Lara said. You can also visit the original Starbucks and Sur La Table.

Hour-long guided tours of the market are available, or just plunge in and wander.

"Honestly, just wandering around all the fresh produce was the best part," Lara said. "Seeing the mountains of berries and veggies—some of which I'd never heard of—was just really, really fun."

pikeplacemarket.org

100

Where the Heart Is

I'M GOING TO END WITH A lovely, wistful response to the question "Where should women go?" from my mother-in-law, Jo Ann Battles.

Jo Ann met her husband, Tom, in Chicago. They were a coupla Catholic-school kids, growing up in the same neighborhood. They fell in love, married, started procreating, and became upwardly mobile, moving several times to follow Tom's jobs. They moved to Glenview, Illinois, then Kewanee, then to Texas, when my husband was 15 years old. When my husband Tom and his three brothers were grown, Jo Ann and Tom moved back to Chicago, to the old neighborhood.

That sort of mobility is, in one way, a quintessential American life, although these days, a husband is just as likely to follow his wife's job. Is there any other nation where people will uproot and cross the country like that? We're a transient bunch, restlessly wandering our homeland. But each time we move, we leave a little part of ourselves behind.

Where should women go?

"The place that says 'home,'" Jo Ann wrote me in an email. "Every woman who has moved with her husband many times has a certain nostalgia for homes and places in her past.

"I have always dreamed of our home in Glenview and what our life might have been there. We visited our old house in

Kewanee, and it was truly falling apart. A dilapidated truck was parked not in the driveway or garage, but in the backyard. Of course the real ache is that one is remembering the time, and no matter where you are, that time cannot be repeated. Revisiting can be bittersweet, and sometimes ends the ache.

"Now we live in the same neighborhood that we grew up in. I guess that's where our hearts were all along."

Index

Acknowledgments

This book has been in the works for a long time. Written in fits and starts and a final desperate frenzy, it was mostly a lot of fun, although also, at times, a tedious slog. For the record: a hundred places is a lot! My gratitude is to those women who provided suggestions and quotes for the content, to friends who cheered me on when I needed it most, and to my husband, Tom Battles, who picked up household slack during those last, desperate few months. I was fortunate to have delightful travel companions for some of my travels, and very fortunate that so many women throughout our nation's history did so many interesting things. I learned a lot, and for that I am truly grateful.

Thanks, too, to Larry Habegger and James O'Reilly for launching Travelers' Tales and keeping it going through good times and lean. I had a piece in the very first Travelers' Tales book and am proud to now have a TT book of my own.

About the Author

Sophia Dembling, who was born and reared in the heart of New York City, discovered her passion for exploring the USA when she was 19 years old, driving cross country with a couple of girl-friends in a baby blue Plymouth Duster.

In the decades following, Sophia crisscrossed the country many times, every which way, by car, by airplane, and by Greyhound bus. She packed up and left New York to move to Texas. She took up travel writing, publishing stories in *The Dallas Morning News*, *The Los Angeles Times*, *The Chicago Tribune*, *American Way*, *Delta Sky*, *World Hum*, and many other publications and websites, including *The Best Women's Travel Writing 2006* and *The Best Women's Travel Writing 2007*. Sophia's other books include *The Yankee Chick's Survival Guide to Texas* and *The Introvert's Way: Living a Quiet Life in a Noisy World*.

Sophia lives in Dallas, Texas with her husband and an ever-changing cast of canines. She remains avid as ever about exploring the USA.